EDITOR'S INTRODUCTION

This book is one of six parts in a system of instructional materials—the McGraw-Hill Basic Skills System: Tools for Learning Success. Designed at the University of Minnesota Reading and Study Skills Center, the Basic Skills System is aimed at college-bound high school students, community college students, college and university students who need to improve those skills necessary for academic and life-experience success. The materials are also viable in adult education programs and training programs offered under the auspices of commercial, governmental, and industrial agencies. The system consists of tests to determine instructional needs and materials designed to meet those needs, plus instructors' manuals to explain the tests and materials and the relationship between them. The purpose of the tests is to determine what instruction a student needs in basic skills; the purpose of the materials is to give the student that instruction. Each student gets what is needed without wasting time on unnecessary tasks.

Six basic skill topics—study, reading, vocabulary, spelling, writing, and mathematics—are covered, and two tests (A and B forms) are provided for each topic. Subscales on the tests are matched to accompanying instructional materials: thus a student with a low score on one or more subscales receives instruction in the corresponding skill. The second form of the test may be used to evaluate progress after instruction.

The materials in the Basic Skills System have been field-tested to provide the best possible results. While most of the materials are self-instructional programs, the tests, of course, are designed for supervised administration.

The testing instructions have been carefully developed and standardized by CTB/McGraw-Hill. The latest research techniques and procedures have been utilized to ensure the highest possible validity and reliability.

The instructional materials are designed to be used separately, if desired, and can be purchased as single units. Most of the materials are suitable for adoption as textbooks in such basic skill courses as Freshman English, Communications, Orientation to College, How to Study, Reading, Fundamentals of Writing, Vocabulary Development, Spelling Improvement, and Remedial or Developmental Mathematics. Individualized diagnosis and instruction are optional in such settings.

With this second edition of *Basic Vocabulary Skills*, improvement has been made to include applications of various occupational areas, incorporate some additional lower-level words, and pinpoint key words throughout the text.

Alton L. Raygor
Consulting Editor
University of Minnesota

Basic Vocabulary Skills

A Program for Self-Instruction

Second Edition

NANCY B. DAVIS
Director
Reading and Study Skills Center
Indiana University

McGraw-Hill Book Company

New York   St. Louis   San Francisco
Auckland   Bogotá   Düsseldorf
Johannesburg   London   Madrid   Mexico
Montreal   New Delhi   Panama   Paris
São Paulo   Singapore   Sydney
Tokyo   Toronto

Library of Congress Cataloging in Publication Data

Davis, Nancy B.
  Basic vocabulary skills.

    Includes index.
    1. Vocabulary. 2. English language—Word
formation. 3. English language—Programmed
instruction. I. Title.
PE1449.D35 1978   428.2   77-6254
ISBN 0-07-044411-0

BASIC VOCABULARY SKILLS

1234567890 DODO 783210987

This book was set in Palatino with Optima Bold
by Black Dot, Inc.
The editors were Donald W. Burden and Barry Benjamin;
the cover was designed by Pencils Portfolio, Inc.;
the production supervisors were Leroy A. Young
and Gayle Angelson.
R. R. Donnelley & Sons Company was printer and binder.

Acknowledgments

Acknowledgment is made for the use of materials from
the following sources:
    Editorial by Nicholas H. Charney, *Psychology Today*,
August 1967, issue, used with permission (pp. 125–127 of
this book)
    Theodosius Dobzbansky, *Genetics and the Origin of
Species,* 3d ed., revised, paperback, Columbia University
Press, New York, 1964, pp. 176–177 (pp. 141–142 of this
book)
    Richard A. Goldsby, *Cells and Energy,* The Macmillan
Company, New York, 1967, pp. 57, 64–65 (pp. 209–211 of
this book)
    Hubert C. Heffner, Samuel Selden, and Hunton D. Sell-
man, *Modern Theatre Practice,* 4th ed., Appleton-Century-
Crofts, Inc., New York, 1959, pp. 60–61 (pp. 138–141 of
this book)
    The Miracle of Language, by Charlton Laird, Premier ed.,
1960, by Fawcett World Library, New York, © 1953 by
Charlton Laird, pp. 62–63 (pp. 293–294 of this book)
    Excerpts from "The Merv Griffin Show," courtesy of
The Westinghouse Broadcasting Company (p. ix of this
book)
    M. J. Sienko, and R. A. Plane, *Chemistry: Principles and
Properties,* McGraw-Hill Book Company, New York, 1966,
appendix A (adapted), p. 575 (pp. 168–178, 180 of this book)

Contents

Preface

The business of being a student is a serious one and rests in great part on skill with words. A way with words may be a talent, but it is a talent that must be developed to a high level for academic work. Just as one can learn to behave in a more intelligent way by developing mental talent, so can one work with words to develop skill in using verbal talent.

This book is intended for students—not for the professional chemist, artist, biologist, etc. It does not teach the subject matter, but rather emphasizes the practical ways to learn and remember the academic vocabulary when one has the responsibility to acquire a high-level vocabulary both in general usage and in technical usage.

This book endeavors to teach *how* to become talented with words. Ample practice material is supplied to develop these skills. In addition, reference sections are included for continuing development after the skills and techniques are mastered.

The content is arranged for self-instruction so that an individual may pursue vocabulary improvement on his own. Full directions for using this programmed format are included.

The content is also adaptable to class instruction. Basic content, special subject-matter content, and the refinements covered in word usage offer sufficient material for a course in vocabulary improvement. If word study is only a part of a larger coverage, then Chapters 1 to 4 can be used, with the subject-matter sections treated as optional work.

Lastly, for those individuals who are not attending school or cannot take course work but who still desire to learn and expand their knowledge, working through this book makes a good beginning.

This second edition represents the benefits derived from the experiences of both students and teachers working with this material. Some frames needed to be clarified, some deleted, and new material has been added—all toward the purpose of serving the needs of the wide range of students now participating in post–high school programs. Grateful acknowledgment is here made to all those people who have contributed to this material from its beginning.

Nancy B. Davis

To the Student

At the end of a world tour Harry Belafonte was interviewed by Merv Griffin. When Belafonte was asked about the problems of communicating with various audiences throughout the world, he made a statement about music being a common language, then added that "part of the repertoire was music indigenous to the region." At which point Orson Bean said, "It means he sang Jewish songs in Israel."

Orson Bean demonstrated his ability to translate formal language into everyday language. Being able to translate formal and technical language into everyday language with meaning you are sure of is an important verbal skill. It is especially important in higher education, where such a vocabulary is in common use. Even admission to college is in part dependent on vocabulary-test scores. And while a person can laboriously memorize the meanings of word lists in preparation for the test (and thereby possibly score sufficiently well to be admitted to academic work), once into the course work the memorized lists are not enough. Skill in handling words becomes a requirement for success.

Skill in handling words means that you can master academic language. You are not overwhelmed by the "big words" but rather have sufficient confidence through knowledge of how words operate to be able to acquire the academic style. This "educated" language will become your everyday language for dealing with matters academic.

The major portion of this book is devoted to learning to use Greek and Latin derivatives because the vocabulary of the academic world is based mainly on word elements derived from these classical languages.

The life sciences use Latin terminology, and even when a new term needs to be invented, it is based on Latin or Greek. Physics and chemistry primarily use Greek as a source for terminology. In the humanities, such as literature, history, and philosophy, classical derivatives are plentiful, for they continue to be the language of educated people. For example, *indigenous, acclivity, propitiatory, peroration.*

You, as a college student, must learn this educated language so that it becomes your everyday language insofar as subject matter is concerned. You must be able to associate some kind of meaning with the words you read and hear. Then, of course, learn to use them yourself in term papers, discussions, and examinations.

Because one classical term is used for many words, it is easier, that is, more efficient, to learn these classical elements than try to learn each word separately. Take for example *mes,* or *meso,* which is Greek for "middle" and is used in the following words:

*meso*blast, the *middle* germ layer of an embryo

*meso*cracy, government by the *middle* class

*meso*morph, the *middle* type of human body form, between endomorph and ectomorph

*Meso*potamia, the country between (*middle*) the Tigris and Euphrates rivers

*meso*thorax, the *middle* segment of the thorax of an insect

In Webster's unabridged dictionary 220 words are entered using *meso* or the alternate *mes.* You may or may not know the remaining part of the word, but recognizing the meaning of *mes* as "middle" can be a clue to combine with the way the term is being used so that you can attach a sensible meaning to the new term.

As knowledge expands, new discoveries and new ideas need to be named. The practice of using Latin and Greek word elements for these new terms continues. Sometimes they are totally formed from classical elements, and sometimes they are of mixed origin. Examples of words only now appearing in new dictionaries are:

Mesoscaphe is a term coined for an apparatus designed specifically for the *middle* depths of the ocean. Perhaps you already know *bathyscaphe,* the name selected for the kind of ship designed for deep-sea exploration. *Bathys* is the form we use, from a Greek word meaning "deep."

Cryosurgery is another new term needed to name a new technique. *Cryo,* meaning "cold" (Greek *kryos*), added to the English word *surgery,* provides the term for the use of extremely low temperatures to destroy or remove diseased tissue.

You are familiar with the word *astronaut* as the name for an explorer of interplanetary space. The literal meaning of the word is "star sailor." The change from the Latin word for sailor (*nautus*) to its use for explorer is not too difficult to understand, since sailors were the early explorers of our world.

New words following the same pattern are *aquanaut* (water sailor) meaning "an underwater explorer" and *chimponaut* referring to the chimpanzees used in space exploration.

These new words use the old word elements and follow the established procedures for constructing words: start with the basic meaning (*naut*), add another element as a prefix (*aqua*) to make the basic meaning more specific, then add the correct suffix to show the function of the word— *aquanaut, aquanautical, aquanautically,* and *aquanautics.*

But "Why not use plain English?" is a question you may well be asking. The answer can be given in two parts. First, the language of higher education is more exact and more efficient. More precise information is conveyed in fewer words. But you must learn the system. Compare these two sentences:

1 Attending to the discriminandum is reinforced by resolution of the task uncertainty.
2 Paying attention to what makes one object different from another object when a difference is to be found is likely to happen more often in the future under the same conditions by successfully finding a difference between the two objects.

Twelve words in sentence 1 compared with forty words in sentence 2 to convey the same information. For example, in the word *discriminandum* you can recognize *discrimin* as being like *discriminate*. The ending *andum* is translated "the thing or person to be. . . ." The verb *is reinforced* is the technical equivalent of "is likely to happen more often in the future under the same conditions."

The second part of the answer to the question "Why not use plain English?" is illustrated by these two sentences:

1 Push that thingamajig sticking out at the corner there. (Plus pointing your finger in all probability.)
2 Press the shutter release.

Things and ideas have names which permit communication with a minimum of ambiguity or confusion. In fact, one of the criteria of a profession is that a formal language does exist in which terms have only one meaning so that communication is as clear as possible. A part of your task as a student is to acquire the language; otherwise you display your ignorance of the subject matter.

In all fairness to the student's point of view, the matter of seemingly overelaborate style of language should be recognized. At times the author's or lecturer's style may seem unnecessarily formal, and rather than use words efficiently he or she seems to go the long way around to get across the message. It is inappropriate in this book to explore the psychological reasons for such a style, but whatever the reasons, the fact remains that the student must be able to handle such language by translating the message into a more understandable form. This translating of messages is a part of the skill needed to handle academic language.

ORGANIZATION OF THIS PROGRAM

This book is organized to cover the basic skills discussed above:

1. Prefixes
2. Roots
3. Suffixes
4. Context clues
5. Application to specific subject matter

The words selected for presentation in this program cover a wide range. Words you already know are used as stepping stones to the more difficult and technical words. Although college professors use ordinary words such as *live, die, love, hate, house,* and *home,* they also use words of a higher level as if such words were also ordinary. And they are intended for the educated person.

The first portion of this program is devoted to the prefixes and roots from Latin and Greek which are used most often in these higher level words (Chapters 1 and 2). Analyzing a word by its basic or literal meaning is an important technique in understanding the words you read and hear. Skill in using suffixes is another part of this analysis (Chapter 3). These skills are combined with various kinds of context clues available to you in the fourth chapter of this book. Chapters 5 to 9 cover application of these vocabulary skills to particular subject-matter areas. Additional prefixes, roots, and suffixes are supplied in reference sections for further work with vocabulary building after you have developed the techniques for achieving vocabulary skill. These reference lists cover general usage and subject-matter terminology and are presented at the ends of chapters for your convenience.

HOW TO USE PROGRAMMED INSTRUCTION

First, take time to leaf through the book to note the features that make up a programmed text. Most of the material has been arranged for self-instruction in steps which are called frames. These frames present certain information, then require you to supply word parts, words, and/or phrases you are in the process of learning. This first stage is followed by practice and then review so that your new knowledge will be remembered.

You will have a card to cover the answers which appear beside each frame. The answers you are to supply are indicated by blank lines. A line of this size _____ or this size _____ indicates each word that is to be supplied, depending on the length of the word. Where only part of a word is to be the answer, a blank line of this size _____ or this size _____ is supplied, depending on the length of the word part.

After you have completed a frame, uncover the answer or answers immediately to check your work. If the frame is a relatively long one, uncover the answers after each paragraph. If you provide yourself with this immediate feedback, errors cannot accumulate. If you have made a wrong answer, reread the frame to see what you have overlooked, then make the correction.

Certain frames are set off by horizontal rules and are numbered for reference. These are called express frames because they enable you to bypass material you may already know. The express frame is designed to find out if you know the meaning of the word element and can use that meaning. The complete word used as an example may well be unknown to you. If so, so much the better since you will then have been tested on the word element itself. And that is the purpose of the express or test frame.

Explanations and special instructions are full page width. These paragraphs should always be read, even though you may be "expressing" through that section of the program.

Both informal and formal reviews are provided. For each formal-review item, the number of the express frame beginning the instruction of that item is included for your convenience.

At the end of each chapter in Part 1 the vocabulary used has been listed alphabetically. These lists provide a quick check on your mastery.

To start the program, begin with the Introduction to Part 1 so that you are familiar with the style of this particular instruction. Then read the first express frame and fill in the blank. If you are correct, skip to the next express frame. If you cannot supply the information asked for in the express frame or are slow in doing so, then work through the intervening instructional frame or frames. Working in this fashion means that you are not bored by tedious repetition of what you already know, but rather you are only working on new material which you need to know.

Courses in how to remember use the technique of association. Use of a word or an image which has special meaning for you is associated with the new information and results in easier remembering. This technique is emphasized in Chapter 1 to start you on your way to easier remembering. An explanation of this technique is found on pages 164–168, Use of Mnemonic Devices.

Recent research in programmed instruction has shown that there can be too many hints offered in a frame, so that the student ends up paying attention to the wrong kind of information. These frames have been carefully prepared and tried out, so that all needed information is present; but you will have to think about what you are doing rather than fill in blanks using nonrelevant clues. This kind of practice means that the work you do in this program more closely resembles the way you will handle words as you meet them in your course work.

Nancy B. Davis

Part 1.
Vocabulary Skills

INTRODUCTION

To ensure your understanding of the way word elements are combined and recombined to build a variety of words, this section begins the program. It serves to introduce you to the skills which you will be learning and practicing throughout the program.

You may already be familiar with certain of the information presented, since you have been exposed to vocabulary study since the early grades, but the section is short. Use it as a quick review of general procedures before starting the learning units.

WORD BUILDING

Vocabulary can be built by combinations of word elements, or parts. These word parts have names: a root, or base, is the basic part of a word; a prefix is fixed before a root; a suffix is fixed after a root.

The prefix of *nonpayment* is _____.

non

The root of *nonpayment* is _____.

pay

The suffix of *illegible* is _____.

ible

Sometimes a prefix and a root together are hard to pronounce, such as *in + legal = inlegal*. In means "not." Say *inlegal* rapidly several times. Hear what happens? We make it easier to pronounce by spelling *inlegal* as *i_l_legal.*

l (illegal)

The process of a letter becoming the same as, or similar to, another letter is called assimilation.

The *n* in *illegal* was a_____ed to an *l*.

ssimilat (assimilated)

The three word elements used to build words are _____, _____, and _____.

prefix/root/suffix

When word elements are joined, some letter combinations are difficult to pronounce. In this case the word is respelled. This change is called _____.

assimilation

TREATMENT OF COMBINING FORMS

Technically speaking, the dictionary enters prefixes, combining forms, and suffixes. In this program, roots will be used instead of combining forms, for the reason that there is less to learn by organizing word elements into prefixes, roots, and suffixes as opposed to learning combining forms.

For example, these entries are made as combining forms derived from Greek *graphein*, meaning "to write":

Combining form	Example of use
grapho	graphology
graph	telegraph
grapher	cartographer
graphy	photography

As used in this program, *graph* is a root to be translated "write." If you compare *graphology* (the study of handwriting) with *telegraph* (writing at a distance), you see that a root may have other forms attached at either end, according to the meaning needed.

In the instance of *grapher* and *graphy*, *graph* is identified as the root and *er* and *y* are suffixes to be used according to the need and attached to any appropriate root.

One aspect of combining forms is especially important for vocabulary skill. *Grapho* from the list above ends with the letter *o*. This vowel is supplied to the root form in order to make certain combinations of word elements pronounceable.

You already know this principle in using the article *a*. "A house," "a boat," but "_____ apple," "_____ egg."

Say "a apple." You must stop between the two *a*'s if you pronounce both words clearly, but "an apple" can be said as if it were one word—no stopping.

an/an

Combine *graph* with *spasm* to make a word meaning "writing cramp": _____.

graphospasm

The vowel *o* is most commonly used in order to make a root combinable with another word element beginning with a consonant sound. Other vowels are sometimes used;

be ready for them. But *o* is the vowel to think of first.

In the Introduction the Greek root for "middle" was used and given with alternate spellings. In addition to *mes* the spelling _____ was given.

meso

To build the technical term for the middle division of the brain, add the correct spelling to *encephalon:* _____*encephalon.*

mes(encephalon)

The noun suffix *on* was added to the meaning "middle" to name a nuclear particle whose mass is typically between the electron and the proton. The name for the middle particle is spelled _____.

meson

Notice what happens in the spelling of roots which end in a single consonant, such as *phon* (sound).

The name invented for Bell's instrument which permitted sound (*phon*) to be heard at a distance (*tele*) was _____.

telephone

The English silent _____ was added to maintain the long vowel in *phon.* Other examples are *telescope, expire, educe,* and *preside.*

e

A part of the vocabulary skill required for handling words consists of recognizing common elements in spite of changes in spelling in order to make the English word easier to _____.

pronounce or say

LITERAL MEANINGS
One more skill in addition to recognizing variations in spelling is needed, and that is the use of literal meanings to help you arrive at a modern meaning.

Examine these words:

port   exportation
portable   purport

porter   reportage
portress   transporter
All of these words share the word element
_____.

                                 port

    The Latin verb *portare*, meaning "to car-
ry," provides the root *port*. Each of the words
listed has a root with the literal meaning of
_____. Prefixes and/or suffixes have
been added to build words with more specific meanings.

                                 carry

Literal meaning is the direct translation of
the word elements. For example, to use the
root *graph* again, *biographer* can be broken
down into:
    bio = life
 graph = write
     er = one who
So that your task is to put the translated
elements into English word order: "one
who writes _____ _____."

                                 a life

The word form meaning "self" is *auto,* so
the word which translates to "one who
writes his own life" is _____.

                        autobiographer

Substitute one word for the words in parentheses in this sentence:
    Although Don Smith claimed that his
novel was fictional, from the known facts
it could be proved that the novel was (as if
he had written his own life) _____.

                     autobiographical

The words "as if he had written his own life" from the frame above point
up a skill necessary for success with words, and it is a skill which some
students overlook. The strictly literal translation of *autobiographical* in
the order of the word elements is "self–life–write–as if." These are the
meanings associated with *auto, bio, graph,* and *ical.* You must adjust these
literal meanings to the context, to the way the word is used, to "as if he
had written his own life."
    This style of free translation is exactly the same kind of adjustment

which is made in translating a modern foreign language into English, say, French into English. The strictly literal translation is only the start. It must be adjusted to the normal way of speaking.

Translating to sensible English includes maintaining the same part of speech needed as well as the tense of the verb needed.

To summarize the skills you will be developing in this program:

1 Building words from prefixes, roots, and suffixes
2 Recognizing assimilated letters
3 Recognizing variations in spelling
4 Adjusting literal meanings to normal English

With this refresher on the *way* words derived from Latin and Greek operate, you are ready to begin.

Chapter 1.
Prefixes and
Roots—
First Group

The prefixes and roots presented in Chapter 1 are those which are commonly found in higher education. Because they are also parts of more familiar words, you will no doubt know many of them. However, since they are the foundation on which to develop vocabulary skill, be certain that you can also use them with the "big" words before bypassing the learning frames.

The chapter begins with English prefixes as a warm-up.

PREFIXES

English

1-1
There was an outpouring of deep feelings at the death of the great man.
    The prefix in the above sentence is _____ and means _____ or _____.

out
external/beyond

The prefix *out* has two meanings, "an external position" and "going beyond a standard or level."
    In the sentence "Captain Harris gave the order to outflank the enemy position," does *out* carry the meaning "external" (position) or "beyond" (a standard)? _____

external

On a farm the buildings which are external to the house are called the _____ buildings.

out(buildings)

In the words *outmaneuver, outmoded, out-rank,* and *outshine* the prefix carries the meaning _____.	beyond

1-2
An unlocked door is not locked.
  The prefix meaning "not" is _____.

un

Un means "not."
  A ghost that is not seen is an _____seen ghost.

un(seen)

  If a problem is uncomplicated, it is _____ complicated.

not

1-3
There is a second prefix *un* which carries a different meaning. In the sentence "Unstop the drain," we get the idea of changing direction, or _____, of a process or condition.

reversal

The second prefix *un* carries the meaning of "reversal," as in *unfasten, unpack, unchain.*
  In the sentence "This pile of yarn needs to be untangled," *un* does not indicate the meaning "_____ tangled"; rather, it tells us that the tangling process must be _____.

not

reversed

The meaning of *un* can be decided by the way the word is used. The two meanings of *un* are _____ and _____.

not/reversal

1-4

The condition of underfed people underlies some of our political problems.

    In *underfed* the prefix meaning is _____ _____.

    In *underlie* the prefix means _____.

too
little
beneath

The prefix *under* carries two meanings, "beneath," as in *underlie*, and "too little," as in *underfed*. It is the opposite of the prefix *over*.

    In the word *underprivileged, under* carries the meaning _____ _____.

    In the word *undertow, under* means _____.

too little

beneath

You may already know the trick of reversing the verb and prefix. Change *underlie* to *lie under*, therefore, *lie beneath*. *Outpouring* becomes a _____ _____. Not a perfect method, but worth trying.

pouring out

These English prefixes are easy because you use them every day. The classical elements need to be equally familiar to you so that you can translate the high-sounding words into everyday words. You do not have to stop to look up each new word, but can understand its meaning as you meet it.

For convenience the classical elements are presented in alphabetical order, first Latin and then Greek. The most important thing to learn is the meaning of each one.

Latin

1-5

Accept, advertise, affix, aggravate, allocate, appreciate, arrears, assist, and *attract* all share the prefix _____ meaning _____.

ad/to or toward

Ad is a prefix meaning "to" or "toward."

"My paycheck is adequate to my needs." The literal translation of this sentence is "My paycheck is equal _____ my needs."

  to

"Vocabulary study will help me *advance* toward my goal of job improvement." Translate: ". . .help me move _____ my goal. . ."

  toward

Notice the repetition in the phrase "adequate _____" and "advance _____." English phrasing often repeats the prefix meaning. Consider "in addition to," "acclimate to," and "accede to." Being aware of such phrases can help you remember that *ad* means _____ or _____.

  to
  toward

  to/toward

The kind of word added to a verb to modify its meaning is called an _____verb.

  ad(verb)

A root meaning "go" is *it*. An exit is a way to go out. The way to go to some place (an entrance) is an _____ it.

  ad(it)

An adequate job is one that is equal to the need. Addition is the process of joining one item _____ another.

  to

Spect means "to look." If you look to one view of a subject, you see one adspect of it. Hard to say? *Adspect*? What happens if you drop the *d*? _____*spect*

  a(spect)

"To go to or yield to another's wishes" can be said in one word: *ad* + *cede*. Spell it so you can say it smoothly: *a_____cede*.

  c (accede)

Spell correctly the word which means "to become hardened to a new climate": _____*climatize*.

  ac(climatize)

Assume that there is a word *clivity*, a noun meaning "a slope," and you want to form a word to describe the upward slope,

the one to the top. You would use the prefix _____ and spell the word _____.

| | ad/acclivity |

The *d* in *ad* changes all the time. The verb
agglutinate literally means "to glue to." The
prefix is really _____ but changed to _____.

| | ad/ag |

"Richards had a tendency to aggrandize
his accomplishments." According to the
prefix of *aggrandize*, did he tend to increase
or decrease the greatness of his accomplishments? _____

| | increase (toward) |

The nerves which convey impulses to
the central nervous system are called
_____*ferent*. This word is made from the
prefix _____ meaning _____ and the
root *fer* meaning "to carry."

| | af(ferent) |
| | ad/to |

A word element that has been fixed to
the root, or basic part, of a word (front or
back) is an _____.

| | affix |

"An allocation of monies has been made."
Monies have been placed _____ each
one's share. The prefix _____ has been
spelled _____.

	to or toward
	ad
	al

"An annotated edition of the statutes has
been printed." An annotated edition means
that notes and comments have been added
_____ the statutes. The prefix _____
has changed to _____.

| | to/ad |
| | an |

Additional information is often hung to,
or added to, a book. We call this part of the
book the _____pendix. Since the *d* of *ad* is
hard to say before *p*, the *d* changed to _____.

| | ap(pendix) |
| | p |

Recognizing prefixes and literal meanings
can help in spelling. The word meaning
"to call to account" is *arraign*. The prefix
is spelled _____ and represents an assimilation of the _____ of _____.

| | ar |
| | d/ad |

"Sam Jones has been arraigned by the

grand jury." He has been called on publicly to _____ for his actions and will be put on trial.

> account

Try saying *ad + similate* (to be like or similar). Easier to say *a____similate*. The *d* of *ad* was made similar _____ the *s* of *similate*.

> s (assimilate)
> to

A will is not valid unless attestation takes place; it must be attested. The root *test* means "witness," so there must be a witness _____ a will. *Ad + test* becomes _____.

> to/attest

Your word or phrase for remembering *ad* is _____ .

> your choice

1-6
Collate, compare, connect, coordinate, and *correct* represent variant spelling of the prefix _____ meaning _____.

> com/with or together

The prefix *com* means "with" or "together."
*Com*pare this prefix _____ the one just learned. Once again the English phrase can be of help in remembering that *com* means _____ or _____. We *com*pare one item _____ another.

> with

> with/together
> with

If you are a person sent or assigned to work with other people for a special project, you are a _____mitteeman, now changed to _____mitteeperson by some people.

> com(mitteeman)
> com(mitteeperson)

*Com*post is the name for decayed organic matter used to fertilize and condition ground. It literally means "matter which has been placed or put _____ ground."

> with

The person who puts together the type for printing is called a _____positor.

"Total compliance with the articles of the treaty was demanded." In this sentence the idea of *with* is repeated in the prefix _____.

com(positor)

com

When people work together toward a common goal, they _____operate.

If two men set up a business as equal partners, we say they have formed a _____partnership. The letter _____ has been dropped.

co(operate)

co
m

The *m* of *com* is difficult to pronounce when followed by certain other consonants. In other words, it _____.

"I suspect that the bank president and treasurer are in _____lusion." But if only one person commits a fraud, he can not be said to have colluded, because *colluded* carries the meaning of_____, which implies more than one person.

assimilates

col(lusion)

together or with

Where two rivers flow together, that point is called a _____flux. The prefix is now _____ changed from _____.

con
con/com

A defect you were born (*gen*) with is a _____genital defect. The letter _____ has been assimilated to _____.

con(genital)/m
n

When the changes in one variable are related with the changes in another variable, the two together are said to be_____related.

A passage in one book which tends to be related with a passage in another book is said to be _____relative. For example, in the Christian Science church service readings from the Bible are followed by _____ _____ passages from Mrs. Eddy's text.

cor(related)

cor(relative)

correlative

The prefix in the three preceding sentences is really _____ changed to _____ .	com/cor
Your clue for remembering *com* is _____ _____ .	your choice

1-7 The city council debated the pro and con of the bond issue. *Con* is short for the prefix_____, meaning _____.	contra against

---

"The pro and con of the proposition were debated far into the night." If you're pro, you're for it. If you're con, you're_____ it. *Con* is short for *contra*, meaning_____.	against against
The well-known phrase "pro and con" could be your clue for remembering that *contra* means _____. Perhaps the word *contrary* appeals to you more. When a child is contrary, he is indeed _____ _____ doing what you have asked him to do.	against against
A device used against fertilization or pregnancy is a _____ceptive. "The final section of the document lists specific acts which contravene the agreement." You can translate *contravene* as "come _____." "There has been no contravention of this treaty in the last five years." The literal meaning of *contravention* is _____ _____ _____.	contra(ceptive) against a coming against
To travel counterclockwise is to travel in a direction _____ normal rotation. Another way of spelling *contra* is _____.	against or opposite counter

Do you suppose a counter in a store is protection against the customers?

Music students study *counterpoint,* which is the technical name for the art of combining melodies. It literally means "the points or notes placed _____ the original melody."

against

The adjective form of *counterpoint* is *contrapuntal* (*punt* is Italian for point). Both *contra* and *counter* mean _____.

against

"The decision made by the committee is controvertible." In other words, the decision is able to be argued _____. Another variant spelling of *contra* is _____.

against
contro

Other words you may know using this prefix are *contraindication, controversy, controversial, counterflow,* and *counteroffensive.* In each case the prefix means _____
____.

against

The clue you have chosen for remembering *contra* is _____ .

your choice

1-8
The prefix of the word depreciate is _____ and means _____.

de
down

The longer you own a car, the more its value *appreciates* or *depreciates* (unless it is a classic or antique). _____

depreciates

The prefix *de* means "down" or "away."
"The military take-over caused the dethronement of King Francis." The King was taken _____ from his throne.

down or away

Knowing that *de* means "down" can serve as a memory device. The denominator of a fraction is the part that is _____, or the _____ part of the fraction.

down
lower or bottom

The degeneracy of young people has been an age-old complaint of their elders. The old folks feel that the youngsters have fallen _____ from the high qualities set by the older generation. And, of course, each younger generation has disagreed with them.

down

A depository is a place where something has been put _____ for safekeeping.

down or away

"The troops had been demoralized by lack of support." In other words, their morale, or confidence, had been taken _____.

away

To say "take away the magnetic power," the word to use is _____*magnetize.*

de(magnetize)

To set down or fix the limits is to _____-limit.

de(limit)

"The problem you have chosen to study is too broad." You must _____limit it.

de(limit)

One can also set or mark down the lines of something by a sketch or drawing. The verb meaning "to set down or mark the lines" is _____*lineate.*

de(lineate)

New words are added to English constantly. Listen for those that use old prefixes. One commonly heard is "Passengers will deplane at 10:20." A short way of saying that passengers will get _____ from the airplane at the arrival time of 10:20.

down

Any of the words used above could serve as a clue to help you remember that *de* means _____. Or you may prefer making up a sentence that associates meaning for you,

down

such as "The denominator is the down part of a fraction." Or, "To degrade is to down-grade."

Your clue for remembering is _____ _____ .

your choice

1-9

The murder victim had been dismembered.

His body was in pieces. This information comes from the prefix _____ meaning _____ .

dis
apart

You already know the prefix *dis* when it means "not," as in *dislike*. Another meaning for *dis* is "apart" or "apart from" (separate).

To cause a mob to scatter or break apart is to _____perse a mob.

dis(perse)

A verb meaning "to separate what has been joined together" is _____*join*. You can form a noun from this verb in two ways: a _____*joining* or a _____*junction*.

dis(join)

dis(joining)/dis(junction)

A synonym for *disjunction* which uses a different root is _____*union*.

The prefix *dis* literally means _____ and indicates a _____tion.

dis(union)
apart
separa(tion)

Dis in the sense of "not" (as in *dislike*) appears in the word *dissimilar*, literally meaning "_____ similar or alike."

not

"Our diplomatic relationships with that country were dissevered in 1960." In the word *dissever*, does *dis* mean "apart" or "not"? _____

apart

The word *dissimulate* means "to conceal or disguise, to be a hypocrite." The root *simul* comes from *simil* meaning "like." In the literal meaning of this word *dis* means _____.

> not

A rambling speaker digresses from his topic; he and his topic go _____. The prefix _____ becomes _____ in the word *digresses*.

> apart or separate
> dis/di

To form one word meaning "to break apart," a root meaning "break" is needed, as well as a prefix to show the direction of the break. The word is _____*fract*. The prefix is _____, and the letter _____ has been assimilated to _____.

> dif(fract)
> dis/s
> f

This literal meaning of "break apart" is applied to the spreading or modification of light and other rays under special conditions.

Have you now noticed that prefixes ending in consonants are the ones which assimilate in order to pronounce the new word more easily? *Ad, com,* and now *dis.*

In addition to the words already used, other familiar words you may want to use to associate *dis* with the meaning "apart" could be *discard, dismiss,* or *disappear.* These words clearly carry the meaning of _____.

> apart

The negative meaning of "not" shows up in such words as *disability, distrust,* or *discontent.*

Your clue for the meaning "apart" is _____. Your clue for the meaning "not" is _____.

> your choice
> your choice

1-10
In the following sentence, supply the missing prefix meaning "out":

A word meaning "to erupt or break out," as with measles, is _____*anthem.*	ex(anthem)

A common prefix is *ex* meaning "out" or "from."

An easy association to make is the word *exit*, the door to go _____ .   →   out

If you need a tooth pulled out, you go to the dentist to have the tooth _____tracted.   →   ex(tracted)

An exorcist is one who drives _____ evil spirits. You may remember the book and movie *The Exorcist.*   →   out

In the case whereby a body has been buried but there remains doubt as to the cause of death, the body may be _____-humed, literally "taken _____ of the ground."   →   ex(humed) / out

To expedite an order literally means "to get the foot (*ped*) _____" and has a dictionary meaning of "to accelerate or speed the progress of." Quit dragging your feet?   →   out

Expatriate, extort, extremity all have something to do with _____ .   →   out

Expatriate means _____ of the native land, an exile.   →   out

Extort means to twist _____ money by illegal means.   →   out

Extremity means the _____ermost part, your foot for example.   →   out(ermost)

Since the letter *x* is a consonant, you can expect _____ to take place when joining *ex* to a root.   →   assimilation

In the words *effect* (to make out or bring about) and *effluence* (the flowing out), the prefix is really _____ but has been assimilated to _____ .   →   ex / ef

In a previous frame (1-5) the word *afferent* was used, showing the assimilation of the prefix *ad* to _____. The opposite of *afferent* is *efferent*. In the term *efferent* the nerve impulses are traveling _____ from the central nervous system.

	af
	out

Escape is another example of assimilation. However, the letter *x* is more often dropped or omitted. Consider these examples:

educate, to lead out
evoke, to call out
elongate, to stretch out

In addition to assimilation, the *x* of the prefix *ex* may be _____ or _____.

	dropped
	omitted

Your word or phrase to associate *ex* with the meaning "out" is _____.

your choice

1-11

The prefix of *inability* means _____; in the word *inspect* the prefix means _____.

	not
	in or into

The prefix *in* means "into," "in," or "on," and usually carries one of these related meanings when used with nouns and verbs. (Not to be confused with the negative "not" — which comes next.)

Fuel injection means that fuel is hurled or forced _____ the combustion chambers of an engine.

in or into

"Willy Jones has been incarcerated." If you know that *carcer* means "prison," translate *incarcerated:* "Willy Jones is _____ _____."

	in
	prison

The opposite of *exhale* is _____.

inhale

To illuminate a room means to throw light into the room. Say *in* + *luminate* to yourself: *inluminate.* Hard? Change the *n* to _____ for smooth saying: _____.

l/illuminate

The root meaning "drink" is *bibe.* If you drink in a liquid, you _____bibe.

im(bibe)

What is the original spelling of the above prefix? _____

in

The word *inhale* could well be a good choice to associate *in* with the meaning "in." But, obviously, the Latin prefix is the same as the English word *in,* so what is there to associate?

A second meaning for *in* is "not." *In* is used frequently with adjectives and nouns to give a negative meaning.

An act that is not decent is _____decent.

in(decent)

"The results of the experiment were of no consequence." They were _____con-sequential.

in(consequential)

"The course of these events is irreversible." Does *in* mean "in" or "not"? _____.

not

The prefix is _____ and has been assimilated to _____.

in

ir

Make these adjectives negative: *secure,* _____ ; *fallible,* _____ ;

insecure/infallible

transitive, _____.

intransitive

Inject, invert, inspect — adjectives? _____.

no

Therefore, *in* probably means _____.

in or into

Invincible, invisible, insane — adjectives? _____. Therefore, *in* probably means _____.

yes

not

Illegal, illegible, illicit. The *n* of *in* does not

combine smoothly with *l*. It is assimilated to _____ in _____*legal*, _____*legible*, and _____*licit*.

l/il(legal)/il(legible)
il(licit)

N and *p* do not join easily; hence something that is not passable is _____passable.

im(passable)

When the way is totally obstructed, whether a road or the meeting of men's minds, an _____passe has occurred.

im(passe)

If you were not already familiar with the meaning "not" for *in* as a prefix, you may want to use an associate word. In addition to the words already used there are also *insomnia, insane, indirect, inconsiderate,* and *inactive.* Choose one that has a special meaning for you. Your associate word is _____ _____.

your
choice

1-12
An interjection such as *Oh!* or *Well!* is a part of speech, thrust _____ the grammatical parts of a sentence, as shown by the prefix _____.

between

inter

The prefix *inter* means "between."

The person who is acting between others, for example, between union and management, is called an _____mediary.

inter(mediary)

Regnum means "rule" or "reign"; therefore, the time between two reigns is called an _____regnum.

inter(regnum)

Here is an example of how knowing the prefix helps with spelling:

The relations between races of people are called _____racial relationships.

inter(racial)

Interregnum is another example of the prefix as an aid to spelling—there are two *r*'s.

An intercom is a communication system
_____ two people.   between

NOTE: *Intercom* is an example of the way we shorten words; *intercom* is
short for *intercommunication system*. The prefix *com* is now serving as a
root. *Gas* for *gasoline* and *tach* for *tachometer* are other examples.

A sentence to associate could be "The interstate highways contain many interchanges." Highways_____ states	between
contain many locations for changing from one highway to another, _____ highways. You may well prefer another word containing the prefix *inter*.	between
Your choice of a word, phrase, or sentence to help you remember that *inter* means _____ is _____.	between/your choice

---

1-13	
Obloquy is unpleasant to hear about yourself since it means speech made_____	against
you as shown by the prefix _____.	ob

Ob means "against."

When you make an objection to an idea or suggestion, you are _____ the idea.	against
A barricade placed _____ your progress on a highway is an_____struction.	against ob
Obverse means "turned against you." The obverse side of a coin is the side turned _____ your view.	against
She remained hardened against all of her family's efforts to persuade her to seek medical help. In a word, she remained _____durate.	ob(durate)

Once again assimilation can be expected
because this prefix ends with a _____ .

consonant

A word meaning "to close against entry"
can be formed by combining *ob* and *clude*
(close). It would be spelled *o*____*clude*.
The prefix is really _____ .

c (occlude)
ob

To offend, or give offense to, literally
means to strike _____ . The prefix is really _____ , but the letter _____
has been assimilated to _____ for easier
saying.

against
ob/b
f

Forces that may be placed or balanced
against each other are *o*____*posable* forces.
Obposable is hard to say; _____*posable* is
easier.

p (opposable)
op(posable)

Occasionally an unusual word has appeal
as an association. What about *obfuscate* (to
darken against, to confuse)? Or you may prefer words you already know but may not
have considered the meaning of the prefix,
such as *oblige* (to bind against, owe a favor
or service). Other possibilities are *obscure,
obscene,* or *obstinate.*
Your way of associating *ob* with the meaning _____ is _____ .

against/your choice

1-14
To peruse a list means to read the first few
items and stop.
　Right or wrong? _____ because
_____ means _____ .

wrong
per/through
or thoroughly

The prefix *per* means "through" or "thoroughly."

If a person shows persistency in his demands, he doesn't ask just once, but literally
stands _____ the whole ordeal
until he gets his way.

through

A perforation is a hole, literally "a boring
_____." To perform is to carry
out _____, to accomplish.

through
thoroughly

For something to be permanent it must
remain through, endure. Perhaps *permanent*
makes an association for you. If not, try "The
tobacco smoke has permeated the air in this
room." The smoke has spread _____
the air.

through

A ticket that allows you to pass through
the admission gate is a _____mit.

per(mit)

Now try a few more difficult words.

"He especially wanted the peroration of
his first speech to be effective." Can you
spot *per* and *oration*—"through speaking"?
Well, the part of the speech that comes when
one is through presenting his message is
the _____; therefore, *peroration*
must mean "a formal _____ to
a speech."

summary or conclusion
summary or conclusion

"His perspicacity saved him from being
cheated; he was able to see_____
their scheme." A beautiful contrast between
the elegance of a derivative (perspicacity)
and the plain talk of literal meanings!

through

The root *tin* means "to hold," so that the
word *pertinacious* can be translated to "holding _____ to a purpose." A syno-
nym would be _____sistent, which also
includes the idea of "through to the finish."

thoroughly
per(sistent)

If you have not yet found an associa-

tion, try *perspiration,* literally: a breathing
through," the substance that passes _____
your pores upon exertion.

    What clue have you chosen? _____

through

your choice

1-15
You may have studied roots and prefixes
previously; if so, you have studied them
_____ now.

    The prefix giving this information is

_____.

before

pre

The prefix *pre* means "before" (time) or
"in front of" (place).

    A word part fixed in front of a root is a
_____fix.

pre(fix)

    Perhaps *prefix* will be your clue word.
Other words which could serve are *preschool,*
predict, or *prepayment.* Or you may prefer a
phrase, such as "be prepared" or "present
arms." Any of these will help you to remember that *pre* means _____.

before

    "The decision was made according to
precedent." That is, examples which had
gone _____ were used as a guide.

before

    In grammar the predicate is that part
of the sentence which is a statement about
the subject, but the subject is that part
which has gone _____ the statement
(*dic* = say).

    Substitute one word for the phrase in
parentheses in this sentence: The subject
(goes before) _____cedes the predicate.

before

pre(cedes)

    From the use of the noun *predicate* above,

can you see where the verb *predicate* means "to affirm a statement or assertion from something which has gone before it"? "These conclusions are predicated on the results of the experiment."

The prefatory section of a book is located in the ——————— of a book, the preface.   front

Precognition means knowing about an event ——————— it happens.   before

The prefix which means "before" is ———————. Your clue for remembering is ———————   pre/your
———————.   choice

1-16

Proposition, proponent, and *procession* share the prefix ——————— meaning ———————,   pro/before
———————, and ———————.   for/forth

The prefix pro means "before" (both place and time), "for" (in favor of), and "forth" (forward).

Promise is an easy clue to use. A promise is an agreement to do something ———————   before
the time you have to do it.

"Pro and con" was used earlier to show the meaning of *con (contra),* against. The phrase can have a double use if you remember that "pro and con" mean ——————— and   for
———————.   against

A familiar word showing the meaning "forth" is *proceed.* When you proceed you go ——————— or ———————.   forth/forward

If you stay flexible about the meanings of *pro,* perhaps just one clue word can serve.

Consider the words used in the express frame:

A proposition is something put _____ a person or group for consideration.

before

The *proponent* of the proposition is the person who is _____ it.

for

The *procedure* is the process through which the person or group goes _____ ; to decide whether or not to accept the proposition.

forth or forward

Hobbes suggests that men have a natural proclivity to hurt each other. Proclivity means they have a leaning _____ hurting each other.

for

A doctor decides the treatment of a disease on the basis of his prognosis. Prognosis means knowing (*gnos*) _____ what is to come.

before

If an early Roman thought the gods were angry with him, he needed to do something so they would be in favor of him, for him. He therefore made sacrifices to make the gods favorable, to _____pitiate the gods. He hoped the sacrifice would be _____pitiatory.

pro(pitiate)

pro(pitiatory)

Something that is before in place is forward; hence something that has been thrust _____ is a _____jectile.

forward/pro(jectile)

In anatomy a muscle which draws a part forward or extends it from the body is called a _____tractor.

pro(tractor)

The adjective *prophylactic* means "guarding against a disease." The prefix _____ shows that steps have been taken before infection.

pro

Pro in the word *prophylactic* means_____; in place or time? _____

before

time

In the following blank write the clue that helps you to remember *pro*: _____ .	your choice

---

1-17 *Re* has two meanings. *Repay* carries the meaning _____, and *reread* carries the meaning _____.	back again

---

The prefix *re* has two meanings. The first one is "back." If you pay back a friend the money he loaned you, you _____pay him.	re(pay)
The bend in a drainpipe prevents the flowing back of sewer gas. It prevents the _____flux of sewer gas.	re(flux)
That which literally sits back, or remains behind, is a _____sidue or _____siduum.	re/re

NOTE: Notice the ending *um* in *residuum*. This ending comes from Latin and is a singular ending; the plural is *a*. For example: *memorandum, memoranda; datum, data*. The plural of *residuum*, therefore, is *residua*.

Reconstituted orange juice is juice which has been put _____ to its original condition.	back
The second meaning of *re* is "again." If you calculate a math problem but make a mistake, you must _____calculate it.	re(calculate)
Recollection is the act of calling_____ ideas — of remembering.	back
When you reread a sentence, you read it _____, but surely not re-reread.	again
The historical period which *re*presented a	

revival of culture is known as the _____nais-
sance (*nais* = born).

Re(naissance)

The word *resurrection* means "a rising
from the dead." It literally means "rising
- _____."

again

Re is such a common prefix that you may
not need a special clue since you probably
first learned it in the second or third grade.
In case you missed it then, maybe one of
these words can serve: *repeat, reproduce,*
or *return.* What helps you? _____

your choice

1-18
The prefix meaning "under" is _____.

sub

    A word said below, or under, voice level
is _____vocal.

sub(vocal)

Sub means "under."
    The easiest way to remember this meaning
is probably the word meaning a ship that
can travel under the surface of an ocean,
a _____. The prefix even serves

submarine

as the name for such a ship, as in the familiar quote "Sighted _____, sank same."

sub

    The part of your mind that is under, or be-
low, conscious level is your_____
mind.

subconscious

Sublunar literally means "_____ the
moon."

under

    Sublunar is an example in which the literal
meaning is only the first step. The context
or way in which *sublunar* is used will tell
you its specific meaning—whether "under
the influence of the moon or within its orbit"

or "under in a physical position, within the influence of the earth, earthly."

"The bleeding was subcutaneous." That is, it was _____ the skin.   under

Submaxilla is the technical term for the upper or lower jaw? _____   lower

NOTE: Do you recall that the ending *a* has been given to you as a plural form from classical Latin? *Submaxilla* illustrates that *a* is also a singular form whose plural is *ae: submaxilla, submaxillae; alumna, alumnae.* These are feminine endings; thus an alumnae chapter is a group of female graduates.

Have you noticed that *sub* ends with a _____? Therefore, you can expect _____ .   consonant
                                                              assimilation

As a general rule, if you see the pattern *su* — — (double consonant) plus the rest of the word, try "under" or "below."

If you fall under the power of the flu bug, you _____cumb to the flu.   suc(cumb)

A word part fixed under a word (at the end, since we write horizontally rather than vertically) is a _____fix.   suf(fix)

The word part fixed before a word is a _____fix.   pre(fix)

If one idea is carried under another idea, making one lead to another, we call it a su_____gestion. The prefix is really _____ but has been assimilated to _____ .   g (suggestion)/sub
                                                              sug

The dictionary defines *supplicate* as "to make a humble entreaty, especially to implore God." Literally, *sub* meaning _____ and *plic* meaning "fold" or "bend"—a proper position in which to implore God.   under

The adjective *surreptitious* literally means

"seizing" or "taking under," hence doing something in secret or by stealth. The prefix _____ has been assimilated to _____.

sub/sur

Harry Harlow is famous for experimentally rearing monkeys with surrogate mothers.

To get at the meaning of *surrogate*, try the general rule: If you see the pattern *su — —*, try the prefix *sub*. That would mean some kind of _____ mother. Can you take the step from "under" to "in place of"?

under

Imagination can help you see how these meanings connect. If a picture in a frame has another picture under it and you remove the top one, then the *under* picture is now *in place of* the top picture. Memory courses depend on making just such mental pictures of two things which you wish to associate. In this instance you associate *under* and *in place of*.

Harlow used substitute mothers in his experiments with monkeys.

In this sentence *sub* has the meaning of
_____ _____ _____.

in place of

What is your associative word to remember that *sub* means _____ ? _____

under/your choice

In this first group of prefixes Latin accounted for most of them. There is only one Greek prefix in this first group.

Greek

1-19
The word *embryo* carries the prefix _____ and means _____.

em
in or inside

The Greek prefix meaning "in" or "inside" is *em*. Its similarity to the Latin prefix *in* should help you remember it.

The word *embryo* literally means "_____ the swelling" (*bryein* = to swell). The term is applied to a young animal or plant while still contained _____ the seed or womb.

A plan which is still in an imperfect state, still being formed, is in an _____bryonic state.

in

in

em(bryonic)

Classical elements are also combined with words of other origin. For example, the English word *power*. A person empowered to act is literally _____ power.

in

A verb meaning "to place a corpse in a tomb" can be built from _____ and *tomb*. *Emtomb*? Change the *m* to _____ for easier saying.

To put into chains is to _____chain. The letter _____ assimilates to _____.

em

n

en(chain)

m/n

The decision to use *m* or *n* is made according to the letter of the root to which the prefix is added. If a *b* or *p* begins the root, then the spelling of the prefix is _____; otherwise the Greek prefix meaning "in" is spelled _____.

em

en

"Typhoid fever is endemic to this region." Typhoid fever is found _____ the people (*dem*) of this region.

in

A variant spelling is *endo*. If a parasite is internal, it is an _____ parasite.

endo(parasite)

Ento is another variation and often interchanges with *endo*, so that an endoparasite may also be an _____parasite.

Zoon is Greek for an animal; therefore, the technical name for an animal living inside or within the body is _____*zoon*.

ento(parasite)

ento(zoon)

The forms *em, en, endo, ento* should give you no special trouble since you already use *in* and *into*—simply the same thing.

What have you chosen as your clue?

_____

your choice

QUICK REVIEW OF PREFIXES

As a quick check on your knowledge of the prefixes studied in this chapter, you are to read the following story as if it were written entirely in standard English. Capitalized prefixes have replaced certain English words. Do not take time to write for this first review, but go through the story substituting the English meaning for the prefixes. If you hesitate or get one wrong, check back to the teaching frames.

Once upon a time there was a little girl who lived IN a cottage at the edge of the woods. Her mother had made PRO her a little red hood which she always wore whenever she went EX. For this reason she was called Little Red Riding Hood.

in
for

out

One day Red Riding Hood was playing COM her dolls SUB the big oak tree when her mother called AD her PER the open window.

with/under
to/through

"Take this basket of goodies to Grandma. She is IN feeling well."

"Yes, mother, right DE."

She propped her dolls CONTRA the tree, promising them that she would be RE very soon.

not
away
against
back

Little Red Riding Hood ran to get the basket, but PRE she left, she put on her red hood.

before

Her mother had packed so many things in the basket that Red Riding Hood had to hold it INTER both arms and close OB her side to carry it. But the little girl was happy to carry the heavy basket because it was for Grandma. DIS from her father and mother, Grandma was her very favorite person.

between/against

apart

And so Red Riding Hood started off to visit Grandma. She followed the path which took her deep EM the woods.

in

ROOTS

Since prefixes are used with roots, it is logical to learn some roots to go with the first group of prefixes you have learned. Clues are supplied for the roots in this section, but wherever a prefix is used which you have already studied, no help is given.

As with the prefixes, most of the roots used frequently in high-level words are from Latin.

Latin

1989388

1-20

In order to intercept a message, a spy has to _____ the message between the sender and recipient.

take or seize

In addition to *intercept*, another word in the sentence above that comes from the same root is _____.

recipient

The root *cept* comes from a Latin verb meaning "to take or seize."

NOTE: Derived roots often have several spellings because Latin verbs have principal parts just as English verbs: *take, took, taken; send, sent, sent; capere, cepi, ceptus.*

Something taken out of the ordinary is ex_____ionable.

cept (exceptionable)

Except means "to take out of the whole"; so if you are an exception to a rule, you _____ yourself out of the whole group and do not need to follow the rules.

take

Instead of "take out," make a word meaning "take to," _____. But if you are not able to take to a suggestion, then the suggestion is _____able to you. The meaning "not take to" is represented by the word elements _____, _____, and _____.

accept

unaccept(able)

un/ac/cept

"Brown's conceptual treatment of the organization was well received." Brown had conceptualized, literally_____ _____, the important features to be considered and had formed one basic plan accordingly, his con_____ of the organization.

taken together

cept (concept)

Under the prefix *contra* you studied the word *contraceptive*. The literal meaning is "something _____ _____."

taken against

The adjective *reciprocal* means "mutual, a giving and taking." The prefix is _____ and means _____. The root is _____ and means _____.
The engine in which the piston is taken back and forth in a straight line is called a _____rocating engine.
Another spelling of *cept* is _____.

re
back/cip
take

recip(rocating)
cip

Cap is also a root but formed from another principal part of *capere* (to take). *Capable* means "having the power or ability to _____."

take

Capacity, capacitate, capacious, capstand, capability—all contain the root _____ meaning _____.

cap
take

Capt is a variation. When an army takes a town, it _____ures the town.

capt(ures)

A reception line is also called a receiving line. Instead of the spelling *cept,* in the word *receiving* the root is _____.

ceiv

To practice deceit is to _____ a person away from the truth. The root *ceit* is another form of _____.	take cept
Deception, capacity, captivity, perceive, recipient—all have roots that carry the idea of _____ing.	tak(ing)
Since principal parts of English verbs can cause problems, then it is no surprise to learn that principal parts of Latin verbs will also need special attention. Straight memorization can succeed as *cap, cep, cept* all mean _____. Associative words can be chosen according to what works for you. What have you decided? _____	take or seize memorization or your choice

---

1-21

The root of *reproduction* is _____ and means _____. A variant spelling is _____.	duct lead or led/duc

---

The root *duct* means "lead" or "led." To lead a group of people together through a museum is to con_____ them.	duct (conduct)
A metal which will not lead electricity through it, that is, transmit electricity, is called a noncon_____or.	duct (nonconductor)
A material or metal that is easily led or worked is _____ile.	duct(ile)
An aquaduct is a structure to lead water (*aqua*). A viaduct is a high, narrow roadway (*via*) to _____ trains across a gorge.	lead
The lacrimal glands discharge their fluids	

by way of tear ducts, pathways to _____ the tears to the eye surface. However, the ductless glands have no way to _____ out their products, but rather discharge them directly into the bloodstream.	lead lead
To reason by induction is to _____ your thoughts from the particular into the general.	lead
To reason by deduction is to _____ your thoughts away from the general to the particular. Associate the prefix only with the general statement.	lead
Another form for lead is *duc*, as in *traduce*. *Traduce* means "to _____ across into disgrace" (shame with slander).	lead
A variation in spelling is *duit*, as in con_____, a pipe for leading electric wires.	duit (conduit)
No reminder of finding an association was given at the beginning of this section. What about the conductor of an orchestra, who con_____ or _____ the musicians? What clue works for you? _____	ducts(conducts)/leads your choice

---

1-22 A facsimile is a copy which has been _____ similar to the original. The root is _____, also spelled _____, _____, and _____.	made fac/fic/fact fect

---

The root *fac* comes from a Latin verb meaning "make" or "do.". If you can make or do something with little effort, you are said to be _____ile.	fac(ile)

A man employed to do all kinds of work is called a _____totum. Did *totum* remind you of *total*, all?	fac(totum)
A task that is not easy to do is dif-_____ult.	fic (difficult)
An act done by a pontiff (bishop) is a ponti_____al act. Another spelling of *fac* is _____.	fic (pontifical) fic
An officer is a person who is assigned to _____ certain things, or duties. To hold office means that you _____ things for other members of the group.	do do
A factor may be a person who makes or does something, say, transacts business. In mathematics, *factor* is the name for any of the numbers or symbols which are mul-tiplied to _____ a product.	make
Still another meaning of *factor* is in this sentence: "Poverty has been a factor in his development." In other words, poverty has something to _____ with his de-velopment. *Factor* carries the basic meaning_____ or _____.	do make do
Many of our tastes in food or drink are factitious. That is, they have been _____; we were not born with them. A variant spell-ing of *fac* is _____. Still another spelling is *fect*. A confection is a sweet_____ by a con_____ioner.	made fact made fect (confectioner)
Infect and *effect* also have the root mean-ing _____.	make or do

The variant spellings *fac, fic, fact,* and *fect* mean that all principal parts of the Latin verb are used in English. As you worked through this section, did you select a clue that has meaning for you?

Did the word *factory* occur to you as an association? A factory is a place where things are _____. What did you do about learning this root? _____

made
your choice

1-23
A coniferous tree _____ cones. The root is _____. A variant spelling is _____.

bears or carries
fer
lat

When a farmer wants his land to bear abundantly, he _____tilizes it.

Have you ever been on a ferryboat? You used it to _____ you across the river.

The root *fer* is most often used with a prefix to show in what direction the carrying is being done.

fer(tilizes)

bear or carry

A conference is a meeting where people _____ ideas together.

carry or bear

A transfer of title to property is a process to _____ title across to the new owner.

carry

A principal part of Latin *ferre* (to bear or carry) is *latus*, from which we get the root *lat*.

To translate a foreign language means to _____ the meaning across from one language to another.

carry

If one idea can be carried back to, or connected with, another idea, we say the ideas are _____ed.

relat(ed)

Supply the words needed in these two statements:

If you bring your wish or desire down so that the wishes of another person take over, you _____ to his wishes. You show _____ence.

defer
defer(ence)

If you are given a choice between two items, you will choose the one that "bears before" the other. In other words you will _____ one item over the other.

prefer

Efferent nerve pathways are those which _____ the nerve impulses _____ from the nervous system.

carry/out

Fer means _____. What is your special clue word for remembering?_____

bear or carry
your choice

1-24
Genealogy is the name for the study of the descent of a person. The root is _____ and means _____.

gen
race, birth, or kind

Since the Greek root for race, birth, or kind is *gen*, then the book of the Bible dealing with the origin of man is appropriately named _____esis.

Gen(esis)

The name for descendants or children, those members of the race brought forth or forward, is _____*y*.

progen(y)

The generic term for Golden Delicious, Winesap, Jonathan, and Roman Beauty is _____; the root meaning "kind" or "race" (class of object) is _____.

apple
gen

The body organs concerned with sexual

reproduction (production of the race, birth) are appropriately named the _____itals.

gen(itals)

A defect present at birth is called congenital. The literal translation of *congenital* is _____ _____.

born/with

Eu means "well" or "good"; therefore, the science of eugenics is concerned with the good or improvement of the _____.

race

When you say "in general" or "generally speaking," you mean that your remarks apply to the whole class or _____ of objects referred to.

kind

The number of people born and living at the same time is called a _____eration.

gen(eration)

A dynamo "gives birth" to electricity. Another name for the machine that produces electricity is _____erator.

gen(erator)

What word in this practice is the clue for you to remember that *gen* means _____, _____, or _____.

birth
race/kind

1-25

The root of *transmitter* is _____ and means _____. The variant spelling is _____.

mitt or mit
send/miss

The root *mitt* (*mit* as a final syllable) means "send."

To commit a criminal to prison is to _____ him in with other criminals.

send

Fire emits heat and smoke; fire _____ out heat and smoke.

sends

Something that "has been sent" is indicated by the Latin verb part *missus*.

Something that has been sent into space is a _____ile.

A missionary is a person _____ out by a church.

miss(ile)
sent

A disease which can be sent across from one person to another is called trans_____ ible.

miss (transmissible)

Both *miss* and *mit* come from the Latin verb meaning "to _____."

send

Sometimes when a suffix is added to the root *mit*, the letter *t* doubles.

A committee is a group of people_____ together to do a particular job.

sent

Spell the word which can be translated "that which you send back": _____*ance*.

remitt(ance)

The common phrase "to transmit a message" could be your clue. Or perhaps you *transmit* over your C-B radio?

Have other words or phrases using *mit* or *miss*, meaning _____ come to mind? Possibly "Mission Impossible," submit, admit, permit? What clue works?_____

send

your choice

1-26

A pose is the position in which you _____ yourself. The root is _____ .

put or place

pos

The root *pos* comes from a Latin verb meaning "to put or place." This Latin verb is *ponere*, whose root is *pon*; however, we will call the root *pos*, since this is the form more widely used in English.

"The English assignment is to put together some words." The instructor wants you to write a _____.

composition

The name of the person who sets up type for printing, literally, one who puts together, is a _____*or.*

composit(or)

The United States Treasury Department uses Fort Knox as a depository for its gold bullion. It has _____, or _____ _____, its gold bullion at Fort Knox.

placed/put
down

Expositor literally means "one who_____ _____." He sets forth for you an explanation; he ex*pos*es the meaning.

puts
out

There is a grammatical construction in which one noun is "placed to" another noun, both of them referring to the same person or thing. In the phrase "the poet Burns," Burns is in _____ition to *poet.*

appos(ition)

A common error in typing is to put one letter in place of another, that is, to place them across, for example, *hte.* The *h* and *t* have been trans_____.

posed (transposed)

Pon is a variant spelling. A proponent is one who _____ himself _____ _____ _____ an issue, that is, one who argues for something. An opponent is the person who _____ himself _____ an issue.

places/in
favor of

places
against

The part of speech called a preposition is that little word _____ before a noun. "The gift is in the box." The word *in* is put before the word *box.*

put or placed

To propose is to _____ _____.

put before

(The word *proposition* was used to introduce the prefix. Did you remember it?) A different version of the verb "to propose" is "to propound." A variant spelling of the root *pos* is _____ .

| | pound |

When two small words are put together to make one word, it is called a _____ word. Bookmark, afternoon, and flashgun are examples of _____ words.

compound

compound

Other things can be compounded, such as when the pharmacist _____ _____ _____ the drugs called for in your prescription.

puts together

Remember the term *exponent* in algebra? It is the symbol _____ outside and to the right of another symbol.

put or placed

What do you call a piece of wood or timber placed upright in the ground? _____
When you place a public notice on display, you _____ it.
Another spelling of *pos* is _____ .

post

post
post

The Latin root meaning "to put or place" appears in *position, propound, exponent,* and *post*. The possible spellings of the root in the four words are _____ , _____ , _____ , and _____ .

pos/pound/pon
post

Pos is another root requiring special attention because of its variant spellings. What clue is helping you to remember? _____ _____

your
choice

1-27

Simplicity literally means "one (*sim*) _____"
—not complicated. The root is _____ . A variant spelling of this root is _____ .

fold
plic
plex

The most unusual root in this chapter is *plic* meaning "to fold."

A problem that has many folds is a com_____ated problem (folded together).

plic (complicated)

To implicate a person in a dispute is to fold him into it. A process making many folds in numbers is multi_____ation.

plic (multiplication)

"Fold" is the meaning for the root _____.
To duplicate a picture is to make it two _____.

plic

fold (twofold)

"The solution to this problem is simplicity itself." The word *simplicity* literally means "one _____" and therefore is uncomplicated.

fold

Uncomplicated can be translated _____ _____.

not
folded together

An apartment complex literally means that several units have been _____ _____.

folded
together

Duplex, perplex, and *simplex* also use the variant spelling _____.

plex

Implicate could be a clue word. Have you not sometimes asked "What are the implications?" What are the hidden factors, those _____ _____?

folded in
your choice

What clue are you using?_____

1-28
A spirometer measures _____. The root carrying this meaning is _____.

breath
spir

The root *spir* comes from *spirare,* meaning "to breathe."

When a person dies, we say he expires.
The _____ has gone _____.
   To breathe in is to inhale or_____.

                      breath/out
                        inspire

   The name for our breathing again and
again is _____*ation.*
   A device which helps us to breathe again
is a _____ator.

                      respir(ation)

                      respir(ator)

   Perspire literally means "to_____
_____," which is what the pores
of our skin do. When breathing is especially heavy, matter is emitted which is
called _____ation.

                      breathe
                      through

                      perspir(ation)

   The Latin noun for a breath was *spiratus,*
coming from this same Latin verb. This
noun gives us the word *spirit,* meaning "a
vital principle which gives life, that is, gives
_____ to."

                      breath

   One association that comes readily to
mind is antiperspirant, certainly a common
term. Or the Holy Spirit, the breath of life.
   What clue has meaning for you to recall
that *spir* means_____?_____

                      breath/your choice

1-29
The conditions obtaining in Paris made
it the cultural center of the world.
   Obtaining contains the root _____ meaning "to _____." Other spellings of
this root are _____ and _____.

                      tain
                      hold
                      ten/tin

The root *tain* means "to hold."
   Obtain means "to hold by effort or occupy, to get possession of"—literally, to
_____ _____.

                      hold against

"The state obtained right-of-way through the courts." If the courts were involved, you can be sure that the state _____ _____ the property owner's wishes.

held
against

"The vote was 37 to 10 with three states abstaining." Three states _____ back their votes.

held

Spelling sometimes changes slightly as the form of the word changes. The sentence above could be reworded to ". . . 37 to 10 with three abstentions." *Tain* has changed to _____.

ten

The good student retains much of what he reads; he _____ it in his mind. In other words, he is re_____tive.

holds
ten (retentive)

The tenets of the church are those beliefs which the members _____.

hold

"I cannot hold with the arguments you have presented." They are un_____able.

ten

The verb *pertain* means "to hold through" —"through" in the sense of "thoroughly." The person who is pertinacious has this quality of enduring or _____ through. An alternate spelling of *ten* is _____.

holding

tain

A synonym for *chastity* is *continence*, meaning literally "a _____ _____ of desires and passions." In other words, restraint.

holding
together

Another use of the literal meaning "hold together" of "hold with" is for the person unable to hold back, or *retain*, the natural evacuations of his body. Since he cannot con _____ himself, he is termed _____ent.

tain (contain)
incontin(ent)

Tin and *ten* are variations of the root _____ meaning _____.	tain/hold
Did any word or phrase in this practice interest you as a clue? What associative device have you chosen? _____	your choice

---

1-30 Tendrils are the leafless parts of certain plants (such as peas or grapes) that _____ or reach to some kind of support. The root of *tendril* is _____. A variant spelling is _____.	stretch tend tens

---

The root *tend* means "to stretch." A tough cord of connective tissue stretched between a muscle and some other part of your body is called a _____on.	tend(on)
A different spelling of *tend* is *tens.* Rubber can easily be stretched; it has a high _____ile strength.	tens(ile)
A *tensor* is a muscle that _____ a part.	stretches
A third spelling *ten* is easily confused with *ten* meaning "to hold." You may need to try both meanings to see which one fits the sense of the sentence. The phrase "extenuating circumstances" means the act was less wrong than it appears. The literal meaning is "weakened" or "_____ out."	stretched
In statistics there is a correction for attenuation of a correlation coefficient. This is a necessary correction because random	

errors of measurement weaken, or _____, this measure between two variables.

stretch

The variant spellings of the root meaning "to stretch" are _____, _____, and _____.

tend/tens/ten

The spelling *ten* also means _____, so that in trying to derive the meaning of a word in context which has the root *ten*, if the meaning "hold" does not fit into the sentence, one can try the meaning _____.

hold
stretch

Do you have a tendency to put off school work? If so, you go in the direction or _____ towards avoiding study. Or do you "stretch to," apply your mind to, in other words _____ to your assignments at the proper time?

stretch
attend

Stretch in the sense of weak or thin may appeal to you, or in the sense of reach or go. Just so you know that *tend* means _____. Clue word or phrase for you? _____

stretch
your choice

1-31
The signing of the nonintervention pact took place at the meeting convened by the President.

Two words in the above sentence represent variant spellings of the same root. The root is _____, also spelled _____ and means _____.

vent/ven
come

Ven is a root meaning "come."

"The members of the new labor union first convened in New York City." That is, they _____ _____ there. | came together

The *ven* root may also have a transitive meaning: "King George convened his ministers." That is, he caused them to _____ _____. | come together

If an event comes between two other events, it is said to inter_____. | vene (intervene)

Build one word to replace the words in parentheses: "The committee's action (comes against) _____ the law." | contravenes

"This committee's unlawful ruling is a contra_____ion of the law." An alternate spelling of the root *ven* is _____. | vent (contravention) / vent

A meeting where members convene is called a _____. | convention

"We will see how things come out." We will see _____ually. | event(ually)

The literal meaning of the word *event* is "a _____ _____"—that which happens. | coming out

Something which comes first and thus stops a subsequent happening is called a pre_____ive. | vent (preventive)

Another name for the street by which you "come to" your destination is an _____. | avenue

Monies coming back to the government in the form of taxes are called _____. The Internal _____ Service has been established to collect the taxes coming back to the government. | revenue / Revenue

The meaning "come" is expressed by the root _____ or _____. | ven/vent

Perhaps you have now practiced this root enough to have learned it for certain. If not, what association have you made? _____	your choice

1-32
Extrovert and *introvert* are psychological terms originated by Carl Jung. They share the root _____ meaning _____. | vert/turn |

Vert is a root meaning "turn."
   The terms *extrovert* and *introvert*, used to describe personality, literally mean "_____ outward" and "_____ inward" respectively. | turned/turned |

   Rights not specifically granted to the federal government revert to the states. *Revert* literally means _____ _____. | turn back |

   "The meaning of this law is incontrovertible." That is, it is so clear that no argument may be _____ _____ it. | turned against |

   "I shall now advert to other matters." *Advert* means _____ _____. | turn to |

   The merchant who wants to turn public notice to his product ad_____ises. | vert (advertises) |

   If one is turned round and round, he becomes dizzy; he suffers _____igo. Heights will also produce dizziness, that is, _____. | vert(igo)

 vertigo |

   The person opposing you is your adversary. He is _____ toward you to defend his side. A variant spelling of *vert* is _____. | turned

 vers |

A verb with the literal meaning "to turn under" is _____, that is, overthrow. The act of subverting is called sub_____ion.

subvert

vers (subversion)

A word meaning "all things viewed as one whole, that is, one turning," is uni_____.

verse (universe)

In logic a universal is defined as affirming or denying something of every member of a class as if they were all _____ as one.

turned

A university is a group of colleges all _____ to one purpose, the teaching of higher branches of learning.

turned

Any departmental funds left at the end of the fiscal year will revert to the treasurer's office. Any funds left will be _____ _____.

turned
back

An accident was averted by his quick thinking. The accident was _____ away.

turned

Any word in this practice of special help for you to remember that the root meaning "turn" is _____? What clue did you select? _____

vert
your choice

1-33

The lecture was presented by video tape. *Video* contains the root _____ meaning _____. Another spelling of this root is _____.

vid
see
vis

The Latin verb *videre* means "to see" and provides the root *vid*.

The root *vid* was used to make a new word for our modern age: *Video tape* means "tape that lets you _____, in other words, television.

see

"Action against aggressors had not been provided for." In other words, officials had not _____ ahead.

seen

From a Latin phrase *ad visum* we get the words *advice* and *advise*. The Latin phrase means "according to what is _____," so that an adviser gives an opinion according to what he _____.

seen

sees

Improvisation literally means "a not_____ ahead" and applies to music or speech which is not planned, but composed on the spot.

seeing

An endorsement on a passport showing that it has been officially seen is a _____a.

vis(a)

A familiar term to serve as a clue could be *audiovisual*, something both heard and _____. Or perhaps the word *vision* will remind you that *vid* and *vis* mean _____.

seen

see

What serves to remind you?_____

your choice

Greek

Only four Greek roots are included in this first group. As explained in the section "To the Student," Greek really comes into its own in technical terminology. The Greek forms given here may be few, but they are important.

1-34
Patriarch is the title given to the founder of a group. This information comes from

the root _____, which means _____, _____ _____, or _____.	arch/begin be first/rule

---

The Greek verb *archein* means "to begin," "to be first," or "to rule." You will have to decide by the context of the sentence which meaning to use. This program is treating *arch* as a root although sometimes it serves in the place of a prefix. For example, an archtraitor is a chief, or _____, traitor.

    first

An anarchist is one who believes in no (*an*) _____ or government.

    rule

    The word *architect* comes from two Greek words, *archi* and *tekton* meaning "a builder." *Architect* literally means "the _____ builder."

    chief or first

    The place where original records or government records are kept is called the _____ives.

    arch(ives)

    A government in which there is only one head or ruler is a mon_____ical form of government.

    arch (monarchical)

    Where there is no ruler or rule of any kind, the government (what there is left) takes an an_____ical form.

    arch (anarchical)

Decide which meaning of *arch* fits in the following blanks:

    An archetype is a prototype; that is, it is the _____ model or pattern.

    first or original

    An archbishop is a _____ bishop.

    chief

    Archaeology is the study of _____ art and customs.

    first or early

    Dictionaries frequently label some defi-

nitions as old, meanings that are now out-
dated. The label used is _____ aic.

arch(aic)

Does the word *architect* serve as an association? The architect is not only the *chief*
builder, the idea of the building was *first*
in his mind, but his plans *rule* the construction workers. If such made-up associations
make sense to you, fine. If not, what clue
are you using? _____

your choice

1-35
Eulogium literally means "a good _____."
The root is _____. Another meaning of
this root is _____.

word or speech
log
reason

Logos is Greek for word, reason, or speech.
As the final syllable in a word the spelling
may be *logue,* as in *dialogue;* however, the
basic root is *log.*
    A speech made at the end of a play (upon
it) is an epi_____.

logue (epilogue)

    A long speech made by one person is a
mono_____.

logue (monologue)

    A duologue is a dramatic piece written
for two (*duo*) _____.

speakers

You may know the word *diarrhea*, a running off of the intestines. A person who
is running off at the mouth can be said to
be suffering from _____rrhea. Did you
maintain the rhythm of the word by including the letter *o* to join *g* with *r*?

logo(rrhea)

Although this program has used roots as
a more efficient way of learning meanings
of word elements (as opposed to combining
forms), the combining form *ology* meaning

"the study of" is so commonly used that *ology* should be recognized.

Biology means "_____ _____ _____ life."

Graph means "write." Build one word meaning the study of handwriting: _____.

A word meaning the study of insects is *entom*_____.

the study
of

graphology

ology (entomology)

The meaning "the study of" suggests that words are used for thinking. This accounts for the third meaning of *log*, "reason."

The word *syllogism* literally means "a _____ing together." A more formal definition is that a syl_____ism is a form of argument consisting of three propositions; the first two are premises and the last is the conclusion.

Such a term comes from the field of *logic*, which word, in turn, carries the literal meaning of "the nature of (*ic*) _____."

reason(ing)
log

reason

Logistic, logomania, logograph, and *sinologue* all share the root _____, which may mean _____, _____, or _____.

log
word/speech/reason

Logos, The Word, the thought, and the will of God, may have special meaning for you. Select something which reminds you that words make speech, and, at least sometimes, speech makes reason. What did you select? _____

your choice

1-36

Monad means "a unit or absolutely simple entity" and has the literal meaning of _____. This information comes from the root _____.

one
mon

Mon, or *mono*, is a Greek form meaning "one" or "alone." This form is frequently labeled a prefix in word study because it is most commonly used as the first part of a word; however, it actually is a root or combining form.

A mournful poem or song for, one voice is a _____ody.

mon(ody)

The word *yes* is a _____ syllabic word.

mono

The technical term for a government ruled by one is _____y.

monarch(y)

A paper written on one particular subject is a _____graph.

mono(graph)

Lith is the Greek root for "stone." So a column made from one piece of stone is a _____.

monolith

From the idea of a column made from one great piece of stone we now use the adjective form *monolithic* to describe something which displays massive uniformity, or _____ness.

one(ness)

The Latin derivative meaning "a solo speech" is *soliloquy*. What would be the English word meaning the same thing but derived from Greek? _____

monologue

Monks live in monasteries where they lead a solitary life or life alone.

The Greek root meaning "one" or _____ appears in how many words in the above sentence? _____

alone

two

Monotony means the same old thing, *monotone*, that one can sing only one tone, what else? What word reminds you that *mono* means _____ or _____.

one/alone

1-37

A theocentric culture is one which is cen-

tered about _____. This information comes from the root _____.	God theo

---

Greek for God is *theos*, from which we get the forms *the* and *theo*.

Belief in one God is _____ism. Belief in many gods is poly_____ism.

	monothe(ism) the (polytheism)

Belief in the existence of God is _____ism.

The concept of the divine right of kings would be what form of government? _____-cracy.

	the (ism) theo(cracy)

The Greek form *pan* means "all." What would be the name of a belief or form of worship which included all gods? _____ism

	panthe(ism)

Pantheism is also the term meaning that God is in all; the whole of the universe is God.

The Pantheon in Rome is a temple built for worship of all _____.

	gods

The root for God is _____, also spelled _____. The clue to remember is _____.

	the theo your choice

QUICK REVIEW OF ROOTS

As in the quick review of prefixes, do not take time to write the meanings of the roots which have been set in capital letters. Merely say the English meaning. Any hesitation in coming up with the English meaning indicates a need to review that root.

Red Riding Hood had to stop often to PON down the basket. It was so heavy to FER. She would TEND her arms and catch her SPIR.

On one of these stops Red Riding Hood FACed friends with a family of squirrels.

	put carry stretch breath
	made

Mr. and Mrs. Squirrel had VEN to VID what
this red creature was. They exchanged
friendly LOGs and Red Riding Hood gave
them some cookies from the basket. Then
she CEPTed the basket in her arms again
and continued to follow the path which
DUCTed to Grandma's house.

come/see

words

took

led

At about the halfway point Red Riding
Hood ARCHed to have the feeling that some-
one or something was following her, always
TENing her in view but never showing
what GEN of creature he was.

began

holding
kind

Red Riding Hood said a little prayer,
"Dear THEO, make him a friendly creature."

God

Suddenly at MONO VERT in the path
there was a big wolf leaning against a tree
with arms PLICed, for all the world as if
he had been waiting for her.

one turn

folded

The wolf's big smile and friendly greeting
dispelled her fears.

"Where are you going, Little Red Riding
Hood?"

"Mother is MITTing these goodies to
Grandma. She's not feeling well today. I
must hurry. Goodbye, Mr. Wolf." And the
little girl hurried on her way.

sending

FINAL REVIEW OF CHAPTER 1

The frames in this section review all of the word elements which you
have learned thus far.

If you make a mistake, go back to the frames covering the word element
you missed. The number of the express frame for the word element is
given in each test frame.

Deducible, conductor, produce, and *reduction*
all share the root meaning _____. (1-21)

lead or led

Name the prefixes used in these four words
and give their meanings:

　　　　　Prefix　　Meaning

deduce (1-8)　　_____ _____

de/down or away

conduct (1-6) _____ _____   com/with or together
produce (1-16) _____ _____   pro/forth or forward
re (1-17) _____ _____   re/back

One *aspect* of vocabulary building is the study of roots and prefixes. Restated: One look _____ vocabulary building is the study of roots and word elements fixed _____ the root. (1-5, 1-15)

     to or toward

     before

Correlate literally means "carry back together." The part meaning "carry" is _____, and the part meaning "together" is _____. (1-23, 1-6)

     lat
     cor (com)

The roots of *intension, distend,* and *extension* convey the meaning of _____. The _____ show the direction of the root. (1-30)
     The prefix of *intension* is _____ and means _____. (1-11)
     The prefix of *distend* is _____ and means _____. (1-9)
     The prefix of *extensive* is _____ and means _____. (1-10)

     stretch
     prefixes

     in
     in or into
     dis
     apart
     ex
     out

An interruption in electric service can cause great inconvenience both to private users and to manufacturers.
     Complete these literal meanings:
     Interruption, a breaking _____ (1-12)
     Inconvenience, a _____ _____ing together (for easy use) (1-11, 1-31)
     Manufacturers, those who _____ things, formerly by hand (*manu*) (1-22)

     between

     not com(ing)

     make

Opposition to the concept of the archetypes proposed by Carl Jung has recurred periodically.
     Opposition is made up of the prefix _____ and the root _____, and literally means _____ _____. (1-13, 1-26)

     ob
     pos
     placement against

The root of *concept* means _____. (1-20)

Archetypes literally means "_____ types." (1-34)

The prefix in *recurred* is _____, and in this sentence it means _____. (1-17)

take or seize

first or beginning

re
again

Many persistent social problems are quite complicated and can generate further misunderstandings before solutions are attainable.

Persistent means "enduring" or, literally, "standing _____." (1-14)

Complicated literally means "_____ together." (1-27)

A literal translation of *generate* in this sentence is _____ _____ _____. (1-24)

The root of *attainable* is _____ and means _____. (1-29)

through
folded

give birth to

tain
hold

Clothing styles often revert to former periods, either as direct copies or as inspirations of earlier styles.

Revert literally means _____ _____. (1-17, 1-32)

Inspirations carries the root _____ and literally means _____. (1-28)

turn back

spir
breath or breathe

George Jessel uses a monocle for correction of vision. One or both eyes need correction?

_____

This information comes from the word element _____. (1-36)

A literal meaning for *vision* is _____. (1-33)

one

mono
seeing

The word *theology* is made up of _____ and _____. Its literal meaning is _____ _____ _____. (1-37, 1-35)

theo
logy/study
of God

Submission to an opposing idea of only minor importance may be the wisest action in order to gain support for your preference in another matter which is directly counter to the negotiating members. *Diplomacy* is the term used for such tactics; in everyday language, horse trading.

Submission literally means that your ideas are _____ _____ those of the opposition. (1-18, 1-25) | sent under

Preference is made up of the prefix _____ | pre
and the root _____. It literally means "that | fer
which is _____ _____." | carried before
(1-15, 1-23)

Counter means _____ and is | against
an alternate form of the prefix _____. (1-7) | contra

CHAPTER 1 WORD LIST

All words used for study in Chapter 1 are listed here. You should be able to recognize the word elements you have learned and be able to supply their meaning. The next step in your mastery is to be able to use each word in a sentence or phrase.

More than one form of the word may be listed, and you should be alert to these changes in parts of speech. If you are not sure of a word ending (suffix), see Chapter 3, "Suffixes."

abstaining	advertise	annotated	arraign
abstention	adviser	antiperspirant	arrears
accede	*ad visum*	appendix	aspect
accept	afferent	apposition	assimilate
acclimatize	affix	appreciate	assist
acclivity	agglutinate	aquaduct	attainable
addition	aggrandize	aquatic	attend
adequate	aggravate	archaeology	attenuation
adit	allocate	archaic	attest
admit	allocation	archbishop	attestation
advance	alumna	archetype	attract
adverb	alumnae	architect	
adversary	anarchical	archives	
advert	anarchist	archtraitor	biology

capability
capable
capacious
capacitate
capacity
captivity
captures
collate
colluded
collusion
commit
committee
committeeman
compare
compliance
complicated
composition
compositor
compost
compounded
concept
conceptual
conduct
conductor
conduit
confection
confectioner
conference
conflux
congenital
coniferous
conjoin
connect
continence
contraceptive
contradict
contraindications
contrapuntal
contravene
contravention
contrary
controversial

controversy
controvertible
convened
convention
cooperate
coordinate
copartnership
correct
correlated
correlative
counter
counteract
counterclockwise
counterflow
counteroffensive
counterpoint

deceit
deception
deducible
deduction
defer
deference
degeneracy
delimit
delineate
demagnetize
demoralize
denominator
depository
depreciate
despiser
dethronement
diffract
digresses
disability
disappear
discard
discontent
disjoin
disjoining
disjunction

dismembered
dismiss
disperse
dissever
dissimilar
dissimilate
distend
distrust
disunion
ductile
ductless
ducts
duologue
duplicate

educate
effect
efferent
effluence
elongate
embryo
embryonic
emits
empowered
enchain
endemic
endoparasite
ensanguined
entomb
entomology
entoparasite
entozoon
epilogue
escape
eugenics
eulogium
event
eventually
evoke
exanthem
except
exceptionable

exclamatory
exhale
exhume
exit
exorcist
expatriate
expedite
expire
exponent
expositor
extensive
extenuating
extract
extractor
extremity
extrovert

facile
facsimile
fact
factitious
factor
factory
factotum
ferryboat
fertilizer

genealogy
general
generally
generate
generation
generator
generic
Genesis
genitals
graphology

Holy Spirit

illegal
illegible
illicit

illuminate	invisible	obstruction	precedent
imbibe	irradiate	obtained	precedes
impassable	irreversible	obtaining	precept
impasse		obverse	precognition
implicate	logic	occlude	predicate (n.)
improvisation	logistic	offend	predicate (v.)
inability	logograph	offense	predict
inactive	logomania	offer	preface
incarcerated	logorrhea	office	prefatory
inconsequential	Logos	officer	prefer
inconsiderate		opponent	preference
incontinent	manufacturer	opposable	prefix
incontrovertible	missile	opposition	prepayment
inconvenience	mission	outbuildings	preposition
indecent	missionary	outflank	preschool
indirect	monarchical	outmaneuver	preventive
induction	monarchy	outmoded	pro
infallible	monasteries	outpouring	procedure
infect	monks	outrank	procession
inhale	monocle	outshine	proclivity
inject	monody		progeny
injection	monograph	pantheism	prognosis
insane	monolith	Pantheon	promise
insecure	monolithic	participate	prophylactic
insomnia	monologue	perceive	propitiate
inspect	monosyllabic	perforation	proponent
inspirations	monotheism	perform	proposal
inspire	monotone	permanent	proposition
interchanges	monotony	permeated	propound
intercom	multiplication	permit	protractor
interjection		peroration	provided
intermediary	nonconductor	persistency	provocation
intermittent	nonintervention	persistent	
interracial		perspicacity	recalculate
interregnum	obdurate	perspiration	receiving
interruption	obfuscate	pertain	reception
interstate	objection	pertinacious	recipient
intervene	oblige	peruse	reciprocal
intransitive	obloquy	polytheism	reciprocating
introvert	obscene	pontifical	recollection
invert	obscure	post	reconstituted
invincible	obstinate	poster	recurred

reducible
reduction
reflux
related
remittance
Renaissance
repay
repeat
reproduce
reread
residue
residuum
residua
respiration
respirator
resurrection
retains
retentive
return
revenue

revert

simplicity
sinologue
spirit
spirometer
subconscious
subcutaneous
sublunar
submarine
submaxilla
submaxillae
submission
submit
subversion
subvert
subvocal
succumb
suffix
suggestion

supplicate
surreptitious
surrogate
syllogism

tendency
tendon
tendrils
tenets
tensile
tensor
theism
theocentric
theocracy
theology
traduce
transfer
translate
transmissible
transmit
transpose

unchain
uncomplicated
underfed
underlie
underprivileged
undertow
unfasten
universal
universe
university
unpack
unseen
untangled
untenable

vertigo
viaduct
video
visa
vision
vista

Chapter 2.
Prefixes and
Roots –
Second Group

Chapter 1 presented the first group of prefixes and roots commonly used in higher education. Chapter 2 presents the group which is next in order of use for this kind of vocabulary.

In Chapter 1 associative words and phrases were suggested to you, as well as the direct question asked as to what you were using as a clue to your remembering. By now it is hoped that you are convinced of the great help this association technique can be for remembering, and that you no longer need a direct reminder to select a special clue. Thus, no reminders will now be given; however, you may want to enter your clue word in the margin.

For convenience the Latin and Greek are given separately. Latin prefixes make the start.

LATIN PREFIXES

2-1
Abduct, abominate, abrupt, and *absent* all share the prefix _____ meaning _____. | ab/from or away

---

Ab means "from" or "away."
If a person's IQ is away from the normal, whether above or below, we call him

_____. | abnormal

If a tribe of people has lived in a place from the beginning–the original inhabitants–we call them ____ origines. | ab(origines)

Ab + *errare* (to wander) = _____*ant,* | aberr(ant)

meaning "a person who has wandered or strayed from the normal or standard."

An _____ banker could wind up in jail.

aberrant

The noun meaning "a wandering away" is _____ation. The concept of a wandering away has been applied to the field of health —"away from the normal condition," "a mental lapse."

aberr(ation)

It also has technical application. For example, in optics if the rays of light do not converge to one focus, that is, if some "wander away," the condition is called an _____ation.

aberr(ation)

In astronomy, there may be diurnal aberration or planetary aberration. Optics also uses the terms *spherical* and *chromatic aberration.* But all carry the basic meaning of _____ _____.

wander away

If you renounce or recant an idea under oath, you literally swear away from it. You _____jure it.

ab(jure)

To lead from, usually by force, is to _____duct, in other words, kidnap.

ab(duct)

The verb *abrade* literally means "to scrape _____" the skin.

from or away

The idea of scraping away or wearing down by friction is applied to things other than skin. An emery cloth is an _____rasive.

ab(rasive)

Under the root *tain* you had the words *abstain* and *abstention,* meaning literally "to _____ _____." In this instance the prefix is spelled _____ in order to join *b* and *t.*

hold from
abs

Another example of spelling *ab* with an *s* is *abstract,* literally, to draw _____.

from

To make an abstract of an article, you literally _____ _____ the entire article the important qualities, a kind of summary.

draw from

The prefix studied in this section is _____, and it means _____ or _____ .

ab
from/away

2-2

Another word for a curse or slander is malediction. The prefix is _____ and literally means _____ .

mal, male
bad or evil

The form *mal,* or *male,* comes from Latin and carries the meaning "bad" or "evil." Although this form is technically a root, it is used almost entirely in the first position of a word and is therefore treated as a prefix.

One of the primary problems to be solved in this modern world is that of poor diet, _____nutrition.

A malefactor is one who does _____ .

mal(nutrition)
evil

Sheridan created a character who misuses words, uses them unsuitably. He gave her the name Mrs. _____aprop (*apropos* = suitable).

Mal(aprop)

From her name has come the term *malapropism* meaning "the _____ use of words." This misuse is usually humorous (although unintentional) in that the error term is similar to the correct term: "But the point we would request of you is; that you will promise to forget this fellow—to illiterate him, I say, quite from your memory." (*The Rivals,* Act I, scene 2.)

bad (i.e., wrong)

We sometimes use the meaning "bad" in

the sense of "naughty" rather than "evil." For example, a word meaning "saucy" or "impudent" is _____apert.	mal(apert)
Maltreatment, maladministration, malodorous, malevolence — all share the word form _____ meaning _____.	mal bad or evil
2-3 *Non* means _____, as in the sentence "The President followed a nonintervention policy."	not

The easiest Latin prefix is *non* meaning "not."
    The word *nonexclusive* can be translated "_____ exclusive."
    Ideas that do not make sense are called _____sense.
 	
This prefix *non* is considered to be less emphatic in meaning than either the English *un* or the Latin *in,* which you have already studied.
	not
	
	non(sense)

2-4 The postscenium is that part of the stage _____ the scenery. This information comes from _____.	after or behind post
The new prefix is *post* and means "after" or "behind." Postgraduate work comes _____ graduation.	after

"The delay in the postmortem examination was unavoidable." The literal meaning of *postmortem* is "_____ death (*mort*)." | after

What would be the name for the movement in painting which came after impressionism? _____ | postimpressionism

You may not realize how often you use *post*. For example, 1:30 P.M. means 1:30 post meridian, the time _____ noon. When you add P.S. at the end of a letter you are adding a *post script*, an item added _____ writing the letter. | after

after

2-5
The opposite of *sublunary* is _____lunary. This prefix means _____ or _____. | super(lunary)
over/above

Super is an easy prefix. It means "over" or "above."
On the lonely heights of the Alps Nietzsche found a new god—the Superman. There is also a cartoon character Superman. In both cases the man is _____ the ordinary human being. | over or above

In Latin *supercilium* means "eyebrow," and if a person raises an eyebrow and curls his lip, we take it as an expression of disdain or sneering. And we call him _____cilious —or perhaps you use plain English and say, "Well, who does he think he is!" | super(cilious)

If a person is superannuated, he's _____ the years (*annu*) and therefore ready to retire. | over or above

The United States and Russia are supereminent in the field of space exploration.

They are _____ other nations in this field.	above
The small letter or figure written directly above and to the right of another word is called a _____script. When such a small letter or figure is written underneath, it is called a _____script.	super(script) sub(script)
You may even have used the expression "It's super!" meaning it is _____ the ordinary.	above or over

---

2-6 *Transfusion, transmarine,* and *transmontane* share the prefix _____ meaning _____.	trans/across

---

A plane that flies across the Atlantic is a _____atlantic plane. To carry the meaning from one language across to another is to _____late. The new prefix is _____.	trans(atlantic) trans(late)/trans
One who or that which carries across is called a _____porter—whether it be goods, passengers, or emotions.	trans(porter)
A transcendent experience is one which has gone _____ or beyond ordinary human experience. A transitive verb is one whose action goes _____ to an object.	across across
One of the cross aisles or wings of a church is called the _____ept.	trans(ept)
If you translated Caesar in Latin class, you may remember that Transalpine Gaul was the part of Gaul (France) _____ the Alps from Italy.	across

To traverse a field is to go _____ it.	across
Another spelling for *trans* is _____.	tra
Traduce can be analyzed to mean "lead _____"—in this instance "across to disgrace"—hence to shame by slander. This is a favorite word on vocabulary tests.	across
Transmit was suggested as a clue word for the root *mit*. Can it do double duty to include *trans* meaning _____?	across

GREEK PREFIXES

2-7 At one time a female medical student was regarded as most unusual. She was not the typical student.	
Say "not typical" in one word: _____*typical*. If joined to a vowel, the prefix becomes _____.	a(typical) an
Nonessential, unlikely, and *inactive* represent three prefixes meaning "not." The two Latin prefixes for "not" are _____ and _____. The English is _____.	non in/un
The Greeks also said "no" sometimes. A person with no morals is amoral, with no feeling is apathetic, with no god is an atheist. The Greek prefix for "not" is _____.	a
To indicate direct reproduction with no sexual action, we use the term _____.	asexual
Frequently you hear two terms used incorrectly, as if they had the same meanings, but literal meanings indicate a difference: atheist = *a* + *theos*, meaning "_____ god"	no

agnostic = *a* + *gnostos*, meaning "_____ know" or "unknowable"	not
What does *aseptic* mean? The *a* means _____. The *septic*? You know *antiseptic*, a product to use against (*anti*) _____, so *aseptic* must mean _____ _____. (*Sepsis* literally means "putrefaction" or "decay.")	not germs no germs
We can say "a car," "a doll," "a tree," but what if we are using *apple* or *egg*? What happens to the article *a*? It becomes _____. The same with the negative prefix *a*; use *an* when the base word starts with a _____.	an vowel
Anarchy means "_____ government." *Anesthetic* means "_____ feeling." The prefix in the above two words is _____.	no no an

2-8

Apostate has the literal meaning of "one who has turned _____," as shown by the prefix _____.	away or from apo

An apogee is that point which is farthest away, as in the orbit of an earth satellite. The new prefix must be _____ meaning _____.	apo away
How does knowing that *apo* is a prefix in the word *apocryphal* help you to remember its meaning? If the word literally means "hidden _____" and was used about writings not to be read to the congregation, does that help you?	away
The Old Testament Apocrypha are those writings of doubtful authorship, hence hidden _____.	away

In general use, one could say, "Some of these paintings are authentic, and some are _____."

apocryphal

The word *apotheosis* has the definition "the glorification of a principle or person." The word can be analyzed into the prefix _____ meaning _____ and the root _____ meaning _____.

apo
from/theo
God

"George Washington has been apotheosized by his countrymen." This is an example of fitting the literal meaning to the context, so that here "away from" has the sense of "away from what he was toward divinity, perfection." _____ may be the highest tribute which can be paid a man or woman.

apotheosis

In scientific terminology *apo* is widely used (see Part 2). For example:
  apomorphine = formed from morphine
  apocope = cutting away the last letters of a word
  apogeotropism = bending away from the ground
Occasionally when *apo* is joined with an *h*, the *o* is dropped, as in *aphelion*, whose literal meaning is "_____ _____ the sun." *Aphelion* is the name of the point of a planet's orbit farthest from the sun.

away from

Apo has both general and technical use. It means _____.

away or from

2-9
In the word *archfiend* the prefix is _____ and carries the meaning _____.

arch
first or chief

Arch has been presented earlier as a root

form; however, it is frequently listed as a prefix. This frame is really review.

One word which means chief traitor is

_____.

archtraitor

2-10

Systole—diastole. Which rhythm of the heart lets the blood through (in order to be pushed onward)? _____ because _____ means "through."

diastole/dia

Dia means "through," as in the diameter of a circle, the measure _____ the circle. This relates to space. "Through" can also relate to time in the sense of "during," and we get the word *diachronic*, literally meaning "_____ time (*chron*)," indicating changes occurring through _____. An example is a diachronic analysis.

through

through

time

Does the *dia* in *diagonal* indicate space or time? _____

space

There is an organ stop called *diapason.* This word was formed from the first two Greek words of a phrase meaning "concord" or "harmony," literally "_____ all the notes."

through

Diabetes is the name of a disease which is marked by an excessive discharge of urine and in which excessive amounts of sugar appear in the urine. It comes from a Greek word meaning "a syphon," literally "a going _____."

through

In the days of witchcraft a diabolic plot

meant one that was devilish — in league with the devil or _____ the devil.	through
"Through" in the sense of "across" or "between" is used for the word *dialogue*, literally _____ _____, a conversation.	words between
Diagonal literally means "_____ a corner."	through
If you picture a square marked with a diagonal line, you can easily see that the line literally "goes_____" the corners of the square.	through
A diagnosis is made _____ knowing (*gnosis*), by recognizing symptoms.	through

2-11 The epicenter of an earthquake is that part of the earth's surface directly _____ the focus of the quake. This information comes from the prefix _____ meaning _____ or _____.	over epi over/upon

The Greek prefix *epi* means "over" or "upon." A speech made upon a play (over and above the play — at the end of it) is an _____logue.	epi(logue)
The layer of skin upon the dermis (inner layer) is the _____dermis.	epi(dermis)
An epitaph is an inscription upon a tombstone. An epigraph is an inscription (writing) _____ a building or statue.	upon or on

In college work you often find the term *epistemology*, the study of knowledge. Over knowledge? Not knowledge as with the facts you know, but above or _____ that level—the theory of knowledge.

over

Episcopacy is the name for the government of the church by the bishops. The term literally means "the looking (*scop*) _____." The bishops supervise, to use a Latin equivalent.

over

Epitomize literally means "to cut (*tom*) _____ in order to condense." The noun *epitome* means "a short summary" or "something that typifies." *Epitome* is an example of use establishing additional meaning. *Epitome* has been misused so often to mean "ideal" rather than "typical" that this meaning is now included in newer dictionaries. However, careful speakers continue to use the meaning "typical."

upon

The prefix studied in this section is _____ meaning _____ or _____ .

epi
over/upon

2-12

The crocus blooms peeping through the snow put me into a euphoric state, since I knew that spring weather was coming.
    You know that the person was in an especially strong state of feeling _____ because of the prefix _____ .

well or good
eu

Eu means "well" or "good."
  We commonly hear the expression *pass away* when a person dies. We say *the underprivileged* or *disadvantaged* rather than use

the harsher term *poor folks*. This process of substituting good words for blunt ones is called _____phemism. The prefix is _____ meaning _____, and *phem* means "sound." We apparently prefer good-sounding words.

eu
eu/well or good

"He played the euphonium euphoniously." What kind of sound is the instrument capable of? _____. What kind of sound did the musician get out of it? _____. This information comes from the prefix _____.

good
good

eu

Words using the prefix *eu* have been given under root study. One was *eugenics*, the study of the betterment of the race. The prefix is _____ meaning _____. The root is _____ meaning _____.

eu/well or good
gen/race

Another word used for root study combined *eu* with the root meaning "word." To speak good words is to _____ize, commonly done at funerals.

eulog(ize)

A topic of considerable controversy is the practice of putting to death painlessly, that is, an easy mode of inevitable death. The proper name for this practice is _____-thanasia (*thanatos*, death).

eu(thanasia)

As a point of interest, consider the words *evangel, evangelical, evangelist*. *Ev* is a variant spelling of *eu*, hence a literal translation of *evangel* is "good messenger" (angel). We commonly speak of the good news or glad tidings.

A monopoly is control by _____ company. The prefix is _____.	one mono
Mon, or mono, is frequently listed as a prefix. For that reason it is mentioned here. The word form meaning "one" or "alone" is _____, or _____.	mon/mono
2-14 Although paranoia is now used to describe a particular kind of mental illness, the Greeks coined the word to mean "derangement" or "madness." Noia means "mind," and para means _____. If _____ the mind, one is out of it, hence mad.	beside/beside

The prefix par, or para, means "beside" or "resembling."
    If two lines are parallel, they are_____ each other, that is, lined up side by side.
    Paraphernalia literally means "beside or beyond a dowry" and referred to former property of a married woman which remained under her own control. We now use paraphernalia to mean "any kind of equipment or miscellaneous accessories _____ or beyond our basic needs."
	beside
	
	beside

An advertising copywriter must often be able to paraphrase technical language so that general readers can understand. From this use of having two versions side by side the meaning "resembling" is often given for the prefix para. A parody is another version of a song. It _____ the original.	resembles

"The magician deals in paraphysical events when he makes the beautiful girl float in thin air." He is dealing with an event that _____ a physical event but without apparent physical cause.

resembles

Paragraph literally means "write (*graph*) _____" and was a line used by the Greeks to mark the change of persons in a dialogue.

beside

Rather than make a mark beside the change of thought as we write our ideas, we show the change or new paragraph by _____.

indenting

A parasite is literally one who is _____ the food or bread. In ordinary language, one who lives at the expense of others but contributes nothing.

beside

An example or model is shown alongside a principle to help explain it. The term for this model presented beside the principle, or rule, is _____*digm.*

para(digm)

NOTE: There is a Latin verb *parare* meaning "to prepare" which supplies a root *para*. For example, a parachute is an apparatus for a prepared fall. A parapet is a bank or wall prepared to protect soldiers from enemy fire.

In using classical word forms, try the meaning you know. If it does not fit, don't force it; there may be a similar form but with a different meaning. If you find the second meaning frequently, then learn it. This does not happen often, but you should be aware of occasional similarity of forms.

2-15
The perimeter of the circle was 2.34 inches.

The perimeter is the measure _____ the circle, as shown by the prefix _____.

around

peri

Watch the vowels. You have just been dealing with *para*. The new prefix is *peri* and means "around."

A periscope is a useful instrument for seeing _____ obstacles.

around

The muscle movement that contracts around the intestinal wall to move the contents along is called _____ stalsis.

peri(stalsis)

"When Don found he knew no one at the meeting, he drifted to the outside of the group and stood around the edge." He drifted to the _____ phery of the group.

peri(phery)

"Mrs. Knight is a good teacher, I guess. She has interesting things to say, but she is so peripatetic!" Since *peri* means _____,
a likely guess on what Mrs. Knight does that seems annoying is to _____
_____ the classroom as she talks. The new word in this paragraph is _____,
and it means _____ _____.

around

move
around
peripatetic
moving around

The term *apogee* was presented under the prefix *apo* meaning _____ _____.
The apogee of the moon's orbit is that point when the moon is farthest from the earth. The term for that point when the moon is nearest to, or around, the earth is _____ gee.

away from

peri(gee)

If you want to indicate "beside" you use _____. If "around," you use _____.

para/peri

2-16
Synthesis and *sympathy* show two spellings of the prefix _____ meaning _____.

syn/together or with

The Greek prefix for "with" or "together"

is *syn*, from a Greek word for yoke, which is certainly together! The consonant *n* will vary according to the next letter; it assimilates.

A word that goes with another word as to meaning is a _____onym.

syn(onym)

The feeling you share with another person who is having difficulties is called _____pathy.

sym(pathy)

Syllable literally means "put_____,"

together or with

which is just what we do with words: we put sounds _____.

together

The combining, or putting together, of separate ideas into a whole is a _____thesis.

syn(thesis)

A connected system or orderly arrangement of word parts is called _____tax, a part of grammar.

syn(tax)

What other word in the above sentence uses the same prefix and means "something brought together"? _____

system

In frame 2-10, systole and diastole were used to indicate rhythms of the heart. The heart contracts in one rhythm to prevent blood flow; the technical term is _____

systole

_____, meaning literally "put _____

together

_____."

QUICK REVIEW OF PREFIXES

Use this review as a check on Chapter 2 prefixes before going on with the roots. This immediate review helps to fix the meanings.

Do not take time to write the answers. Read this installment of "Red Riding Hood" and substitute English meanings for the prefixes which are capitalized.

But this was really an MAL wolf. He wasn't

evil

as friendly as he had ARCH seemed to Little

first

Red Riding Hood. As soon as the little girl had gone APO, the wolf cut TRANS the woods and reached Grandma's house EU ahead of Red Riding Hood.

away/across
well

He knocked at the door.

Since Grandma was MONO and sick in bed, she could AN come to the door, but instead called out, "Who's there?"

alone
not

"It's Little Red Riding Hood, Grandma. I've brought some goodies AB home." The wolf had made his voice PARA a little girl's. Anyway, Grandma's years of good hearing were POST her, and she accepted the voice as that of her granddaughter.

from
resemble

behind

"Lift the latch and walk in."

At sight of the wolf, Grandma leaped SUPER the end of the bed and went DIA the back door.

over/through

The wolf had NON planned on Grandma's being so spry, but went ahead SYN his plan. He rummaged PERI in the dresser and found a nightgown and bed cap. After he had put on Grandma's nightdress, he hopped into bed and pulled the covers EPI him. All he had to do was wait for Little Red Riding Hood.

not
with
around

over

ROOTS

2-17
"Her diction was remarkable."

Restated: Her _____ was remarkable, as shown by the root _____ meaning _____.

speech
dict
say or speak

The root meaning "speak" or "say" is *dict*, or *dic*.

"His downfall could not have been predicted." *Predicted* literally means _____ _____.

said
before

The root in *predicate* is _____, and this word also has the literal meaning_____ _____.

dic
said
before

NOTE: You can remember the distinction between *predict* and *predicate* by remembering the grammatical predicate. The predicate part of a sentence is that which is said about what went before, the subject. Therefore, to predicate means to affirm, say something about what has gone before, even preach.

An edict is an order issued by a king or lawgiver. *E + dict* literally means _____ _____. A dictum is a _____ing, an authoritative opinion. "Good will triumph" is a _____um.

speak
out/say(ing)

dict(um)

Diction, dictate, dictatorship, dictionary, dictograph—all are related by the root_____ meaning _____.

dict
say or speak

2-18
A fine has come to mean a sum of money paid as settlement. The root of *fine* is _____ and literally means _____.

fin
end

The root *fin* means "end" or "limit."
"The court imposed a $10,000 fine as settlement of the lawsuit." The fine made an _____ to the matter.

end

Final examinations, or finals, are those which _____ a course of study, as shown by the root _____.

end
fin

The end or concluding piece in a concert is the _____ale.

fin(ale)

"Her gift of land for a playground was the finial of a life made up of many noble

deeds." Here *end* (finial) would be used in the sense of _____	highest
"The lecturer went on ad infinitum." In other words, he went on without _____.	end
Infinitude is a countless number, a quantity that has _____ _____.	no end
Using the meaning "limit" for *fin*, what is the name of a verb form which is not limited by person or number?_____. Finis of *fin*.	infinitive

---

2-19 *Mobility, motion, movable*—all represent forms of the root _____ meaning _____.	mo/move

---

From the Latin verb *movere* meaning "to move" we get various related spellings. All mean "move."	
One problem many students experience is *motivation*, or lack of it. How strongly are you *motivated* to study? In other words, can you _____ yourself to study when you should?	move
A home which can be moved from place to place is a _____ home. In case you answered "motor home," remember that motors also set things in motion.	mobile
If a person has become immobile through illness, he cannot _____ .	move
Something within a person which stirs him to action is a _____tive.	mo(tive)
Eye motility is one way to study reading; your eyes _____ a great deal while you are reading.	move

A promotion is an advancement. *Promotion* literally means "a_____ _____."	move forward
Since the third letter varies (*mob, mov, mot*), treat the root as *mo* meaning_____.	move

---

2-20
"There was a renascent interest in classical architecture."

The interest was _____ again, as shown by the root _____.	born
	nasc

Nasc and *nat* are roots coming from the Latin verb *nasci* meaning "to be born, to begin."

A nascent interest is one which is in the process of _____ _____, whereas a renascent interest is one which is_____ _____.	being born
	born
	again

Your natal day is your _____day.	birth(day)
"The natality figures have been showing a decline." The _____ rate has been declining.	birth

Research has now shown that prenatal learning can occur. This is learning_____ _____.	before
	birth

Although you are familiar with the terms *nation, international,* and such, it may help to understand their full meaning if you realize that the root is _____ and means that there was a beginning or_____; nations did not always exist.	nat
	birth

2-21

The root in the word *denominator* is _____, and means _____.	nomin
	name

Nomin means "name." *Nomen* is a variant spelling.

To nominate for office is to _____ .

The nominee is the one who has been _____ .

name

named

The terminology of science is composed of a system of names. A synonym for *terminology* is _____ clature. The *i* of *nomin* has changed to _____ .

nomen

e

Your cognomen is your "together _____ ," that is, the name you share with other members of your family: *co + (g)nomen*.

Co + (g)nomen is from *(g)noscere*, to know. To know is to name. If you can't name it, you don't really know it.

In algebra a quantity consisting of two names or terms is a bi _____ ial. The *in* of *nomin* has been _____ .

name

nom

dropped

A nominalist follows the doctrine that general terms have no corresponding reality either in or out of the mind, being merely words. Words are only _____ , not the real thing. "Sticks and stones may hurt my bones. . ."?

names

Nominal, trinomial, and *nomenclature* show the three spellings of the root _____ meaning _____ .

nomin

name

2-22

Your paternal grandmother is the mother of your _____ , as shown by the root _____ .

father

pater

Pater is Latin for father. The forms *pater* and *patri* are both in use.

"The lawsuit dealt with the paternity of the child." It sought to establish who was the _____.

father

The father or head of a household is called the _____familias.

pater(familias)

A *paternoster* is another name for the Lord's Prayer. It comes from the first two words of the prayer in Latin, *pater noster*, our _____.

Father

Pauline as a girl's name is patrilinic. It is a name adapted from the name of the _____.

father

Other related words are *patron, patriotic,* and *expatriate,* all sharing the root _____ meaning _____. The combining form is frequently spelled _____.

pater
father
patri

Along with father you should also know mother, *mater. Maternity, alma mater.*
If a woman is head of the family, she is called a _____arch.

matri(arch)

The murder of one's own mother is _____cide.

matri(cide)

The murder of one's own father is _____cide.

patri(cide)

To complete the family:
Frater means "brother"—*fraternity, fratricide.*
Soror means "sister"—*sorority, sororicide.*

2-23
A new blue ribbon depended from her straw hat.

The ribbon was _____ down from her hat, as shown by the root _____. The other meaning of this root is _____.

hanging
pend
weigh

The meaning of the root *pend* you can guess from *pendulum* and *pendant*. Patents pending and matters pending are _____ing fire, that is, awaiting final action.

hang(ing)

Try using prefixes with the root *pend*:
Something that hangs down, thus leans on, _____.

depends

Something hung to the main part of a book is an _____ix.

append(ix)

Presumably *pend* is also related to the meaning "weigh." Matters pending final action are hanging fire, but also, the waiting might weigh heavily. A summary of a larger work, things weighed together, is a _____ium.

compend(ium)

A weight attached at one point will hang down under the point of attachment—it is _____ed.

suspend(ed)

When you are under a weight of uncertainty, you are in a state of _____.

suspense

The noun form of suspend is _____.

suspense

The gold pendant was _____ from a black ribbon.

hanging or hung

"Appendant to this action, the committee has filed a minority report." The report has been _____ _____ the action.

hung to

2-24
The stenographer transcribes her shorthand notes.
She _____ across from the shorthand to English. Variant spellings of this root are _____, _____, and _____.

writes

scrip/script/scriv

A scribe is one who writes. A scriber is that which writes, a tool for writing or marking. A root meaning "write" is _____.

scrib

Principal parts once again: *scrib, scrip, script, scriv.* Be flexible!

The word *scribble* comes from a diminutive form of the Latin verb and literally means "one who _____ little or small."

| writes |

We now use *scribble* to mean "little" in the sense of "worthless." An author who has little to say is called a _____bler.

| scrib(bler) |

A spelling coming from another principal part of the Latin verb is *script.*

A manuscript originally meant "a document _____ by hand (*manu*)."

| written |

The word for the writings of the Bible is _____*ure*, which originally meant anything written.

| script(ure) |

Another spelling is *scrip.*

We use the root as a word, *scrip*, to mean "a _____ing," as a certificate or document.

| writ(ing) |

The Sheaffer Pen Company made up an appropriate trade name for writing ink—Skrip. From *scribe* to *scriv* isn't a big step.

A *scrivener* is a professional or public _____, a notary. The next time you need the services of a notary, ask for the scrivener!

| writer |

Circumscription, prescriptive, superscribe— all share the root _____ meaning _____.

| scrib/write |

2-25
Only the most sentient subjects can be used in this experiment.

The word *sentient* contains the root _____ meaning _____.

| sent |
| feel |

The Latin verb *sentire* meaning "to feel" provides the root *sent.*

Dissenter is the name given to one who

has seceded from an established church. His _____ are _____, or different from those of the group.	feelings/apart
A vague foreboding, or feeling beforehand, is a _____iment.	present(iment)
A sentimentalist is one who regards _____ as more important than reason.	feeling
A sensitive person has the capacity for _____. Another spelling of the root *sent* is _____.	feeling sens
Sensualism is the belief in indulging in _____. The adjective *sensual* is used to describe this indulgence in the pleasures of the senses with the meaning of "lewd, sexy."	feelings
The adjective *sensuous* means "full of feelings," being _____itive, but not in a lewd way. You can remember this difference by the *a*—sensual. Does an association with Hawthorne's *The Scarlet Letter* help?	sens(itive)
There are two spellings of the root meaning "feel"; they are _____ and _____.	sent/sens

---

2-26

Residuum is a word meaning "a remainder, that which is left behind." The root of *residuum* is _____ and means _____.	sid/sit

---

A residence is literally that place where you may sit back, may remain. The root is _____ and means "sit."	sid
A residuary is the person to whom the residue of an estate is willed. He receives what remains behind, literally what _____ _____.	sits back
A presiding officer is one who _____	sits

_____ a group, usually to lead and exercise control over the group.	before
The name given to this position is _____ent.	presid(ent)
To sit to or at something would indicate constant attention or diligence. The word with the literal meaning "sit to" is _____uity.	assid(uity)
Remember the assimilation of *d* to *s*. An assiduous student is one who _____ to his work and gets it done.	sits
The root studied in this section is _____ and means _____.	sid sit

---

2-27

"The extortioner was arrested in Mexico." *Extortioner* literally means "one who _____ out," as shown by the root _____. Alternate spellings of this root are _____ and _____.	twists or twisted tort tors/torqu

---

The third principal part of the Latin verb *torquere*, to twist, supplies the commonly used forms of this root. *Tort* from *tortus*, twisted. A later form of Latin spelled this participle *torsus*, from which we derive *tors*.	
Yes, Latin changed in form and spelling during the centuries it was widely used, as do all languages.	
To contort the features is to _____ them.	twist
A contortionist is one who can assume _____ postures. The part of his body which can twist is called the _____o.	twisted tors(o)
There is a family of small moths called Tortricidae. They were originally named in Latin as Tortrix because of their habit of	

_____ leaves to make a nest. This is an example of the way a literal meaning can help you to remember a name or characteristic.	twisting
Another spelling of this root is *tors*. If a rod is twisted, it tends to untwist, or return. This force is called _____ion.	tors(ion)
A twisted cord used as a hat ornament is a _____ade.	tors(ade)
The spelling *torqu* is found mainly in the word *torque* and is used most commonly as a term in physics meaning "the _____ing or rotary force of a mechanism."	twist(ing)
"The new racing engine had high torque." It had a lot of wind.	
Another meaning for the word *torque* is "a necklace of metal rings _____ together." A torque was a neck chain worn by the ancient Gauls, Germans, and Britons. A current style of necklace could well be called a torque.	twisted
The root meaning "twist" may be spelled _____, _____, or_____.	tort/tors/torqu

2-28 The literal meaning of *retract* is "_____ back," as shown by the root _____.	draw tract

The root *tract* means "draw." A farm tractor _____ the tools necessary to work the ground.	draws
A trucking rig is made up of a semitrailer and a _____or to _____ it.	tract(or)/draw

Under conditions of low temperature your skin contracts; it _____ together.	draws
"Draw together" is also used in the sense of "to agree." A con_____ is an agreement, a _____ing together.	tract (contract) draw(ing)
An adjective form meaning "having the power to draw together" is con_____ile.	tract (contractile)
"The Senator demanded a retraction of the columnist's statement." He demanded that the columnist _____ _____ his statements.	draw back
If the columnist had made statements which tended to draw down the Senator's image, his statements could be called _____ive.	detract(ive)
To draw out is to _____. We draw out from many areas—mathematics, mining. We even draw out a passage from a book or, chemically, draw out the essence of a substance.	extract
The new root is _____ meaning _____.	tract/draw

QUICK REVIEW OF ROOTS

Use this final installment of our fairy tale as an immediate review of the roots which you have just covered.

As you read, the English meanings of the capitalized roots should come to mind immediately. Any hesitation is a sign that you should go back to the learning frames.

Soon Red Riding Hood knocked on the door. "Who's there?" ROGed the wolf, making his voice sound like Grandma's.	asked
"It's me, Grandma. I've brought you some goodies," DICed Red Riding Hood. "Lift the latch and walk in."	said
Little Red Riding Hood went in and SIDed down beside the bed.	sat
The wolf TRACTed the covers closer and waited.	drew

"My goodness, Grandma! What big eyes you have!"

"The better to see you with, my dear."

"And what long ears you have!"

"The better to hear you with, my dear."

"And, Grandma, what huge teeth you have, PENDing from your mouth!"   hanging

"Ah, yes. The better to eat you with, my dear."

And the wolf MOed out of the bed and   moved
started after Red Riding Hood. But just then
the door burst open, and there was the
strong woodsman NOMINed Adolph with   named
his ax. He chased the wolf out the door
and into the woods.

Grandma had sent Adolph to the rescue.
After things had quieted down and Grandma
was SENTing recovered from her run in   feeling
the woods, Red Riding Hood took Grandma
home with her so they could tell PATER   father
and MATER about their adventurous day.   mother
Red Riding Hood told her dolls all about
it, too.

The FIN   end

P.S. Although some people give a Freudian
TORT to this ancient tale, this version is   twist
the way it was SCRIBed down many cen-   written
turies before you were NASC.   born
P.P.S. Do you know the meaning of the
name Adolph?

FINAL REVIEW OF CHAPTER 2

The quick reviews served to fix the English meanings associated with
the word elements. This formal review offers practice in context so that
literal meanings are included.

The number of the express frame is supplied for easy reference in the
case of an error. Be sure that you can use these word elements.

Appended to the document was an abstract
of the discussion recorded at the final

session of the committee. This atypical procedure was followed in an effort to prevent distortion of the facts.

Appended literally means "_____ to." (2-23)

The word *abstract* is made up of the prefix _____ and the root _____, and means _____ _____. *Abs* is a variant spelling of _____. (2-1, 2-28)

Final comes from the root _____ meaning _____. (2-18)

Atypical translates to _____ _____. (2-7)

The root of *distortion* is _____ meaning _____. (2-27)

	hung
	abs/tract
	drawn from
	ab
	fin
	end
	not typical
	tort
	twist

Transplanted human organs are now becoming a reality. Perhaps the time will eventually come when perinatal replacement can be made.

A *transplanted* human organ is one which has to be taken _____ from the donor body to the receiving body. (2-6)

Perinatal replacement would be replacement at a time _____ _____. (2-15, 2-20)

across

around birth

The term *apostle* comes from a Greek word meaning "messenger," literally "to send _____," as shown by the prefix _____. (2-8)

away/apo

When a message is added to a letter after the closing signature, it is called a P.S. This abbreviation stands for _____, literally _____ _____. (2-4, 2-24)

Cases of medical malpractice are matters of serious intraprofessional concern.

Malpractice translates to "_____ practice." (2-2)

Nominating conventions precede the pres-

postscript
after writing

bad

idential elections by approximately three months, yet indirect campaigning may have begun a year or two earlier.

Nominating conventions are those which _____ the candidate for the office of President, the office which literally _____ before all others. (2-21, 2-26)

name
sits

Japan is frequently an epicenter of earthquakes.

Translate: Japan is frequently _____ _____ _____ of earthquakes. (2-11)

above
the center

Diarrhea is the correct term for the condition in which an unusually frequent discharge flows _____ (*dia*) the intestines. (2-10)

through

Paragraph, parody, parapsychology, parascenium — all share the prefix _____ meaning _____ or _____. (2-14)

para
beside/resembling

The eucalyptus tree was so named because the buds are _____ covered (*calypt*). This information comes from the prefix _____. (2-12)

well

eu

Sensual, sensation, sensum, sentient, and *sentimentality* are examples of words conveying the meaning of _____. The root may be spelled _____ or _____. (2-25)

feeling
sens/sent

Motivational research frequently dictates the style which advertising assumes. As evidence accumulates on the appeals which motivate or _____ people, then that evidence dictates, or _____, what form the advertising message should take. (2-19, 2-17)

move
says

Symposium is a quite respectable term for

a meeting where several speakers gather
to discuss a topic. But isn't it interesting
that the term also applies to the party which
often follows a banquet!

The term *symposium* is made from the
prefix _____ and a Greek word meaning
"to drink." Its literal meaning is "a drink-
ing _____." (2-16)

sym

together

CHAPTER 2 *WORD LIST*

All of the terms covered in Chapter 2 are listed for convenience for further
practice. Go through the list and identify the prefixes and roots which
have been covered thus far. This will also include some word elements
from Chapter 1. Being able to supply a literal meaning is the first step
of mastery, and will permit you to understand the basic meaning of words
you read and hear. The final step of mastery is for you to be able to use
each of the words in your own writing and speaking.

abduct	apogee	contort	dictum
aberrant	apogeotropism	contortionist	dissenter
aberration	apomorphine	contractile	distortion
abjure	apostate	contracts	
abnormal	apostle		edict
abominate	apotheosis	denominator	epicenter
aborigines	appendant	depended	epidermis
abrade	appended	detractive	epigraph
abrasive	appendix	diabetes	epilogue
abrogate	archfiend	diabolic	episcopacy
absent	archtraitor	diachronic	epistemology
abstain	aseptic	diagnosis	epitaph
abstention	asexual	diagonal	epitome
abstract	assiduity	dialogue	epitomize
ad infinitum	assiduous	diameter	eucalyptus
agnostic	atheist	diapason	eugenics
amoral	atypical	diarrhea	eulogize
anarchy		diastole	euphemism
anesthetic	binomial	dictate	euphonium
apathetic		dictatorship	euphoric
aphelion	circumscription	diction	euthanasia
apocope	cognomen	dictionary	evangel
apocryphal	compendium	dictograph	evangelical

evangelist
expatriate
extortioner
extract

final
finale
fine
finial

immobile
inactive
infinitive
infinitude
international

maladministration
malapert
malapropism
malediction
malevolence
malnutrition
malodorous
malpractice
maltreatment
manuscript
matriarch
matricide
mobility
monopoly
motility
motion
motivated
motivation
motivational
motive
movable

nascent
natal
natality

nation
nomenclature
nominal
nominalist
nominate
nominating
nominee
nonessential
nonexclusive
nonintervention
nonsense

paradigm
paragraph
parallel
paranoia
paraphernalia
paraphrase
paraphysical
parapsychology
parascenium
parasite
parody
paterfamilias
paternity
paternoster
patriarchal
patricide
patrilinic
patriotic
patron
pendant
pending
pendulum
perigee
perimeter
perinatal
peripatetic
periphery
periscope
peristalsis

postgraduate
postimpressionism
post meridian
postmorten
postscenium
postscript
predicate
predict
prenatal
prescriptive
presentiment
president
presiding
promotion

renascent
residence
residuary
residuum
retract
retraction

scribble
scribe
scriber
scrip
script
scripture
scrivener
sensation
sensitive
sensual
sensualism
sensum
sensuous
sentient
sentimentalist
sentimentality
superannuated
supercilious
supereminent

superlunary
Superman
superscribe
superscript
suspended
suspense
syllable
symbiosis
sympathy
symphony
symposium
synchronize
synapse
synonym
syntax
synthesis
synthetic
system
systole

torque
torsade
torsion
Tortricidae
tractor
traduce
transalpine
transatlantic
transcendent
transcribe
transept
transfusion
transitive
translate
transmarine
transmontane
transplanted
transporter
traverse
trinomial

unlikely

REFERENCE SECTION—GENERAL

Chapters 1 and 2 presented the word elements most commonly used at higher educational levels. This reference section lists the remaining word elements used in this special group of words. By going through the list systematically, you can expand your vocabulary rapidly. Set a schedule which is reasonable, say, three items per day. Be sure to include time for review. The list can also be used for convenient reference. Whenever you notice a word element repeating in the words you meet, refer to this list for meaning and other examples. Lists of word elements used for technical terms in subject-matter fields will be found at the end of the section treating the particular subject area.

As explained in the Introduction, combining forms are treated as roots, and only the basic form is given; however, the examples have been selected to show the vowels used to combine with other word parts. These examples also show variant spellings. An asterisk indicates that the item has been presented in Chapters 1 and 2. The abbreviations L, G, and E in the "Meaning and Source" column stand for Latin, Greek, and English respectively. This section is divided into "Prefixes," "Roots," and "Numbers."

PREFIXES

Word element	Meaning and source	Examples
*a	not (G)	anachronism, anonymity, anathematize
*ab	from, away (L)	abasement, abortion, abstemious
*ad	to, toward (L)	adequacy, accretion, affiance
ambi	both, around, about (L)	ambidextrous, ambient, ambulatory
ante	before (L)	antediluvian, antechamber, anterior
anti	against, opposed (G)	anticlimax, antisocial, antipodes
*apo	from, away (G)	apologia, apostrophize, apoplectic
bene	well, good (L)	benefactress, benignity, benediction
bi	two, twice (L)	bigamous, bipartisan, bilateral
cata	down, downward (G)	cataclysmic, catafalque, catastrophic

Word element	Meaning and source	Examples
circum	around, about (L)	circumambient, circumnaviga-tion, circumlocution
*com	with or together(L)	compulsive, congruence, complaisance
*contra	against, opposite (L)	contrariety, contretemps, countersign
*de	down, from (L)	desecrate, decrement, deodorize
*dia	through (G)	diaphanous, diagnostic, diathermy
*dis	apart from, separation (L)	discordance, disservice, differential
*em	in, inside (G)	embroilment, emblazonment, enraptured
*epi	upon, above (G)	epidemical, epithet, epileptic
*eu	well, good (G)	euphemism, eulogize, euphoria
*ex	out (L)	exacerbate, exculpate, effectuate
extra	outside, beyond (L)	extracurricular, extravaganza, extradite
hemi	half (G)	hemispherical, hemicycle, hemimorphic
hyper	above, excessive (G)	hyperbole, hypersensitive, hypertension
hypo	under, less (G)	hypodermic, hypothesis, hypocrisy
*in	in, on (L)	involution, inhere, impinge
*in	not (L)	immaturity, infinitude, illicit
*inter	between (L)	interact, interject, internecine
mal	bad, evil (L)	maltreatment, malodorous, malevolence
mis	wrong (E)	misstate, misdoing, misquote
mono	one, alone (G)	monasticism, monochrome, monograph
multi	many, much (L)	multiform, multilateral, multifarious
non	not (L)	nonintervention, nonexistence, nonpareil
ob	against, facing (L)	obduracy, obscenity, opprobrium
*out	external, beyond (E)	outbid, outmoded, outflank
over	over, above (E)	overladen, overhand, overdo

Word element	Meaning and source	Examples
pan	all, every (G)	pantheism, panoramic, pandemonium
*para	beside, resembling (G)	parapsychology, parable, parentheses
post	after, behind (L)	postlude, postdoctoral, posterity
*per	through, thoroughly (L)	permutation, perforation, peroration
poly	many (G)	polyandry, polytheism, polyglot
*pre	before (L)	preferential, prescient, prescriptive
*pro	for, forth, in favor of (L)	procreant, promiscuity, proselytism
pseudo	false, counterfeit (G)	pseudonym, pseudoscience, pseudoclassic
*re	back, again (L)	receptivity, resiliency, reincarnation
retro	back, backward (L)	retrospection, retroversion, retrograde
se	apart, away (L)	secretive, secularization, seducer
semi	half, partly (L)	semiarid, semifinal, semi-precious
*sub	under, below (L)	subservience, substantiation, supplicate
*super	over, above (L)	superscribe, superpower, superpose
*syn	with, together (G)	synchronous, synthesize, symphonic
*trans	across, beyond (L)	transferable, transcendental, trajectory
ultra	beyond, excessively (L)	ultramarine, ultramontane, ultramundane
*un	not, reversal (E)	unmitigated, unorthodox, undeceive
*under	below, beneath (E)	undercover, underprivileged, underlie
uni	one, once (L)	unicorn, universality, uniqueness
vice	instead of, in place of (L)	vice-presidency, vice-regent, vicarious

ROOTS

Word element	Meaning and source	Examples
ag, act	to do or drive (L, *agere, actum*)	actualize, agency, interact
amb	walk (L, *ambulare, ambulatum*)	ambient, ambulatory, per-ambulator
anim	breath, soul, spirit (L, *anima*)	reanimate, animalism, animation
annu	year (L, *annus*)	semiannual, biennial, annuity
anthrop	man, a human being (G, *anthropos*)	anthropomorphic, anthropoid, misanthropic
*arch	to begin, rule, be first (G, *archein*)	archaism, exarch, archangel
aud	to hear (L, *audire, auditum*)	audibility, audio, audition
auto	self (G, *autos*)	autointoxication, autopsy, autobiographical
bibl	book (G, *biblion*)	bibliophile, bibliographical, Biblical
calc	lime, stone (L, *calx, calcis*)	calcify, miscalculate, calcimine, calculus
capt, capit	head (L, *caput, capitis*)	captaincy, decapitate, recapitulation
*cep, cap	to take (L, *capere, captum*)	perceptive, misconceive, captivate
ced, cess	to go, move along (L, *cedere, cessum*)	precedency, secessionist, intercessor
cent	a hundred (L, *centum*)	centenarian, centigram, centenary, centipede
chrom	color (G, *chroma*)	monochrome, achromatic, chromo
chron	time (G, *chronos*)	anachronism, chronometer, synchronous
cid	to cut or kill (L, *caedere, caesum*)	concise, excise, homicide
civi	citizen (L, *civis*)	civics, incivility, uncivil
clud, clus	to close or shut (L, *claudere, clausum*)	closure, occlude, exclusiveness
cord	heart (L, *cor, cordis*)	cordiality, discordance, concordant

Word element	Meaning and source	Examples
corpor	body (L, *corpus, corporis*)	corporeal, corpulent, incorporeal
cred, credit	to believe, put trust in (L, *credere, creditus*)	credo, discreditable, credibility
cur	care, to take care of (L, *cura; curare, curatum*)	curative, insecurity, procurer
cycl	circle, wheel (G, *kyklos*)	cyclical, cyclone, bicycle
dem	the people (G, *demos*)	epidemical, democratize, demography
derm	skin (G, *derma*)	dermis, epidermal, dermatologist
*dic, dict	to say, tell, or speak (L, *dicere, dictum*)	interdiction, dedicatory, malediction
*duc, duct	to lead (L, *ducere, ductum*)	seducer, reducible, educative
equ	equal, even (L, *aequus*)	equivocate, equipoise, equability
*fac, fic	to do or make (L, *facere, factum*)	benefactress, ineffaceable, disqualification
*fer, lat	to carry or bear (L, *ferre, latum*)	transferable, inferential, collate
*fin	end, limit (L, *finis*)	finis, undefined, infinitude
flex, flect	to bend or turn aside (L, *flectere, flexum*)	flex, inflexibility, reflective
flu	to flow (L, *fluere, fluxum*)	fluency, reflux, affluence
*gam	marriage (G, *gamos*)	bigamist, monogamy, exogamy
*gen, gener	birth, race, kind (L, *genus, generis*)	degeneracy, congener, congenital
gnos	knowing (G, *gnosis*)	agnostic, diagnostic, prognosticate
grad, gress	to step or go (L, *gradi, gressum*)	gradient, regress, congresswoman
graph	to write (G, *graphein*)	monograph, ideograph, typography, graphic
hem	blood (G, *haima*)	hemorrhage, hemoglobin, hemophilia

Word element	Meaning and source	Examples
her, hes	to stick or cling (L, *haere, haesum*)	cohesive, cohere, inhere, incoherence
hetero	other, different (G, *heteros*)	heterodoxy, heterogeneous, heterosexual
hydr	water (G, *hudor*)	hydrant, hydraulics, hydroelectric
idio	personal, peculiar, private (G, *idios*)	idiomatic, idiocy, idiosyncrasy
ject, jact	to throw or hurl (L, *jacere, jactum*)	ejection, projectory, objector
judic	to judge (L, *judicare* = *jus dicare*, to speak justice)	injudicious, adjudicate, unprejudiced
junct	to join (L, *jungere, junctum*)	conjuncture, disjunction, junta
liber	free (L, *liber*)	liberalize, illiberal, libertine
liter	a letter (L, *litera*)	literacy, literate, alliteration
*log, logy	word, speech, reason (G, *logos*)	antilogarithm, apologia, archaeologist
loqu, loc	to speak (L, *loqui, locutum*)	loquacity, obloquy, circumlocution
luc, lumin	light, source of light (L, *lux, lucis; lumen, luminis*)	luminosity, lucidity, elucidation
man	hand (L, *manus*)	manipulative, manicurist, emancipator
med	middle (L, *medius*)	mediate, intermediary, immediacy
meter, metr	measure (G, *metron*)	diametrically, metrical, perimeter
*mit, miss	to send, let go (L, *mittere, missum*)	commital, admissible, noncommissioned
*mo	to move, set in motion (L, *movere, motum*)	demote, unemotional, unmovable
mort	death (L, *mors, mortis*)	mortuary, morbidity, mortgager
*nasc, nat	to be born, begin (L, *nasci, natum*)	nascent, prenatal, nationalize

Word element	Meaning and source	Examples
*nomin	name (L, *nomen, nominis*)	nominalism, renomination, pronominal
not, gni	to know (L, *noscere, notum; gnoscere*)	notional, cognize, precognition
nov	new (L, *novus*)	innovate, novitiate, renovation
ord, ordin	order, arrangement (L, *ordo, ordinis*)	inordinant, insubordination, ordinal
omni	all (L, *omnis*)	omniprescence, omniscient, omnivorous
path, pass	feeling, suffering, disease (G, *pathos*; L, *pati, passum*)	pathos, passionless, pathologist
ped	foot (L, *pes, pedis*)	pedal, expedite, velocipede
pell, puls	to drive or force (L, *pellere, pulsum*)	repellent, compulsive, pulsation
*pend, pens	to hang, to weigh (L, *pendere, pensum*)	compendious, compensatory, pendulous
phil	loving, friendly (G, *philos*)	philharmonic, philter, bibliophile
phon	sound, tone (G, *phone*)	antiphonal, symphonic, phonetic
plac	to please (L, *placere, placitum*)	placable, complaisant, placidity
*plic, plex	to fold, lay together (L, *plicare, plicatum*)	explicable, complicity, pliancy
popul, public	people, of people (L, *populus; publicus*)	populousness, publicize, depopulate
port	to carry (L, *portare, portatum*)	transporter, supportable, opportunist
*pos	to put or place (L, *ponere, positum*)	disposable, superpose, predispose
reg, rect	to rule or direct (L, *regere, rectum*)	regicide, rectorship, registrar
rog	to ask or beg (L, *rogare, rogatum*)	abrogation, interrogator, derogatory
rupt	to break or burst (L, *rumpere, ruptum*)	erupt, corruptible, disrupt

Word element	Meaning and source	Examples
sacr, secr	holy, sacred (L, *sacer, sacrum*)	sacrosanct, desecration, reconsecrate
sal	health, safety, salt (L, *sal, salis*)	salutatory, salary, salubrity
*scrib, script	to write (L, *scribere, scriptum*)	superscribe, transcription, prescriptive
*sent, sens	to perceive or feel (L, *sentare, sensum*)	sensualist, nonsensical, presentment
sequ, secut	to follow (L, *sequi, secutum*)	inconsequence, consequential, consecutive
serv	to serve (L, *servire, servitum*)	subservience, disservice, servility, serfdom
sign	a mark or sign (L, *signum*)	insignificance, signatory, countersign
spect	to see, look at, or watch (L, *specere, spectum; spectare, spectatum*)	retrospection, spectacled, perspicuity
*spir	to breath; breath of life, soul (L, *spirare, spiratum; spiritus*)	spirituous, uninspired, inspirational
stat, sist	to stand; cause to stand (L, *stare, statum; sistere*)	statical, substantiate, consistence
tang, tact	to touch (L, *tangere, tactum*)	tangibility, tactile, contingent
tele	far off, distant (G, *tele*)	telepathic, telephoto, telegraphy
tempor	time (L, *tempus, temporis*)	temporality, contretemps, extemporize
*ten, tain	to hold or keep (L, *tenere, tentum*)	attainment, tenant, retention
*tend, tens	to stretch (L, *tendere, tensum*)	extenuation, tensile, tenseness
*theo	God, deity (G, *theos*)	theosophist, monotheist, apotheosis
*tors, tort	to twist or wind (L, *torquere, tortum*)	extortioner, contort, torsion
*tract	to draw or pull (L, *trahere, tractum*)	retractor, intractable, extractive

Word element	Meaning and source	Examples
val	to be strong, to be worth (L, *valere*, *valitum*)	invalidate, convalesce, evaluation
*ven, vent	to come (L, *venire*, *ventum*)	eventuate, adventurous, supervene
vert, vers	to turn or change (L, *vertere*, *versum*)	transversal, perversion, inconvertible
*vid, vis	to see (L, *videre*, *visum*)	video, prevision, envisage
vital	life, relating to life (L, *vita*; *vitalis*)	vitals, devitalize, vitalism
voc	to call or summon (L, *vocare*, *vocatum*)	vocalize, vociferate, provoking
volv, volut	to roll (L, *volvere*, *volutum*)	evolutionist, devolution, revolve

NUMBERS

Latin		Greek
uni	1	*mon, mono*
universal		monastic
university		monocular
uniformity		monograph
du	2	*di*
duplex		dichotomy
duplicity		dilemma
dualism		diphthong
tri	3	Same as Latin
trinity		
trident		
thrice		
quat, quad	4	*tetra*
quaternity		tetragrammation
quadrivium		tetraploid
quadricycle		tetratheism

Latin		Greek
quin	5	*penta*
quinary		Pentagonese
quintessence		Pentateuchal
quinquennial		pentathlon
sex	6	*hex*
sextuplicate		Hexateuchal
sexangular		hexode
sexadecimal		hexad
Sept	7	*hept*
September		heptad
septenary		
septime		
oct	8	Same as Latin
octal		
Octateuch		
October		
nov	9	*enne*
November		ennead
novena		
dec	10	Same as Latin
decade		
decalogue		
decimate		

NOTE: For larger numbers see the end of the chapter on the physical sciences, page 190. Metric numbers are also given.

Chapter 3.
Suffixes

To complete the translation of unknown words, it is necessary to know the meanings of suffixes, the third part of words. You must be able not only to recognize the basic meaning of a word but also to distinguish its various uses as indicated by the suffix, as in *variability, variable, variance, variant, variate,* and *variation.* Being able to deal with these changes in the basic word is especially important in higher education. A term may be introduced and explained if the professor thinks it an unusual word, but from then on he will use it in any appropriate form and expect you to understand. Being able to cope with the rapid changes in form of a word is a part of vocabulary study.

The suffixes appearing in this section are those found most often in the list of higher-level words. Because many of the same suffixes are also used with more common words, you may already know many of them. For this reason express frames are used to guide you to those needing your special attention. You will also need to use the prefixes and roots you have already studied.

3-1 The suffix of the word *hydrometer* is _____. Use the meaning of this suffix to complete a literal translation of hydrometer: _____ _____ measures water. Another meaning for this suffix is _____ _____. Other spellings of this suffix are _____ and _____.	er that which one who ar or
The most common way to indicate the doer of an action is to use the noun suffix *er.* It may be translated "one who" or "that which" does the action shown in the base of the word. The literal meaning of *nutcracker* is "_____ _____ cracks nuts." A saloonkeeper is _____ _____ keeps a saloon.	that which one who

The registrar is in charge of the records of college students. He is the _____ _____ registers students.

one
who

Build one word for each of these literal meanings:

one who grants   _____

that which leads together _____

one who daubs   _____

one who bears tales   _____

grantor
conductor
dauber
talebearer

The suffix which shows agency, that is, the doer of some action, is _____. Also spelled _____ and _____.

er
or/ar

For each of the following verbs form the noun which will show who or what performs the action:

polarize   _____

versify   _____

slander   _____

construct   _____

escalate   _____

adduce   _____

contrive   _____

polarizer
versifier
slanderer
constructor
escalator
adducer
contriver

3-2

One who practices plagiarism is called a _____. The practice of, or belief in, plagiarizing is shown by the suffix _____.

plagiarist

ism (plagiarism)

Not all roots combine easily with *er, or,* or *ar* to show the agent or doer. *Cyclist* and *novelist* use the suffix _____.

ist

This suffix also indicates specialized skills or a profession. One whose special field is biology is called a _____.

biologist

One who specializes in writing satire is called a _____.

satirist

Yet another refinement in the meaning of *ist* indicates one's belief in a certain doctrine or theory.

One who supports the theory of evolution is called an _____.

evolutionist

One who emphasizes a material point of view is a _____.

materialist

A Communist is a believer in commun _____.

ism (communism)

Socialists are adherents of social_____.

ism (socialism)

The belief or theory which is followed is indicated by the suffix _____.

ism

Amorist, capitalist, pacifist, hedonist, Darwinist, and *ventriloquist* — the suffix indicates, not *what*, but _____.

who

If we want to show what they believe in or the area of specialization, we switch from _____ to _____.

ist/ism

3-3

Warner's writing is marked by an earthi_____ which has had wide appeal.

ness (earthiness)

An individual who is conscious of his own nature represents attain_____ of the human goal.

ment (attainment)

A synonym for *discord* is *disson_____*.

ance (dissonance)

Helium, neon, and argon are examples of elements showing low reactiv_____.

ity (reactivity)

These four suffixes mean _____, _____ or_____ _____.

state
condition/quality of

There are several ways to indicate state, condition, or quality of. Consider:

quality of being offensive _____

offensiveness

condition of being enslaved _____

enslavement

state of being incandescent _____

incandescence

quality of being masculine _____

masculinity

Add the appropriate suffix to the forms
below to indicate state or quality:

periodic_____	ity (periodicity)
belliger_____	ence (belligerence)
devil_____	ment (devilment)
inevitable_____	ness (inevitableness)

Without learning highly technical aspects of language, one can develop
an "ear" for language. By paying close attention to the words you see
and hear, you can become familiar with the appropriate suffix to select
as well as the correct form of the root. Remember that verbs have more
than one principal part. For example, the adjective form of *protrude* is
protrusible.

One ending sounds "right" because you have heard that particular
form of the word before. It is much easier to remember things you have
noticed and even have repeated to yourself. In other words, having an
ear for language means simply that you have listened and paid attention
to "what goes with what."

The next two frames offer an opportunity to try out your ear. Mistakes
in these frames are a sign that you need to do some listening.

Use the suffixes *ity, ance* or *ence, ness,* and
ment to complete the following:

1   This essay lacks coher_____.   ence (coherence)

2   Occasionally by some unknown
    means a man manages to write a
    great book despite his intellectual
    vacu_____.   ity (vacuity)

3   Test cases in the courts serve to estab-
    lish the valid_____ of a law.   ity (validity)

4   But your picture is all angles! Its
    angular_____ disturbs me.   ity (angularity)

5   Tensions have been created through-
    out the world by the immin_____   ence (imminence)
    of nuclear war.

6   This program is planned for the
    further_____ of your word skills.   ance (furtherance)

Here are more:

7   Spencer calls architecture, sculpture,
    painting, music, and poetry the
    effloresc_____ of civilized life.   ence (efflorescence)

8 His harsh judgments have now been tempered by mellow_____.	ness (mellowness)
9 Ruthless_____ has been the mark of tyrants.	ness (ruthlessness)
10 Rome is a memorable city. Its impressions were nearly beyond my powers of receptiv_____.	ity (receptivity)or ness (receptiveness)
11 The accident caused a disfigure_____, but its psychological effect was even stronger than the physical.	ment (disfigurement)
12 The entrench_____ of the establishment is the problem to be overcome.	ment (entrenchment)

3-4

Apis is the Latin name for "bee." An apiary is a place where bees are kept. This information of *place* comes from _____. The suffix is _____ and is also spelled _____ and _____.	ary ary/ory ery

A library is a _____ for books.	place
A crematory is a _____ for cremating.	place
A perfumery is a _____ for making perfume.	place
The suffix *ary, ery,* or *ory* must mean "a _____ for" and is an ending for a _____ (part of speech).	place noun

Ery also has the meaning of the collective qualities which display a certain character, as in *knavery, chicanery, buffoonery.* It is the equivalent of the noun suffix *ness.*

Rather than the word *rogueness* we have *rogu_____.* Rather than *prudeness* we have *prud_____.*	ery (roguery) ery (prudery)

But then there are words such as *shimmery, ornery, circulatory, exploratory, binary,* and *unsanitary.* Still *ary, ery,* and *ory,* but the

suffix now indicates use as an _____ (part of speech) and carries the meaning "belonging to" or "connected with."	adjective

3-5

News of the cease-fire produced jubi-lat_____ throughout the country. The suffix to be added is _____ and carries two meanings: (1) _____ and (2) _____.	ion (jubilation) ion act or process state or condition

A noun suffix to name an act or process is *ion*. The process of laminating is a lami-nat_____.	ion (lamination)
The name of the action shown by the verb *to genuflect* (literally, bend the knee) is a *genuflect*_____.	ion (genuflection)

The suffix *ion* is also commonly used to name the state or condition of a person, a thing, or an event.
    The condition resulting from inadequate eating is malnutrit_____.
    Pleasure is a synonym for *delectat*_____, denoting a delightful _____.
	ion (malnutrition)
	ion (delectation)
	state or condition

Name the act or process shown by these verbs:
    render   _____
    predicate _____
    preempt   _____
    sublimate_____
    connote   _____
	rendition
	predication
	preemption
	sublimation
	connotation

Name the state or condition associated with these verbs:
    prognosticate _____
    subfuscate   _____
	prognostication
	subfuscation

deplete _____	depletion
amputate _____	amputation
subvert _____	subversion
retrogress _____	retrogression

NOTE: Verbs ending in *ate* form nouns by using *ion*: *Castigate* becomes *castigation* as a noun. The related noun ending for verbs ending in *ify* is *ication*: *emulsify, emulsification; saponify, saponfication; indemnify, indemnification.* Verbs ending in *ize* use *ation* to make the noun: *mechanize, mechanization; polarize, polarization, demobilize, demobilization.*

3-6 UFO stands for unidentified flying object. 　The suffixes in the above statement are _____ and _____ and indicate _____ (part of speech).	ed/ing/adjective

NOTE: No instructional frames are written for the suffixes *ed* and *ing*. You know these and use them but need to be reminded that they are suffixes — *ed* to form the past tense of verbs and as an adjective, *ing* to form adjectives and nouns.

3-7 Your remarks are peripher_____ to the argument. Please confine yourself to rel-ev_____ remarks.	al (peripheral) ant (relevant)
The observation tower offers a pan-oram_____ view of the harbor.	ic (panoramic)
The suffixes in the above sentences are used to form _____ (part of speech) and carry a meaning of _____, _____ _____.	adjectives of, related to

There are three adjective suffixes commonly used in the higher-level words to indicate "related to, of, having the character of." Consider:	

An evening of music is a music_____ evening.

al (musical)

Two points which are of equal distance from a third point are equidist_____ points.

ant (equidistant)

The policy of a government having the characteristics of imperialism is an imperialist_____ policy.

ic (imperialistic)

Complete these words by adding an adjective suffix meaning "related to, of, having the character of":

Statements of conjecture are conjectur_____ statements.

al (conjectural)

A person who cognizes a situation is cogniz_____ of the situation.

ant (cognizant)

A process which occurs in cycles is a cycl_____ process.

ic (cyclic)

One word meaning "related to a category" is *categorical.* One word meaning "of or related to rabbis" is *rabbinical.*

A variant of the suffix *ic* is _____.

ical

Note that both forms are frequently used for the same word: *rabbinic* or *rabbinical; systematic* or *systemat_____; apostolic* or *apostol_____.*

ical (systematical)
ical (apostolical)

The suffix *ic* may also be used as a noun suffix. The noun indicates the one related to or having the character of. You can distinguish noun or adjective by the use of the word as you find it in a sentence. For example:

"My mother is a diabetic." Used as a(n) _____.

noun

"My mother is in a diabetic coma." Used as a(n) _____.

adjective

NOTE: The suffix *ics* is a noun suffix meaning "the study or knowledge of" certain events or phenomena. You have already had *ology* meaning "study of," as in *biology.* The other suffix in common use with a similar meaning is *ics,* as in *physics, phonics, numismatics, diatetics, eugenics.*

3-8 Another way to say, "She had the characteristics of a coquette," is to say, "She was _____." The suffix is _____ and means _____ _____.	coquettish ish/characteristic of or typical of

The meaning "characteristic or typical of" is indicated by the suffix *ish*.
    Blackish means _____ _____ _____ _____ _____.
 	
    Clannish means _____ _____ _____ _____ _____.
 	
    Pinkish, rakish, foppish, and *swinish* may all be translated _____ _____ the idea which is carried in the base word.
	characteristic or typical of black
	characteristic or typical of a clan
	
	typical of or characteristic of

3-9
He accepted the prestigious if somewhat onerous assignment as chairman of the committee.
    His assignment was literally _____ _____ prestige.
    Another word in the sentence using this same suffix is _____.
    The suffix forms a(n) _____ (part of speech).
	full
	of
	
	onerous
	adjective

"Full of" or "abounding in" is conveyed by the suffix *ous*.
    United States relationships with Russia have at times been most tenuous; that is, they have literally been _____ _____ stretch, that is, weak.
 	
    A calamitous situation _____ _____ _____ calamity.
	full of
	
	is full of

Weak vocabulary skills are disadvantageous to a student. They present a situation which is _____ _____ disadvantage.

full of

Make adjectives from the following nouns which mean "full of":

slumber	_____	slumberous
vermin	_____	verminous
idolatry	_____	idolatrous
sedition	_____	seditious
acrimony	_____	acrimonious
felicity	_____	felicitous
blasphemy	_____	blasphemous
glamor	_____	glamorous

3-10
John was at an age to be impressible.
   The suffix in the above sentence is _____
and means _____ _____.
The more common spelling of this suffix
is _____.

ible
capable of or able to

able

Able or *ible* is the suffix used to convey the information "capable of" or "able to."
   If something is not able to be worked, it is unwork_____.
   If an idea can be discredited, it is discredit_____.

able (unworkable)

able (discreditable)

Write one word which is equivalent in meaning to each of the following phrases:

not able to be recovered	_____	irrecoverable or nonrecoverable
able to be demonstrated	_____	demonstrable or demonstratable
able to be taught	_____	teachable
not able to be escaped	_____	inescapable
able to be reversed	_____	reversible
not able to communicate	_____	incommunicable

The suffix is _____ or _____ and means _____ _____.	able/ible capable of, able to

3-11

Word study is an educat_____ process. The suffix is _____ and means _____ _____ _____ _____ _____. This suffix indicates _____ (part of speech).	ive (educative) ive/performs or tends toward an action adjective

To show that something tends toward an action or performs that action, the suffix to use is *ive*. When the action is regular or lasting, this is particularly the suffix to use.

"Childhood is the period during which habits and character are formed." These are the format_____ years.   ive (formative)

Evidence tending to help draw a conclusion is conclus_____ evidence.   ive (conclusive)

You cannot learn what you have not paid attention to. You must be attent_____.   ive (attentive)

For each of the following phrases build one word which has an equivalent meaning:

tends to intrude _____	intrusive
that correlates _____	correlative
tending to repress _____	repressive
expressing in terms of quantity _____	quantitative
expressing in terms of quality _____	qualitative
tending to regenerate _____	regenerative
that permits _____	permissive

NOTE: The something which performs or tends toward the action is also indicated by *ive*. Then it is a noun suffix. Examples are *abrasive,* either describing or naming that which performs the abrading action, and *fixative,* that which fixes. But the adjective use is more common.

3-12 Sleep that is without dreams is dream_____ sleep. The suffix is _____ and means _____.	less (dreamless) less without
The suffix *less* means "without." 　Glands which have no ducts, or are without ducts, are duct_____. 　A horse without a rider is rider_____. The suffix *less* is an easy one, since its meaning is conveyed in and of itself. 　A chicken less, or minus, its feathers is feather_____, or _____ feathers.	less (ductless) less (riderless) less (featherless) without
3-13 In the word *irregular* the prefix was originally *in*, but the *n* has been assimil_____ to an *r*. 　He had resharp_____ his knife to get a better cut. 　"This ground has been set aside for religious use." The ground has been sanct_____. 　The three verb suffixes given above are _____, _____, and _____. The fourth, and very common, suffix used to form a verb is _____.	ated (assimilated) ened (resharpened) ified (sanctified) ate/en/ify ize
You have probably heard the language purists complaining and weeping over modern use of a very common verb suffix. A whole new crop of verbs has come about. For example: 　To become familiar with or to make familiar is to _____. 　To make final is to _____. 　If you make your house up-to-date, you _____ it.	 familiarize finalize modernize

When you yield to the tempo of the times, you _____.	temporize
If you commit all these word elements to memory, you _____ them.	memorize
To cause to be free or to make free is to liber_____.	ate (liberate)
To make something longer is to length _____ it.	en (lengthen)
To make a deed glorious is to glor_____ it.	ify (glorify)
Three more verb suffixes are _____, _____, and _____.	ate en/ify

---

3-14
The suffix commonly used to form an adverb is _____ and means _____ _____ _____ _____.

ly/in the
manner of

Ly is the adverbial suffix commonly used. It means "in the manner of" whatever is supplied in the base word. Sometimes you must first form the adjective before you add *ly*.

A person who performed in the manner of being without fault performed fault-less_____.

ly (faultlessly)

"In a manner which tends to suggest" is expressed in the word *suggestive*_____.

ly (suggestively)

Express the following phrases as single adverbs:

in a manner full of ostentation

_____

ostentatiously

in a manner showing hesitation

_____

hesitantly

in the manner of an idiot

_____

idiotically

in a manner not able to conform

_____

unconformably

in a manner displaying obliqueness

_____

obliquely

in a manner without time

_____

timelessly

Although *ly* is most commonly used as an adverbial suffix, please note "a crawly insect," "a queenly woman," "a crumbly cookie," "a wifely act." *Ly* may also be used as a(n) _____ (part of speech). However, it still has the idea of manner. A queenly woman is one who is like a queen in manner.

adjective

3-15
Trigonometry, monogamy, smutty, seaworthy — all contain the suffix _____ which may be used to indicate the parts of speech_____ and _____ .

y
noun
adjective

The use of *y* as an adjective suffix is already familiar to you. *Shifty, sweaty, wordy,* and *zany* are words you have used. A formal meaning for *y* as an adjective suffix is "characterized by."
   A person who displays grumpiness is grump_____ .

y (grumpy)

The most common use of *y* as a noun suffix is to name a state, condition, or quality — it has the same meaning as the noun suffixes in 3-3. The *y* is frequently added to a root to make a combining form.
   The root *log* has a *y* added to mean _____

_____ _____ .

the
study of

Tom means "cut." To cut the appendix is to perform an appendec_____ .

tomy (appendectomy)

The Greek word *kratos,* strength or power, gives us the form *cracy,* meaning "the form of government." A state having one person

in power is a _____. If the people hold the power, the state is a demo_____.	monocracy cracy (democracy)
The root *gam* means "marriage." The state of being married to only one spouse is _____. If there are two spouses, the noun is *bi*_____.	monogamy gamy (bigamy)

REVIEW OF SUFFIXES

In the following article you are to supply the missing suffixes. Not all suffixes have been deleted, but a sufficient number have been deleted to offer you a review and a check on your skill in handling them. You can judge your success by how accurately and how rapidly you can complete this exercise. An article is used so that you will have the advantage of a connected passage.

People are afraid of machines—and right_____ so—and the machine that tops the blacklist—and rightly so—is the comput_____.	ly er
The computer is often seen as an invis_____, superhuman force that perme_____ our lives, robb_____ us of our ident_____ and human_____. Names are replac_____ by numbers, and the numbers are fed into computers, and our lives are controlled by this outside account_____ *extraordinaire* who sends home our school grades, tells us how much we owe Carte Blanche, computes our bank bal_____, and keeps track of our phone calls.	ible ates/ing ity/ity ed ant ance
Giv_____ the fact that a computer is really no more than a giant adding machine, performing faithful_____ and quick_____, why is it that people become upset by a timesaving machine which makes their lives so much easier and pleasanter? (Even the complain_____ Berkeley student might want his IBM number back if he found how long he would have to wait in lines without it.)	en ly/ly ing
I think the reasons why people are afraid	

of machines are quite clear—and they are
not the most import_____ reasons. First,
people are often afraid of machines because they feel inferior to them—machines
can do so many things faster and more accurately.

ant

Second, people are insecure about their
own human warmth and feel_____ and
worry that in many ways they are like a
machine—no soul, no compass_____, no
free will. And third, people blame machines
for ills that really result from other sources—
impersonal_____ results when large
numbers of people are thrown together;
yet machines, in trying to cre_____ order
out of potent_____ chaos, become scape-
goats for those who are unsure of their
own ident_____.

ings

ion

ization

ate
ial

ities
ically

And so, iron_____ enough, as the world
gets smaller and the number of people gets
larger, human contact increases and human
security decreases. Is the computer at fault?
I doubt it.

Why, then, should people be afraid of
computers?

Given their aston_____ capac_____
for doing numer_____ calculat_____,
computers can become quite powerful—
even in the role of serv_____ to man. As
time goes on and computers are used more
and more to solve complex mathemat_____
equations which pertain to the regulation
of our econom_____, our defense system,
and our polit_____ system—only then does
the fear of computers become legitim_____.

ishing/ity
ical/ions

ant

ical

y
ical
ate

For example, what happ_____ if one of
these mathematical equations or models is
inaccurate or incomplete? What happens if
there is poor judg_____ in deciding what
data to give the computer? What happens
if—Machine forbid—the electron_____ wiz-
ard makes an err_____? Probably nothing

ens

ment

ic
or

would happen. The miscalculation would be caught, correct_____ and everything would proceed without a hitch.

But as computers become even better, mathematical models more accurate, and mistakes fewer, people might begin to rely on the Machine's answers more and more.

Eventual_____ the computer would be making calculations of such a complex and detail_____ nature that the quantitat_____ transformations would result in qual-itat_____ differ_____ between the input and the output. Then errors would be dif-ficult, if not imposs_____ to recogn_____.

The ultimate danger might come if the output of the computer were tied directly into regul_____ and mod_____ the system —just the way computers are used today to make instantane_____ decis_____ in guiding a rocket to a safe landing. Thus, a futur_____ society guided by a self-generat__•___, self-regulat_____computer could compound an even minor miscal-culation into something grotesque—long before the consequ_____ could be rec-ogn_____ or averted.

And so, weep not that the computer does not weep, nor that you do not weep—but weep when you ask the comput_____ to weep for you.

ed
ly
ed/ive
ive/ences
ible/ize
ating/ifying
ous/ions
istic
ive/ory
ences
ized
er

CHAPTER 3 WORD LIST

The words used for study in Chapter 3 are listed for your use in further practice. Try changing the form of the word. For example, *abrasive, abrasiveness, abrasively*. The final level of mastery means that you also know other related forms, in this instance, *abrade, abrasion*.

abrasive	amorist	appendectomy	attentive
accountant	amputation	assimilated	
acrimonious	angularity	astonishing	balance
adducer	apiary	attainment	belligerence

bigamy
binary
biologist
blackish
blasphemous
buffoonery
calamitous
calculations
capacity
capitalist
castigation
categorical
chicanery
circulatory
clannish
cognizant
coherence
communism
compassion
complaining
computer
conclusive
conductor
conjectural
connotation
consequences
constructor
contriver
coquettish
corrected
correlative
create
crematory
cyclic
cyclist

Darwinist
dauber
decisions
delectation
demobilization
democracy

demonstrable
depletion
detailed
devilment
diabetic
diatetics
differences
disadvantageous
discreditable
disfigurement
dissonance
dreamless
ductless

earthiness
economy
educative
efflorescence
electronic
emulsification
enslavement
entrenchment
equidistant
error
escalator
eugenics
eventually
evolutionist
exploratory

faithfully
familiarize
faultlessly
featherless
feelings
felicitous
finalize
fixative
foppish
formative
furtherance
futuristic

genuflection
given
glamorous
glorify
grantor
grumpy

happens
hedonist
hesitantly
humanity
hydrometer

identities
identity
idolatrous
idiotically
imminence
impassible
imperialistic
impersonalization
important
impressible
incandescence
incommunicable
indemnification
inescapable
inevitableness
instantaneous
intrusive
invisible
ironically
irrecoverable

jubilation
judgment

knavery

lamination
legitimate
lengthen

liberate
library

malnutrition
masculinity
materialist
mathematical
mechanization
mellowness
memorize
modernize
modifying
monocracy
monogamy
musical

novelist
numerical
numismatics
nutcracker

obliquely
offensiveness
onerous
ornery
ostentatiously

pacifist
panoramic
perfumery
periodicity
peripheral
permeates
permissive
phonics
physics
pinkish
plagiarism
plagiarist
polarization
polarizer
political

potential
predication
preemption
prestigious
prognostication
prudery

qualitative
quantitative
quickly

rabbinical
rakish
reactivity
receptivity
recognize
recognized
regenerative
registrar

regulating
relevant
rendition
replaced
repressive
resharpened
reversible
riderless
rightly
robbing
roguery
ruthlessness

saloonkeeper
sanctified
saponification
satirist
seaworthy
seditious

self-generative
self-regulatory
servant
shifty
shimmery
slanderer
slumberous
smutty
socialism
subfuscation
sublimation
subversion
suggestively
sweaty
swinish

talebearer
teachable
temporize

tenuous
timelessly
trigonometry

unconformably
unsanitary
unworkable

vacuity
validity
ventriloquist
verminous
versifier

wordy

zany

REFERENCE SECTION – SUFFIXES

An intensive study of suffixes is well worth the effort. Word endings not only indicate the part of speech but also convey meaning. This list includes the suffixes covered in Chapter 3 (marked with an asterisk) as well as additional endings. Endings are listed alphabetically for your convenience. Suffixes used in chemistry are covered under the nomenclature of chemistry, pages 168–181.

Suffix	Meaning	Part of speech	Example
*able	capable of, able to	adj.	exchangeable
ac, acious	of, related to	adj.	cardiac
age	collection, action, place of	n.	coverage
*al	of, related to, like	adj.	developmental
al	action, process	n.	rebuttal
an, ian	of, belonging to	adj.	reptilian
an, ian	one who, one skilled in	n.	obstetrician
*ance, ancy	action, state, quality	n.	superabundance
*ant	of, related to, like	adj.	ascendant
ant	one who	n.	celebrant
ar	of, related to	adj.	vehicular

Suffix	Meaning	Part of speech	Example
*ar	one who	n.	registrar
ard	one who	n.	laggard
arium	place where	n.	herbarium
ary	of, belonging to	adj.	precautionary
*ary	place where	n.	seminary
ate	having, being	adj.	insensate
ate	office, rank	n.	doctorate
ate	one who	n.	advocate
*ate	to act upon, cause	v.	federate
ation	action, process	n.	verification
ble	able to be	adj.	soluble
cy	state, quality	n.	fervency
dom	state, quality	n.	freedom
ee	one who is	n.	advisee
eer	one who	n.	auctioneer
elle, ella	little	n.	organelle
en	like, having	adj.	wooden
en	little	n.	kitten
*en	to cause, come to be	v.	strengthen
*ence, ency	state, quality	n.	presidency
ent	one who	n.	president
*er	one who, that which	n.	modifier
ern	related to	adj.	southern
ery	place where	n.	perfumery
ette	little	n.	dinette
ful	full of	adj.	playful
hood	state, quality	n.	boyhood
*ible	capable of, able to	adj.	legible
*ic, ical	of, related to, like	adj.	demonic
ice	that which	n.	service
id	being	adj.	placid
ie	little	n.	doggie
ier	one who	n.	furrier
*ify	to make, perform	v.	amplify
ile	like, related to	adj.	servile
ine	like, related to	adj.	feline
*ing	action, process	n.	reading
*ing	ongoing	v./adj.	arresting
*ion	action, process; state or condition	n.	validation
ise	to make, perform	v.	criticise

Suffix	Meaning	Part of speech	Example
*ish	characteristic or typical of	adj.	swinish
*ism	state, belief	n.	positivism
*ist	one who	n.	militarist
ite	one who is	n.	favorite
*ity	state, quality	n.	depravity
*ive	performing, tending toward	adj.	manipulative
*ive	that which performs or acts	n.	sedative
*ize	to make, perform	v.	epitomize
kin	little	n.	pipkin
*less	without	adj.	hopeless
let	little	n.	droplet
like	like, related to	adj.	sportsmanlike
ling	little	n.	duckling
*ly	like, related to	adj.	queenly
*ly	in the manner of	adv.	profoundly
*ment	state, quality, act	n.	estrangement
mony	that which	n.	testimony
mony	state, quality	n.	matrimony
*ness	state, quality	n.	astuteness
oid	like, resembling	n.	humanoid
or	state, quality	n.	demeanor
*or	one who, that which	n.	factor
*ory	place where	n.	factory
*ory	belonging to, connected with	adj.	respiratory
ose	full of	adj.	verbose
osis	state, quality	n.	acidosis
*ous	full of, abounding in	adj.	perilous
ship	state, quality	n.	statesmanship
some	characterized by	adj.	lithesome
tude	state, quality	n.	fortitude
ule	little	n.	pustule
ulent	full of, abounding in	adj.	opulent
ure	that which is	n.	picture
ure	act	n.	departure
ward	toward	adv.	forward
*y	characterized by	adj.	grumpy
*y	state, quality	n.	liberty

Chapter 4.
Vocabulary in Context

Learning the meaning of a word through its use in a sentence is the most practical way to build vocabulary. Considering the thousands of words you must be able to understand, it can be safely said that only a relatively small number of words must be given precise definitions by you, that is, such definitions as would be found in a dictionary. What you must be able to do is to make sense out of the sentences you are reading or hearing. Certainly, during a lecture you do not have time to look up an unknown word in the dictionary, and in your reading you do not want to take time to look up each unknown word.

Skipping the hard word and hoping that its meaning will become clear later on is a risky business, particularly with academic material. A technical term will be defined the first time it is used. From then on you are expected to know it, not wait for the meaning to become clear. With nontechnical words in an academic context, you are expected to understand them.

Learning as you read, then, is the practical skill worth acquiring. You understand as you read because you can derive sufficient meaning from even unknown words so that the text makes sense.

This chapter presents six kinds of context clues commonly used to derive the meaning of unknown words. Clues are those bits of information which can help you get at meaning. You no doubt began lessons in the use of context clues in the early grades, but experience has shown that you may not really be alert to actual clues and, therefore, have no way of making the clues pay off.

The purpose of this chapter is to offer practice in using context clues rather than to make you able to talk about them by name. Once alerted to the various ways words within a sentence help give information about another word in the sentence, you can take advantage of this practical approach.

There are no express frames in this section because you are not required to learn the names of clues or recognize them as such. Rather, the emphasis is on your being able to use the information contained in a sentence; therefore, do not use a dictionary. You are training yourself to use all the clues in the sentence. You are to work all the frames in this section. There is no one correct answer. You will have to judge whether or not the word or words you supply do mean the same as the suggested answers given. However, these answers do represent synonyms that were commonly used by students in preliminary tryouts of the program. Additional practice can be found in each of the special subject matter areas, Part 2.

SIX KINDS OF CONTEXT CLUES

1   *Definition.* The term will be formally defined, or a sufficient explanation will be given within the sentence for the meaning to be available.

The majority of organisms are aerobic; that is, they require oxygen to release the energy needed for life functions.

Aerobic means _____ _____.

requiring oxygen
clue: that is

After age forty some men increase their amount of bed rest to the point where it actually becomes enervating. The man who gets more than eight or nine hours of sleep will probably have less energy than the man who gets fewer hours of sleep.

Enervating must mean _____ _____ _____.

loss of energy
clue: less energy

2   *Analysis.* The parts used to construct the word can be a direct clue to meaning. The first three chapters of this program have offered practice in using the elements most commonly found to construct higher-level English words. Strictly speaking, analysis is not a clue from the rest of the sentence, but it is a practical way of knowing the meanings of words as you read.

Because government has become an important factor in income and investment activities, it is necessary for a manager to previse governmental fiscal action in developing his plans.

Previse means _____ _____.

look ahead
clue: *pre* = before
vis = look

As the disease progresses, nervous and mental symptoms supervene even the most noticeable physical symptoms.

Supervene means _____.

overcome
clue: *super* = over
ven = come

3   *Experience.* Either from an experience of your own or one that you can imagine, the meaning of a word is made clear.

A person may hold a certain philosophy but not be able to articulate it, at least not always in words.
    Articulate means _____ _____.

speak clearly
clue: not be able . . .
in words

It is likely that both olfactory and taste sensitivity are involved in food selection. The problem of taking that first bite of Limburger cheese serves as an example.
    Olfactory means _____ _____
_____.

sense of smell
clue: Limburger cheese

4   *Contrast.* By contrasting terms, you may find that one term will help clarify or explain another. This assumes, of course, that you know one of the terms.

Meditation is generally favored by the Roman Catholic, but in general the Protestant will abjure it.
    Abjure must mean _____.

reject, avoid
clue: favored . . . but

The term *sea* usually implies that waters are saline, but the Sea of Galilee is not salty.
    Another word for *saline* is _____.

salty
clue: but . . . not salty

5   *Inference.* Sufficient clues are available for you to make an educated guess at meaning.

In his lectures Sullivan typically eschewed the obvious in favor of the obscure.
    Eschewed means _____.

passed over, shunned
clue: in favor of

Important pedagogical purposes can be served by the essay-type examination because students learn to organize their ideas and improve their style of expression.
    Another word for *pedagogical* is _____.

teaching, educational
clue: students learn

6   *Combination of analysis with one of the other four.* Modern usage may

have grown away from the literal meaning of the word elements, but clues within the passage will enable you to go from the literal meaning to the modern meaning.

In this kind of experiment the next step is to extirpate the median nerve cord and the lateral nerves to see if the heart beats without these.

    Another way of saying *extirpate* is _____ _____.

> cut out
> *clue: ex* = out, without

The records of our penal institutions show that bribes and threats, and punishments and rewards are only moderately effective — for prisons are full of recidivists.

    Recidivists means _____.

> repeaters, relapsers
> *clue: re* = back or again;
> only moderately

PRACTICE WITH THE SIX CLUES

This next section offers practice with these various kinds of clues. They are labeled so that you can gain experience in using a particular type of clue before trying regular material where the clues are mixed.

Definition

The great religions all share the common purpose of producing a *metanoia*, a change of spirit.

    Metanoia means _____ _____ _____.

> change of
> spirit

The characters created and developed by a writer need not be based on actual people, but they must have verisimilitude, or plausibility.

    Verisimilitude must mean _____, that is, _____ _____ _____.

> plausibility
> appearance of truth

Energy is defined as the ability to do work.

    Energy means _____ _____ _____.

> ability to
> do work

Analysis

Doctors who came in contact with sleeping sickness adduced that changes of personality were a result of brain damage caused by this disease.

Adduce means_____

_____ _____ _____ .

present as proof or example (*ad* + *duc* = lead to)

Pittsburgh has experienced a renaissance due to the creative vision of architects.

Renaissance means _____ .

rebirth (*re* + *nais* = born again)

An author may deal with a modern theme but set his story in another time in order to obviate certain assumptions about current times which his readers may hold but which are not useful in understanding his story.

Obviate means _____ .

prevent (*ob* + *via* = against the way)

Experience

If you outline the major bodies of water, you will automatically delineate the land masses.

Delineate means _____ .

mark, represent

His sin was envy. It caused him to denigrate the work of others for his own glorification.

Denigrate means _____ .

downgrade, belittle

One fear about the discoveries in the use of drugs is that some future dictator might use them for nefarious purposes.

Nefarious means _____ .

evil

Contrast

The pictorial aspect of art may be important, but it is not the significant factor which separates mundane art from great art.

Mundane means _____ .

ordinary

Many an amateur artist has discovered that he had latent talent once he started to paint.

Latent means _____ .

undiscovered, hidden

We can now summarize our discussion by

this statement: that which is used develops, and that which is not used atrophies.

Atrophy means _____.

waste away, deteriorate

Inference

Your assigned reading consists of a collection of papers dealing with the topic Learning. They have been categorized under the rubrics of Acquisition, Transfer, and Retention.

Rubrics means _____.

titles, headings

At the next level down the hierarchy of a political party is the state committee.

Hierarchy means _____.

levels, rank

The writing of Voltaire was so vitriolic that he seemed to have dipped his pen in acid.

Vitriolic means _____.

caustic, biting

Combination

Heredity and environment are synergic. Even the most gifted individual must be in a favorable environment to reach his fullest achievement.

Synergic means _____.

work together (*syn* = together)

Why study literature? Most of us would agree with Arnold that it is a major purpose of literature to illumine human experience.

Illumine means _____.

enlighten, clarify (*il* = not, *lumin* = light)

There are about four thousand species of living reptiles which herpetologists recognize.

Herpetologist means _____
_____ _____.

one who studies reptiles (*olog* = study, *ist* = one who)

GENERAL PRACTICE

The six kinds of clues you have been working with are the ones which are generally most useful. The purpose of naming and explaining each kind was to make you aware of the various clues available to help you to make sense out of your reading by developing the skill of using context clues effectively. Using a dictionary would defeat the purpose of this chapter. In regular text material these clues are not isolated or sequenced in any kind of order. You must be ready to use any kind of clue available.

When you come upon an unknown word, you must be able to translate to terms you do know. This section presents excerpts from two college texts of contrasting subject matter, drama and genetics. Your task is to translate each of the italicized words into plain English. Since your answers may not be identical with the key, you must decide if you have said the same thing.

In addition to the clues you have just practiced, you will also find an accumulative effect, or building up of clues to help you. This means that your first translation may be only tentative, but the accumulative effect will confirm your choice or provide sufficient information to correct your choice of meaning. For convenience of your practice the text material is broken into small sections.

Notice that in actual use, deriving word meanings from context clues blends into reading comprehension. One is a part of the other.

Drama

1 Melodrama, sometimes called low tragedy, is not a type of
2 tragedy but belongs to that third form of drama whose action and
3 powers differ from tragedy. The action of melodrama is seemingly
4 serious or temporarily serious. It poses a threat to a *sympathetic*
5 individual or individuals and hence *engenders* fear for their hap-
6 piness and well being. Usually that threat is initiated and manip-
7 ulated by an *antipathetic antagonist* or villain whose *machinations*
8 arouse hate. The distinctive powers of this third form are the
9 arousal and *purgation* of fear and hate. Pity enters into our re-
10 action usually in the form of *pathos* as a means of increasing the
11 antipathy and hate and not as a distinctive power in itself. For
12 the proper purgation the third form should have a double ending—
13 reward for the sympathetic and punishment for the antipathetic
14 individuals.

Line 4—*Sympathetic* literally means "feelings _____." The character in the melodrama is joined by the feelings of the _____. They suffer _____ (*sym*).

with

reader or audience
together

Line 5—Substitute a word for *engenders*
which also has to do with causing_____
(*gen*): "and hence _____ fear."

birth
begets or produces

Line 7—The prefix of *pathetic* is now _____.
It is contrasted with _____ and means
_____.

anti
sym or with
against

    A synonym for *antagonist* in this context
is _____. The clue is _____.

villain/or

Line 7—Does your mental picture of a villain
in melodrama include a man twirling the
ends of a black mustache while gloating
over the crafty schemes he has plotted
against the hero or heroine? If so, then you
can translate *machinations*_____ _____.

evil schemes or tricks

Line 9—*Purgation* of fear and hate follows
arousal. Once aroused, something must be
done about the fear and hate. A synonym
for *purgation* is _____.

cleansing, eliminating,
or ridding

    Perhaps you know the term *purge* as an
old-fashioned term for laxative and from
this association can apply the proper meaning to another situation.

Line 10—*Pathos* is a form of _____.

pity

15   The characters in this third form, unlike those in tragedy
16   but like those in comedy, are *static* in that they have made
17   their fundamental moral choices before the action begins. In the
18   course of the action they do not make successive fundamental
19   moral choices and hence do not grow and develop in the way that
20   characters do in tragedy. Though we may learn successive new
21   things about them, they do not change their fundamental natures.
22   The hero remains essentially good and sympathetic throughout
23   and the villain remains evil to the last. In the end of the play he
24   may, as a part of his punishment, be convicted of his evil nature
25   and ways and allowed to repent but the form is more satisfying if
26   he is turned over to justice, beaten to death, or pumped full of
27   lead. Melodrama should produce that relief of fear *averted* or

28   escaped and that enjoyment of vengeance achieved. In its final
29   effects it comes close to that of certain comedies. In fact this third
30   form may be conceived as lying between tragedy and comedy and
31   sharing some of the formal characteristics of both. It resembles
32   comedy in that its characters are static, its final effects somewhat
33   similar, and its structure may be loose and *episodic*. It resembles
34   tragedy, among other ways, in that its action is for a time serious
35   and one of its powers, fear, is the same as a power of tragedy.

Line 16—*Static* means _____.	stationary or unchanging
If you did not know the meaning of the root *stat*, stand, you could have derived the meaning by the contrast with tragedy signaled by the cue word _____.	unlike
Line 27—*Averted* is made up of the prefix _____ and the root _____. Its literal meaning may be substituted so that the phrase reads "relief of fear which has been_____ _____."	a or ab/vert turned away
Line 33—*Episodic* means situations occurring _____ (epi) the way (sod) that may be enjoyed separately but still are a part of the story.	upon

36   There is a wide tendency to use the terms *tragedy* and *melodrama*
37   in a *prejudicative* sense. This must be understood and
38   guarded against in reading critical studies. Tragedy may be good
39   tragedy or bad tragedy; melodrama may be good melodrama or
40   bad. Simply because a tragedy is not in the ranks of the great mas-
41   terpieces is no reason for obscuring an examination of its form
42   by denying the name tragedy to it. Moreover, a good melodrama
43   may be *aesthetically* better than a bad tragedy.

Line 37—*Prejudicative* literally means "judging _____."	before
Although *prejudicative* is not in common use, did you think immediately of a similar and more familiar term? _____.	prejudice

This meaning is confirmed in the remaining portion of the paragraph.

Line 43 — A sensible substitute for *aesthetically* in this context would be _____.
This synonym fits the subject matter of drama.

artistically

Genetics

1 The fundamental units of racial variability are populations and
2 genes, not *complexes* of characters which *connote* in the popular
3 mind a racial distinction. Much confusion of thought could be
4 avoided if all biologists would realize this fact. How important it is
5 may be illustrated by the following analogy. Many studies on hy-
6 bridization were made before Mendel, but they did not lead to the
7 discovery of Mendel's laws. In *retrospect*, we see clearly where the
8 mistake of Mendel's *predecessors* lay: they treated as units the
9 complexes characteristic of individuals, races, and species and
10 attempted to find rules governing the inheritance of such complexes.
11 Mendel was the first to understand that it was the inheritance of
12 separate traits, not of complexes of traits, which had to be studied.
13 Some of the students of racial variability consistently repeat the
14 mistakes of Mendel's predecessors.

Line 2 — *Complexes* literally means _____
_____ and implies several units
as contrasted with the _____ (number)
named. The clue word signaling contrast
is _____.

folded
together
two

not

Line 2 — *Connote* literally means "to note
_____." The extra meaning of
"racial distinction" is carried along _____
(*con*) the basic meaning intended in listing
racial characteristics.

with or together
with

Line 7 — For "in *retrospect*" may be substituted "in _____ _____."
Apparently nothing beats hindsight — even
in science!

looking back

Line 8 — *Predecessors* can be translated to

"those who have gone (*cess*) _____   before
(*pre*)."

15 An endless and notoriously *inconclusive* discussion of the "race
16 problem" has been going on for many years in the biological,
17 anthropological, and sociological literature. Stripped of unnecessary
18 *verbiage*, the question is this: is a "race" a concrete entity existing
19 in nature, or is it merely an *abstraction* with a very limited useful-
20 ness? To a geneticist it seems clear enough that all the *lucubrations*
21 on the "race problem" fail to take into account that a race is not a
22 *static* entity but a process. Race formation begins when the fre-
23 quency of a certain gene or genes becomes slightly different in one
24 part of a population from what it is in other parts. If the differentia-
25 tion is allowed to proceed *unimpeded*, most or all of the individuals
26 of one race may come to possess certain genes which those of
27 the other race do not. Finally, mechanisms preventing the
28 *interbreeding* of races may develop, splitting what used to be a
29 single collective *genotype* into two or more separate ones. When
30 such mechanisms have developed and the prevention of interbreed-
31 ing is more or less complete, we are dealing with separate species.
32 A race becomes more and more of a "concrete entity" as this
33 process goes on: what is essential about races is not their state of
34 being but that of becoming. But when the separation of races is
35 complete, we are dealing with races no longer, for what have
36 *emerged* are separate species.

Line 15—The root of *inconclusive* means "to
close." Translate the kind of discussion
which has been going on: "one which tends
_____ _____ _____ _____."   not to close together

    The suffix is _____ and denotes what   ive
part of speech? _____   adjective

Line 18—*Verbiage* means _____,   wordiness
that is, _____ _____. The word   excess words
implying an excess amount is_____.   unnecessary
The word *stripped* also gives the same hint.

Line 19—*Abstraction* is contrasted with the
word _____, and literally means   concrete
"a _____ _____ the real   drawing from

world certain characteristics or features for special attention."

Line 20 — *Lucubrations* is an example of the accumulative effect of context. Having noted "endless and notoriously *inconclusive*" in line 15, then "for many years" and the mention of *three* professional areas, lines 16 and 17, a good guess on the meaning of *lucubrations* is _____ _____.

laborious study or thought

This author thinks much or little of all the work and discussion done heretofore? _____

little

Line 22 — A synonym for *static* which fits this sentence is _____. See above, line 16 of "Drama."

unchanging

Line 25 — A literal translation of *unimpeded* is "_____ with the foot _____ the way." A more ordinary way of expressing this idea is _____ _____.

not/in

without interference or blocking

Line 28 — The prefix of *interbreeding* is _____, so that the idea expressed here can be translated to "breeding _____ the races."

inter

between

Line 29 — The term *genotype* refers to characteristics of an individual or group inherited through the genes or by _____ (*gen*). *Genotype* is often paired with the contrasting term *phenotype* from Greek *phainein*, to show. *Phenotype* means "the appearance or showing of characteristics resulting from an interaction between the environment and the genotype."

birth

Line 36 — In place of *emerged*, the last clause can be reworded to "for what have come

_____ are separate species." *Emerged* is literally translated as "dipped _____."

out
out

CHAPTER 4 WORD LIST

Use this list for review and practice. If the meaning of a word escapes you, try to recall the context in which it was used. Having a meaningful example of the word in actual use can be helpful in remembering it.

The vocabulary used in Chapter 4 represents a fairly difficult level. For each entry try to supply a synonym or phrase which will help you to understand the word. Also use these words for practice with suffixes so that you not only are familiar with all the forms when you meet them but also can use such words yourself when appropriate.

abjure	energy	lucubrations	purgation
abstraction	enervating		
adduce	engenders	machinations	recidivist
aerobic	episodic	metanoia	renaissance
aesthetically	eschewed	mundane	retrospect
antagonist	extirpate		rubrics
articulate		nefarious	
atrophy	genotype		saline
averted		obviate	static
	herpetologist	olfactory	supervene
complexes	hierarchy		sympathetic
connote		pathetic	synergic
	illumine	pathos	
delineate	inconclusive	pedagogical	unimpeded
denigrate	interbreeding	predecessors	
		prejudicative	verbiage
emerged	latent	previse	vitriolic

Part 2.
Application to Subject Matter

INTRODUCTION

In beginning courses the vocabulary peculiar to the subject being studied is the primary learning task. After basic concepts are introduced, each next step is built on a preceding one. Each concept and each process have labels or names which must be learned. Not all concepts can be grasped immediately, and it may be several courses before they are completely understood, but from the first day the concepts are introduced their names are used and must be known by students. These names, then, may be in the form of words or symbols; both forms are the vocabulary to be learned.

Textbook authors and lecturers are most careful to explain or define a term when first used, but from that time on the student is expected to recognize and use the term, know its meaning, and handle the various forms in which it may appear. For example, in a chemistry class you might hear the lecturer say, "This demonstration you have just seen was for the purpose of showing that electric energy can be used to produce chemical change. The process is called electrolysis. As a second example of chemical change produced electrolytically we shall consider what happens when aqueous sodium chloride is electrolized." In this example the term *electrolysis* has been used as a noun, as an adverb, *electrolytically*, and as a verb, *electrolized*. A student could reasonably expect the adjective form, *electrolytic*, to show up while he is studying electrolysis.

This example is used to emphasize the need for mastery of suffixes (Chapter 3) so that students can handle the various forms in which the term appears.

A student has no trouble identifying or locating these terms which he must learn; they are printed in boldface type or italics when introduced. The problem is to learn and remember them. This problem is made greater because of the rapid rate at which these terms are introduced. One term is scarcely learned before there are several more to be mastered. Rote memorization of a list of terms and definitions is the least satisfactory way to master this vocabulary. The more meaning something has, the easier it is to learn and remember. Specialized vocabulary comes from several sources, and it is these sources which provide the clues to use for learning and remembering:

	Source	*Clue for remembering*
1	Derivatives of Latin and Greek or other languages	Meaning of the individual word elements

Example: *ovipositor* = that which places eggs

ovi = eggs

pos = put or place

or = that which

2   Names after the discoverer   The discoverer or circumstances
                                                of the discovery
    Example: pasteurize, from Pasteur
3   Acronym   Each letter of the acronym
    Example: *laser* = *l*ight *a*mplification by *s*timulated *e*mission of
                  *r*adiation
4   Any word not included above   Mnemonic device, an artificial
                                                or arbitrary association
    Example: stala*c*tite, emphasis on *c* for ceiling
             stala*g*mite, emphasis on *g* for ground

In addition to the technical terms which must be learned, two other kinds of vocabulary pose problems in special subject areas:

1   One is the nontechnical language which is not used in ordinary conversation. These words are mostly derived from Latin and Greek. The word elements most useful for dealing with such words were presented in Chapters 1 and 2 of this book, and are the foundation for deriving meaning in general; however, practice in using these elements within a subject-matter context is required for ease in handling the language of a field.
2   The other kind of vocabulary problem within a subject area deals with ordinary words used in special ways, that is, ordinary words with technical definitions.

Physics is a good example of a field where technical definitions are applied to ordinary words—*heat, impulse, temperature*. In an effort to reduce ambiguity the term may be defined mathematically: pressure is $p = F/A$, where p is pressure, F is force, and A is area.

Such a situation comes about when a term is already in wide use, then must be defined in as exact a manner as possible so that one member of the profession can communicate with another member and keep ambiguity to a minimum.

These subject-matter chapters are organized to follow the basic plan of this book. The first two sections of each offer practice in applying the prefixes and roots from Chapters 1 and 2 to a particular subject field. Only those word elements used frequently in the field are included. Where only one or two examples could be found, the word element was omitted, since it is easier in such cases to learn the term directly.

The next section provides practice in using context clues from text material in the particular subject field. The amount of context practice offered is sufficient to give you experience in applying the clues studied in Chapter 4 to a particular content. This section does not pretend to be enough practice for complete mastery, since specific clues vary with authors and subject content. Your *real* practice is to use the *real* text material you are reading for course work. The six kinds of clues studied in Chapter 4 will be there—look for them.

The final section of each chapter is a reference section listing the prefixes, roots, and numbers commonly used in the technical terminology of the subject area. This list will be directly useful in applying the techniques covered in this book for mastery of vocabulary.

The matter of mnemonic or memory devices (number 4 above) is apparently an individual matter. Some people find such a scheme extremely helpful, while others do not advocate this approach. If you already like such an approach or want to learn about it, see pages 164–168, where the scheme is applied to remembering the symbols for chemical elements. The process is the same for any area.

Chapter 5.
Physical Sciences:
Chemistry,
Mathematics,
Physics

The physical sciences make extensive use of derivatives from Latin and Greek. This is true whether the term was originally formed in an earlier day when all students also studied Latin and Greek or is a term that had to be created today. Many of the newer terms continue to use the system of classical derivation.

The first two sections of this chapter use the word elements taught in Chapters 1 and 2 of this book but apply them to technical terminology. Even though the definition you are required to give in a course or on an exam might include more than the literal meaning, remember that the reason for knowing the derivatives is that you will then have a clue for remembering the more formal definition, the characteristics, or whatever it is you are to remember. The purpose of this practice is to show you how to use the literal meaning of the word element as a clue to the technical use.

Since the original list of prefixes and roots was taken from all subject-matter fields, you will not find each prefix and root in a given subject area. However, since the selection was made as both useful and worthwhile learning, you will find that most of them are used in all subject areas.

Prefixes begin the practice, and they are arranged alphabetically. The reference number is the express frame which introduced the word element.

PREFIXES
a, an (2-7)
The term *achromatic* literally means"_____ _____ color (*chrom*)."

Achromatic lens means "an optical lens corrected so that its focal length does not depend on the color of light being used."

The two words in the definition of *achromatic lens* which correspond to the literal meaning of the term are _____ and _____.

no or without

not
color

The term *anhydrous* literally means "_____ water (*hydr*)."

no

If you are dealing with hydrogen peroxide (H_2O_2), you may have to distinguish between anhydrous H_2O_2 and an aqueous (water) solution of H_2O_2. The *an* of *anhydrous* reminds you that there is _____ water in this form of the compound.

no

If you heard the phrase "anelastic strain," you might misinterpret it if you were not alert to the negative prefix *an* because the phrase would mean "a strain which is_____ an elastic one" rather than the reverse.

not

ab (2-1)
The term *aberration* literally means "a wandering _____."

away or from

Applied to optics this would be a wandering _____ _____ the perfect image, that is, a defect of optical images.

away from

An *abrasive* is a substance which wears (*ras*) _____ a surface.

away

Abscissa literally means "cut _____";
it is a perpendicular _____ a given point to the *y* axis.

from

from

A substance which has the capacity to take up another substance, that is, literally to suck from, is called _____ sorbent.

ab(sorbent)

com, con (1-6)
The term *commutative* literally means "changed _____."

with

The term applies to an axiom of algebra stating that $ab = ba$, $a + b = b + a$, the terms exchange _____ each other.

with

A number consisting of a real number together with an imaginary part is called a *complex* number, literally _____ _____.

folded together

Conservation means "a saving _____," that is, without loss. Additional examples of terms using this prefix are *converge, convert, convection,* and *convex.*

together or with

dia (2-10)

The term *dialysis* literally means "loosening _____" and refers to the process of separating substances in solution because of the fact that one substance will diffuse _____ a semipermeable membrane.

through

through

The term *diathermancy* is an example of a technical term that is not widely used but occasionally must be dealt with. Knowing the meaning of the parts will permit your understanding the unusual term even so. *Diathermancy* is the term for the property of transmitting heat. In other words, the heat gets _____.

through

A diamagnetic substance has a magnetic permeability of less than unity and is feebly repelled by a magnet. The meaning of *dia* as _____ can be associated with permeability as a clue in remembering the definition.

through

The diameter of a sphere is any straight line which passes _____ the center of the sphere and ends at the surface. Literally, the measure (*meter*)_____.

through

through

epi (2-11)

The technical definition of *epicycloid* is quite long, yet the clue to remembering it is that the curve rolls _____ a fixed circle. The term is opposed to *hypocycloid,* rolling under (*hypo*) the fixed circle.

over

Chemistry uses the term *epoxy,* which

was formed by combining *epi* and *oxygen.* An epoxy compound is generally described as one which contains oxygen attached to two different atoms which are already united in another way. In other words, the oxygen is attached _____ the atoms already attached.

over or above

mono (1-36)
Monomolecular means "consisting of or involving only _____ molecule."

one

   Monomial is an algebraic expression meaning "_____ term." It literally means "_____ _____ (*nom*)."

one
one name

   Monochromatic literally means "_____ color." The more precise meaning is "only _____ wavelength."

one

one

   Mer is a root widely used in chemistry. It means "a part." A simple chemical compound is a _____mer as opposed to polymer (*poly* = many).

mono

non (2-3)
Noncoplanar forces are those whose lines of action do _____ lie in the same plane.

not

   Nonelectrolyte and *nonferrous* both share the prefix _____ meaning _____.

non/not

peri (2-15)
Period is the term used to indicate the time required to complete a cycle or for something to run its course. Literally, a way (*od*)_____.

around

   You may know the Latin derivative *circumference,* which literally means "a carrying around." The Greek way to say "a carrying around" is _____*phery*. The Greek way to say "a measuring around" is _____ *meter.*

peri(phery)
peri(meter)

   Pericyclone is the term applied to the ring of rising pressure which is _____ a cyclone.

around

super (2-5)

A supernatant liquid is literally the liquid that swims _____. The clue to remember is the *super*, because the term applies to the clear liquid which lies above a residue in the bottom of a container.

over or above

Supersaturation refers to the state of containing more of a substance than is required for a state of saturation; it is _____ saturation.

above

Supersonic refers to any speed which is _____ the velocity of sound. A more precise meaning could be stated in terms of speed or relative to a mach number.

over or above

syn (2-16)

Synchronous means "having the same phase or period," literally, "taking place_____."

together

If a collection of things are arranged together so as to present a general view, they are said to be _____optic.

syn(optic)

Asymptotes are lines which extend infinitely. Although they approach nearer to a curve than any other line, they never meet. "Never meet" comes from the two prefixes _____ and _____.

a/sym

trans (2-6)

To indicate the action of changing the sign in an equation and putting it across to the other side, one uses the term _____*pose.*

trans(pose)

Aeronautical speeds are called transsonic if they are between 600 and 900 miles per hour, that is, any speed from subsonic _____ to supersonic velocities. Although *transonic* is also a correct spelling, you can remember this category of speed more easily if you retain the complete prefix *trans* and spell the word _____ *sonic*.

Transuranic is a term made up to designate those elements _____ uranium on the periodic table.

ROOTS
cept, cap (1-20)
Capacitor is the name for a device which permits electricity to be stored temporarily, which permits electricity literally to be _____ temporarily.

Capacitance is the name of the property permitting such a storage system.

The word *acceptor* is literally translated as _____ _____ _____ _____ _____.

Proton acceptor is the term in chemistry to apply to a substance which _____ to it (gains) a hydrogen ion (H^+). This term is opposed to *proton donor*, literally, that which gives a proton.

dic, dict (2-17)
Prediction is the goal of scientific work, that is, to be able to _____ beforehand what will happen.

duc (1-21)
Conduction can be translated literally as "a _____ _____."

Conduction is the term used for the flow of, say, heat or sound along or through a substance. The substance is that which leads together, or a _____.

A product in mathematics is the result of multiplying two or more quantities. Literally, a product is what is _____ _____.

Deductive and *inductive* are terms frequently used. *Deductive*, to _____ from

---

trans(sonic)

across or beyond

taken or seized

that which takes to it

takes

say

leading together

conductor

led
forth

lead

the general. *Inductive,* to _____ into
the general.

fac, fic (1-22)
Calcification is the technical term for the
deposition of insoluble calcium salts. It
literally means "_____ calcium."

    You could be asked to factor the quantity
40. You could answer "5 and 8"; literally,
"That which _____ 40 is 5 and 8."
    Factor is also used to mean "any circum-
stance that influences events," literally,
_____ _____ _____.

    Magnification means "_____ great
or large." *Petrifaction* means "_____
into stone." These two words share the
root meaning _____.

fin (2-18)
Finite means "having limits or bounds,"
literally, "having an _____."
    A finite straight line is a straight line
which has an _____.
    A finite series is a series that _____
at some assigned term.

Infinity is used in mathematics to mean
"greater than any assignable quantity,"
literally, "something without _____."
    The symbol for infinity is ∞. Have you
noticed that this symbol is also without
_____?

In chemistry atoms have a tendency to select
one element rather than another with which
to unite. This selectivity is called affinity,
literally, _____ _____ _____.

gen (1-24)
The literal meaning of the chemical element
hydrogen is "produces water." It was so

lead

making

makes

that which makes

make
made

make or do

end

end
ends

end

end

to the end

named by Lavoisier from the fact that water is produced from its combustion, _____ (*gen*) from its combustion.

A group of chemical elements that form compounds with metals, like common salt, are called halogens. *Hals* means "salt"; *gen* means "to _____ _____."

Photogenic organisms are those which _____ light (*photo*).

log (1-35)

The term *aerology* literally means "the _____ _____ air " — more precisely defined as the _____ _____ the free atmosphere.

Radiology is the _____ _____ radioactivity.

There is a branch of chemistry called pathological chemistry. This doesn't mean that chemistry has suddenly gone berserk; rather, pathological chemistry is an area which _____ the chemical effects of disease.

matr (2-22)

The term *matrix* literally means _____. It can be applied in anatomy to mean "the womb." A more general form of this meaning would be "the cavity in which things are imbedded." Applied to mathematics it means "a rectangular array of terms arranged so as to facilitate the study of the relations among the terms." From this "mother" may be born many problems for further study.

mit (1-25)

Alpha emitter may be remembered by its literal translation, "that which _____ out an alpha." The term applies to radio-

born

be born (produce)

produce

study of
study of

study of

studies

mother

sends

active change through the emission (the
_____ out) of an alpha particle.

The sending out of electrons from an
electrode into the surrounding space is
called electron e_____ion.

sending

miss (emission)

mo (2-19)
Greek is the language mostly used for words
indicating motion (*kine;* see page 186); however, there are these Latin derivatives:

Moment is defined as the product of force
and distance and literally means _____.

Momentum is the measure of mass in
_____.

move or moving

movement or motion

nomin (2-21)
Binomial means "two terms" or "two
_____."

Denominator literally means "that which
_____ the number below (*de*) the line
in a fraction."

names

names

Nomenclature is the system of_____,
a basic part of a field which must be learned.
The nomenclature of chemistry is the system
of giving _____ to chemical processes
and must be learned. See pages 168–181 for
instruction in the nomenclature of chemistry.

names or naming

names

plic (1-27)
Explicit means "distinctly stated or expressed, not merely implied." *Explicit* literally means _____ _____, where-
as *implied* literally means_____ _____.

folded out
folded in

pon, pos (1-26)
A composite number is one in which several
numbers have been _____ together.
The factors into which this quantity can be
divided are called com_____ents.

put or placed

pon (components)

A variant spelling of *pon* is *pound.* A

chemical compound is a substance made up of two or more elements _____ together. Once again such a definition must be refined, but this literal meaning makes a start.

put or placed

The exponent in algebra is the symbol _____ outside and to the right of another symbol.

put or placed

Synonyms for *proposition* are *theorem* and *problem*; however, the term *proposition* literally means "something which has been _____ forth."

put or placed

sens, sent (2-26)
Something which feels, or senses, light is described as photo_____itive.

sens (photosensitive)

The sensible atmosphere is that part of the atmosphere which may be _____; that is, it offers resistance.

felt

If an instrument or machine is slow to feel a change in input, it is said to have a low degree of _____itivity.

sens(itivity)

tend, tens (1-30)
Strain produced by tension is called tensile strain. A translation would be, "Strain produced by _____ is called tensile strain."

stretching

An extended source of light is any source of light that is not regarded as a point source; that is, it has been literally _____ out.

stretched

tain, tin, ten (1-29)
Tenacity means "_____ power."
   Applied technically tenacity means "the maximum tensile stress which a material

holding

can withstand." In other words, it means "how much stretch a material can _____."

hold

tort, tors (2-27)
In optics the term *distortion* is often used to apply to any aberration or lens defect. *Distortion* literally means "a _____ apart," that is, out of shape.

twisting

The term *torsiometer,* meaning literally "the measure of the _____," is a good example of using the context to apply the literal meaning in a sensible way. A torsiometer is an instrument for measuring the amount of power transmitted by a twisting (rotating) shaft.

twist or twisting

Although you may have to use formal language, if you were required to define *torsional wave,* you know that your definition would have to include something about _____.

twisting

tract (2-28)
One particle holds *attraction* for another particle; that is, one particle _____ another to itself.

draws

The extraction of a root consists of the operation of _____ out a root of a given quantity.

drawing

Contraction literally means "a _____ _____." It is a term used to refer to the shrinkage in solids as a result of the _____ _____ of the atoms. This is the opposite process to expansion, a spreading out.

drawing together

drawing together

vert, vers (1-32)
A reversible reaction is one which is able to be _____ back.

turned

Other terms using this root are *inverse, inversion, inverted,* and *reversed,* all sharing the root meaning _____ .

turn

vid, vis (1-33)
We see an image on a television receiver. A small camera tube which transforms the original image into electric signals for transmission to a TV set so that we can *see* the image is called a _____ *icon.* This term was coined from *video* and *iconoscope.*

vid(icon)

Stereovision means "_____ in depth or three dimensions."

seeing

Double vision, visual angle, and *visibility* are other terms used in which the cue is *vis* meaning _____ .

see

CONTEXT–CLUE PRACTICE

Even though scientific writing is in a generally tight style, wasting no words, context clues do exist. By paying close attention to the words surrounding an unknown term, you can deduce a meaning which will enable you to continue reading or listening with good comprehension.

The six kinds of clues presented in Chapter 4 are used in the frames below for your practice in applying them to the physical science area. The easiest clue, of course, is when the term is defined or explained, but other clues are by analysis of the word elements, something you have experienced or can imagine, by contrast, by inference, or some combination.

This next sequence of experiments is called a stochastic process because the outcome of each experiment depends on some element of chance.

Stochastic involves the idea of _____ .

chance

Where the metal becomes a superconductor, the magnetic field is expelled. In other words, the metal starts up its own current to push the field out.

In other words, *expel* means _____

_____ .

push
out

These examples are all examples of finite sets, that is, sets having a finite number of elements.

Finite means _____.

end or limit (*fin* = end)

The existence of Brownian motion contradicts the idea of matter as a quiescent state.

Quiescent is contrasted with _____; therefore, it must mean _____.

motion
quiet or still

Some oxides are able to neutralize both acids and bases. Such oxides are called amphoteric.

The combining form *ampho* must mean _____.

both

Gases are said to be miscible; that is, they can mix in any proportion.

Miscible translates to "able to_____."

mix

We now come to a situation where quantum mechanics shows its own characteristic effects on a large, or macroscopic, scale.

A synonym for *macroscopic* is _____.

large

The rate of motion of a particular oil droplet is measured by observing it in a transverse light beam.

Transverse is analyzed to mean _____ _____.

turned
across

Not all solids are crystalline in form. Glass, for example, does not have the ordered crystalline state. These substances are called amorphous solids.

An amorphous solid is _____ crystalline in _____.

The word *amorphous* analyzes to *a* meaning _____ and *morph* meaning _____.

not
form

no/form or shape

Thus *p* or *q* or both is called the inclusive disjunction, while *p* or *q* but not both is called the exclusive disjunction.

Match the definitions to the names:
Inclusive refers to _____.

Exclusive refers to _____ _____.

Disjunction refers to _____.

both
not both
the word *or* of *p* or *q*

Point *P* can be described in terms of any noncoplanar set of axes.

In other words, a set of axes which are _____ _____ in the same _____.

not/together
plane

Thus far we have been able to show a similar or parallel operation with traditional physics, but let me show you another way to measure the momentum of a particle which has no classical analog.

Analog must mean "something which is _____."

similar or parallel

Instead of breaking with the formation of flat faces and angles between the faces, glasses show conchoidal fractures.

Conchoidal is contrasted with _____ and _____; therefore, it must mean _____.

flat
angles
curved (like a conch shell)

A typical trapezoidal partitioning is shown below.

What would you look for? A part in the shape of, or like, a _____.

trapezoid

NaCl can be pictured as a cubic close-packed array of chloride ions with the sodium ions fitting into interstices between the chloride layers.

A synonym for *interstices* is _____.

spaces

A characteristic property of gases is their thermal expansion. All gases increase in volume when their temperature is raised.

Thermal translates literally to "related to _____."

heat

The temperature at which molecules coalesce to form a liquid is called the liquefaction temperature.

The words in the above sentence which are equivalent to *liquefaction* are _____ _____ _____ _____.

to
form a liquid
(*fact* = make)

Coalesce must mean_____ _____.

draw or come together
(*co* = together)

Optical isomers occur when two species differ only in that one is the mirror image of the other.

You have looked in a mirror. What happens? Your right side is now your_____.

left

Except in this one respect, the two images are _____, or _____ _____, or isomeric.

equal/the same

NONTECHNICAL TERMS

In studying the elements of Group II of the periodic table we find a decrease in ionization potential as we go down the group except for radium. This anomaly has not been explained.

A synonym for anomaly is_____.

irregularity, deviation

To explain this next result, we must invoke yet another rule.

Invoke means _____ _____.

call in or on

Since water of hydration is often omitted from chemical equations, we can write the equation more simply with the tacit understanding that all species are hydrated.

Tacit means _____.

unspoken, silent, implied

Your estimate of 4 is a fortuitous result since the true slope at $x = 1$ is actually 4.

A synonym for *fortuitous* is _____.

lucky, fortunate

Determination of the structures of liquids is very difficult, since the molecules are not arranged in a repetitive order; nevertheless,

liquids do exhibit a vestigial order inter-
mediate between solids and gases.

    Vestigial must mean _____, or _____
_____.

    trace/minute
amount

For this particular section of the text we will
make the convention that all calculations will
be worked to the fourth decimal place.

    A synonym for *convention* is _____.
The literal meaning is _____ _____
_____.

    agreement
a coming
together

Traditionally this last formula is excluded
because it is convenient to maintain the
sanctity of the octet rule.

    Although you may ordinarily associate
sanctity with a church, rules may sometimes
take on the aspect of _____, but
admittedly for convenience.

    sacredness,
inviolability

On the basis of his experiments Rutherford
was led to postulate the existence of the
nucleus.

    A synonym for *postulate* is _____.

    hypothesize, claim

USE OF MNEMONIC DEVICES

Since there is disagreement on the benefit of mnemonic devices, this
section is optional. If you like such an approach, you will find the section
helpful. If you are not familiar with memory schemes, try this section
and then decide if you want to follow it.

    The purpose of mnemonic devices is to obtain some kind of meaning-
ful association with things to be learned and remembered. We know that
meaningful items are more easily learned and remembered; therefore,
when no association is already established, we arbitrarily make one.
The word *mnemonic* is derived from the name of the Greek goddess of
memory, Mnemosyne.

    Memory experts use such arbitrary associations. They associate some
feature and visualize it strongly, so that whenever the item to be remembered occurs, this strong visual association comes and the item can be
recalled. Such artificial associations are personal; therefore, the ones
given below may not be the associations you would make. But they will
serve to show how the system operates, and they can stimulate you to
make your own associations.

To illustrate the technique, some of the common chemical elements with their symbols will be used. If such symbols were all written out, textbooks would be at least twice as large as they are—that is one reason for symbols—and they must be learned.

If you use certain symbols frequently, they become permanent knowledge and you no longer have to resort to mnemonic devices, but such devices help you to get started. Some feature of the symbol can be used, or a personal experience. The secret of such associations is that you build strong mental images of the association which strikes you as distinctive.

The frames present the associations useful for the author. If you have one which is more meaningful for you, use it. The purpose here is to show the technique.

Some feature of the item to be remembered can be used to make an association.

The symbol for lead is Pb, from Latin *plumbum*. A chunk of lead is commonly used on the end of a string as a PlumB BoB. Another association is *plumber*, but emphasize the *b*: plumBer.

Plumbers work with _____ pipe. | lead
A plumb bob is made of _____. | lead
Pb is the symbol for _____. | lead

The Latin *plumbum* also supplies derived forms such as *plumbic, plumbite, plumbous.*

The symbol for tin is Sn. Tin SNips is an easy association to make. Say "tin snips" several times, picturing SN in some special way, as if in flashing lights.

The Latin word for tin is *stannum*, which supplies the stem *stann*, to which you must add appropriate suffixes: *stannate, stannic, stannite, stannous.*

Sn is the symbol for _____. | tin
The compound SnS is read as _____ous sulfide. | stann(ous)

Personal experience can provide the source of a needed association.

A young man worked in a chemical plant and had the job of slicing bricks of metallic sodium on a power saw. He grew careless and cut off three fingers. It was a NAsty accident.

NAsty associates with Na as the symbol for _____.

                                            sodium

The term sodium is used in naming compounds. For example, Na_2O_2 is _____ peroxide.

                                            sodium

The term *soda* may be more familiar to you:

    Na_2CO_3 is washing _____.

                                            soda

    $NaHCO_3$ is baking _____.

                                            soda

    The symbol Na stands for _____.

                                            sodium

Knowing a "fancy" word may make the association for you. In the case of iron, try *ferriferous*. Ferri*ferous* rocks, ferri*ferous* ore. The form *ferri* means "iron."

The root *fer* means "bear or carry" (see express frame 1-23). Ferriferous ore is iron-_____ ore; such ore contains _____.

                                        bearing/iron

The first two letters of the word make the symbol. The symbol for iron is _____.

                                              Fe

The Latin word is *ferrum* and provides the stem to which suffixes are added for naming compounds:

    $Fe(OH)_2$ is _____ous hydroxide.

                                            ferr(ous)

    $BaFeO_4$ is barium _____ate.

                                            ferr(ate)

General knowledge you already possess can be a source of making associations.

Say the word *alkali*. Do you hear how strong the letter *k* is? K is the symbol for potassium, a member of the alkali metal group.

A common form of the element is called potash (potassium carbonate from wood ashes). Does the association *potassium* to *potash* to *alkali* to K work for you?

K is the chemical symbol for the element _____.

                                        potassium

Potassium can also be used to illustrate the story of discovery. This element was

named by Davy in 1807 when he extracted
the element from plants which he burned
in pots, called pot ashes (our present word
potash). But then we are back to *potassium*
to *potash* to *alkali* to _____.

K

Some of the associations you make may
seem ridiculous or farfetched. So much
the better, perhaps. The criterion of a suc-
cessful mnemonic device is that it works!

Another tactic to use is to group or organize
items into groups. For chemical elements
try lining up all names beginning with the
same letter. The first two letters of the element are used for the symbol where possible,
but since this rule does not always hold, the
grouping tactic applies. As you practice
them, emphasize the letters in their names
which show the symbols. Say the name but
draw out the clue letters. This is the same
tactic you already use with spelling demons.
There is little danger of mispronouncing
the term in regular use because you know
why you mispronounce it when you are
trying to memorize the symbol.

For example, what are the symbols for
the B group?

BBBoron	_____	B
bAAArium	_____	Ba
berKKKelium	_____	Bk
bEEEryllium	_____	Be
bIIIsmuth	_____	Bi
bRRRomine	_____	Br

Other elements, especially those discovered
in modern times, have been named according to their conditions of discovery, in honor
of a person, or by geography. The standard
Latin ending *ium* has been added.

Try these:

Fm was named after Enrico Fermi. The
element is _____.

fermium

Bk was discovered by Berkeley scientists and named _____ .

berkelium

The Curies named their discovery Ra because of its power to give off rays, or *radii*. The element is _____ .

radium

Ekeberg finally tracked down the element Ta in 1802. One story goes that he found the task so difficult but so tantalizing that he named the element _____ .

tantalum

You may recall the story of Tantalus from Greek mythology. He was sent to Hell, where food and drink always stayed just beyond his reach.

THE NOMENCLATURE OF INORGANIC CHEMISTRY

The basic principles of chemistry deal with the nature of the elements and the processes through which these elements combine to form compounds.

In order for us to talk about the elements and their compounds they have names, and these names follow a system or code using prefixes, roots, and suffixes. In the same way that the word *exporter* can be analyzed to arrive at its literal meaning of "one who carries out," so can the names of compounds be decoded to arrive at the information contained in the name. The reverse process can also be done. If you must name the compound you have been working with, then you follow the system or code.

Elements

In this system of naming chemical compounds by using prefixes, roots, and suffixes, the names of the elements serve as the roots. The names and symbols of the more common elements must be learned. That is one of the early assignments in a course. For example, the symbols replace the names in printed matter, but you "read" the name. "The bond in BrCl consists of an electron pair shared unequally between Br and Cl." You decode this language to "The bond in bromium chloride consists . . . between bromine and chlorine."

If you are taking your first chemistry course or have never really mastered the names and symbols of the elements, refer to the section on mnemonic devices for techniques of learning them, pages 164–168.

The following frames are arranged according to the principles or rules for naming compounds, that is, the system of prefixes and suffixes used with the names of the elements as roots. There are express frames for each of the rules involved. If you can complete the express frame successfully, then move to the next express frame. Any time you cannot complete the express frame, that is your signal to learn to use the rule. In that case do each of the frames immediately following the express frame which you have missed.

None of the express frames requires that you state the rule; rather, they require that you *use* the rule. However, if you cannot apply the rule, then you must learn it, and that is what goes on in the instruction frames.

Compounds from Two Elements (Binary: Bi = Two)

5-1 The compounds hydrogen chloride, calcium oxide, and aluminum nitride are so named to show that each compound is made from _____ elements.	two
In the compound hydrogen chloride, hydrogen is named first because it is the more _____ of the two.	electropositive
In binary compounds the suffix _____ is the standard ending given to the _____ _____.	ide less electropositive
The name of a compound composed of but two elements is formed from the names of the elements, with the more electropositive element named first.	
In the compound sodium chloride (NaCl) the two elements are_____ and_____.	sodium/chlorine
Calcium oxide (CaO) is made up of the two elements_____ and_____.	calcium/oxygen
In the compound aluminum nitride (AlN) you know that the more electropositive element is _____ because it is named _____.	aluminum first
In the compound sodium chloride (NaCl) the more electropositive element is_____.	sodium
In naming a two-element compound, the second element is given the suffix _____.	ide

Supply the chemical names for each of these compounds (the elements are named in the correct order):

potassium + chlorine = _____ — **potassium chloride**

calcium + oxygen = _____ — **calcium oxide**

zinc + sulfur = _____ — **zinc sulfide**

aluminum + nitrogen = _____ — **aluminum nitride**

To review, in naming the binary compounds the more electropositive element is named _____. The element named second is given the suffix _____. — **first** / **ide**

There are a few exceptions, but the rule holds generally and is therefore worth learning as a guide.

NOTE: Further review is supplied by returning to the express frame. These special frames can also serve for review in the future.

5-2
Supply the technical names for the following binary compounds:

N_2O_4 _____ — **dinitrogen tetroxide**
Na_3P _____ — **trisodium phosphide**
Cr_2O_3 _____ — **chromium sesquioxide (also chromic oxide)**

If more than one atom of an element is involved in the two-element compounds, a prefix denoting the number is used. These prefixes follow the Greek numbers and apply generally to compounds of two nonmetals. (See page 172 where metals form more than one compound.)

The rule states, "If more than one. . . ." Therefore, you would not expect a prefix designating the number one (1) to appear.

You would expect in the compound calcium oxide (CaO) that only _____ atom of each element is involved.

one

However, there are exceptions, as there are apparently in all rules of language. The rules take care of most cases, so if you use the rule you will probably be right. If you find an exception, take special note of it. For example, CO is carbon _____oxide. But, in general, play the probabilities.

mon(oxide)

Di is the prefix indicating two (2).

In the compound iron dichloride, how many atoms of each element are involved?

iron _____ chlorine _____

one/two

The compound N_2O_4 is properly named _____nitrogen tetroxide.

di(nitrogen)

SO_2 is read as sulfur _____.

dioxide

The empirical formula of carbon dioxide is CO_____.

2 (CO_2)

Tri is the prefix meaning three (3).

The name sulfur trioxide shows that there are how many atoms of oxygen?

_____

three

To write the name of the above compound using symbols, one would write SO_____.

3 (SO_3)

The symbol form Na_3P can be read as _____sodium phosphide.

tri(sodium)

Greek for four (4) is *tetra*.

The symbols N_2O_4 can be read as _____ nitrogen _____oxide.

di(nitrogen)
tetr(oxide)

The compound dinitrogen tetroxide contains how many atoms of oxygen?_____

four

Ru is the symbol for ruthenium. RuO_4 is read as _____ _____.

ruthenium tetroxide

One method for getting zirconium as a pure metal is the thermal decomposition of the tetriodide, ZrI_____, on a hot tungsten wire.

$4\ (ZrI_4)$

The prefix *penta,* or *pent,* means five (5).

If a compound contains five atoms of a particular element, then the prefix _____ will be used.

penta or pent

In the compound dinitrogen pentoxide the number of oxygen atoms is _____.

five

Ta_2O_5 is read as tantalum _____oxide.

pent(oxide)

The pentoxide of niobium is Nb_2O_____.

$5\ (Nb_2O_5)$

The most important compound of vanadium is probably V_2O_5, the _____oxide.

pent(oxide)

The fifth prefix in common use is *sesqui* meaning one and one-half (1½). You may know this prefix from *sesquicentennial*. When a town or state has reached 150 years (1½ centuries), it celebrates its sesquicentennial. This same relationship is applied to compounds containing three atoms when combined with two of another.

The symbol N_2O_3 may be read as either _____nitrogen trioxide or as nitrogen _____oxide.

di(nitrogen)
sesqui(oxide)

Chromium sesquioxide is written in symbols as Cr_2O_____.

$3\ (Cr_2O_3)$

NOTE: These number prefixes are the most common ones. If you do not already know the number prefixes for higher numbers, see page 190.

5-3

When two elements form more than one compound, there are three systems of distinguishing among them. Under the symbol headings given below fill in the blanks according to the three systems:

$FeCl_2$	$FeCl_3$
iron _____chloride	iron _____chloride

di(chloride)/tri(chlorride)

_____ chloride	_____ chloride	ferrous/ferric
_____ chloride	_____ chloride	iron(II)/iron(III)

Since the same two elements can frequently form more than one compound, a way of distinguishing among them must be made. The use of prefixes has been covered above (5-2).

A second system is to use the endings *ous* and *ic* to denote the lower and higher oxidation states respectively. Although this system is becoming obsolete, it is still in wide use, and you should recognize the system.

Compare nitrous oxide (N_2O) with nitric oxide (NO). The lower oxidation state of nitrous oxide as compared with nitric oxide is designated by the ending _____ .

ous

If you see the compound name *ferric chloride* you immediately will guess that there is a ferr_____ chloride.

ous (ferrous)

The compound with the higher oxidation state of these two iron compounds is _____ _____, as shown by the ending _____ .

ferric
chloride
ic

Examine the compounds ferric oxide (Fe_2O_3) and ferrous oxide (FeO). Write the formula of the compound with the lower oxidation state: _____ .

FeO

The system replacing the ous-ic system is called the Stock system, wherein Roman numerals in parentheses indicate the oxidation states.

In the compound iron(II) chloride the oxidation number is _____ .

two

In the compound written as iron(III) chloride the oxidation number is _____ .

three

The compounds iron(II) chloride and iron(III) chloride may also be named respectively as _____ chloride and _____ chloride.

ferrous
ferric

Compounds Containing More than Two Elements

The names of compounds containing more than two elements depend upon whether the compound is a base, an acid, or a salt. These names are more complicated than the simpler compounds, but there are guidelines to follow.

5-4

Supply the names of the following compounds:

NaOH _____

$Ca(OH)_2$ _____

$As(OH)_3$ _____

sodium hydroxide
calcium hydroxide
arsenic trihydroxide

The common term used in the above compounds is _____, and it is used as the group name because most _____ contain the _____ ion.

hydroxide
bases
hydroxide

Since most bases contain the hydroxide ion (OH^-), they are generally called hydroxides.

Once again note that the rule can only be stated for the most probable event. It is still better to be right most of the time than never to know what to do. Use these rules as guidelines.

In the compound NaOH the symbol OH is a clue for the word _____.

hydroxide

The word *hydroxide* or the symbol OH is a clue that the compound is a _____.

base

Likewise, the word *base* should immediately lead you to expect the word _____ or the symbol _____.

hydroxide
OH

Complete the following statements:

$Fe(OH)_2$ is read as ferrous _____.

$Mg(OH)_2$ is read as magnesium _____.

hydroxide
hydroxide

Fill in the missing information:
 calcium hydroxide, Ca(_____)₂
 lead hydroxide, Pb(_____)₂
 chromium _____, $Cr(OH)_3$

OH [$Ca(OH)_2$]
OH [$Pb(OH)_2$]
hydroxide

5-5
Fill in the necessary prefixes and/or suffixes to give the correct names for these compounds:
 $HClO$, _____chlor_____ acid
 $HClO_2$, chlor_____ acid
 $HClO_3$, chlor_____ acid
 $HClO_4$, _____chlor_____ acid

hypo/ous
ous
ic
per/ic

In the naming of acids, when there are only two common oxyacids of a given element, the ending *ous* refers to the lower oxidation state and the ending *ic* to the higher. This is the same designation made for compounds from two elements (5-3 above).

In distinguishing between sulfurous acid (H_2SO_3) and sulfuric acid (H_2SO_4), the one with the lower oxidation state is _____, as indicated by the suffix _____.

sulfurous (H_2SO_3)
ous

HNO_3 has a higher oxidation state than HNO_2. Name these compounds:
 HNO_3 is nitr_____ acid.
 HNO_2 is nitr_____ acid.

ic (nitric)
ous (nitrous)

When there are more than two oxyacids of different oxidation states, then the distinction "lower and higher" is not sufficient. One way to make further distinction is to add the prefixes *hypo* meaning "under" and *per* meaning "through"—in this context "through to a higher designation."
Examine the following series of acids:
$HC1O$ hypochlorous acid
$HC1O_2$ chlorous acid
$HC1O_3$ chloric acid
$HC1O_4$ perchloric acid

The series is ranked by oxidation state. If there had been only two common oxyacids, their names would have been _____ and _____ .	chlorous chloric
Since there are more than two, the way to designate the acid whose oxidation state is below chlorous is by the name _____ .	hypochlorous
The way to designate an oxidation state higher than *ic* is to add the prefix _____ .	per
The general guideline, then, for compounds which form more than _____ oxyacids and are of _____ _____ _____ oxidation states is:	two higher and lower
To indicate an oxidation state lower than that of an *ous* acid, use _____ .	hypo
To indicate an oxidation state higher than that of an *ic* acid, use _____ .	per
In naming acids, prefixes and suffixes show the relationship among _____ _____ .	oxidation states

5-6
Use the correct endings in writing the names for the following sodium salts:

Na_2SO_3, sodium sulf_____	ite (sulfite)
Na_2SO_4, sodium sulf_____	ate (sulfate)
In the case of salts derived from more than two oxyacids, the system for distinguishing among them is as follows:	
$NaClO$, sodium _____	hypochlorite
$NaClO_2$, sodium _____	chlorite
$NaClO_3$, sodium _____	chlorate
$NaClO_4$, sodium _____	perchlorate

The names of salts derived from oxyacids follow the same system to show relationship as did the names of the acids. The exception is that the ending *ous* is replaced by *ite* and the ending *ic* is replaced by *ate.*

In naming salts derived from oxyacids, the suffix indicating "lower" is _____, and the suffix indicating "higher" is _____.

ite
ate

For the following two compounds supply the correct ending:
Na_2SO_3, sodium sulf_____
Na_2SO_4, sodium sulf_____

ite (sulfite)
ate (sulfate)

Where the salts derive from more than two oxyacids, the designation for a still lower salt follows the prefix system of the acids. *Hypo* means "below" and in this context means "below lower." *Per* is used once again to mean "higher than higher."
The following four compounds are arranged in order. Supply their names so that this order of relationship is shown by the names:
$NaClO$, sodium _____
$NaClO_2$, sodium _____
$NaClO_3$, sodium _____
$NaClO_4$, sodium _____

hypochlorite
chlorite
chlorate
perchlorate

5-7
The names of salts derived from polyprotic (more than one proton) acids usually include the name of the element_____ as well as the prefix indicating the_____ of its atoms left _____.

hydrogen
number
unneutralized

Salts derived from polyprotic acids (polyprotic = yielding more than one proton) are best named so as to indicate the number of hydrogen atoms left unneutralized.
For example, the name of the salt monosodium dihydrogen phosphate indicates that _____(how many?) atom(s) of _____ remain(s)_____.

two
hydrogen/un-
neutralized

The salt NaH_2PO_4 will include in its name the H₂ designation as _____ .

dihydrogen

The name for the salt Na_2HPO_4 is *disodium* _____ *phosphate*.

monohydrogen

Although the prefix *mono* (for one) is frequently omitted, remember that the purpose here is to indicate number.

Translate the first line of the following rule:
For monohydrogen salts of diprotic acids, the presence of hydrogen may also be indicated by the prefix *bi*.

"For _____ hydrogen atom left unneutralized salts of acids yielding_____ protons. . . ."

one
two

An example is $NaHSO_4$, called sodium _____sulfate. Under the preferred designation $NaHSO_4$ would be called sodium _____ sulfate. This prefix is often omitted but is understood.

bi(sulfate)

monohydrogen

NOTE: Rules and principles are frequently stated with one example in some section of the text or in the appendix. This programming on nomenclature is being done to make such rules easier to learn because the formal statement of rules can be formidable, therefore discouraging. However, you can teach yourself such formal rules using the example in the following way.

Here is another rule from chemical nomenclature:
"Complex cations, such as $Cr(H_2O)_6^{+3}$, are named by giving the number and name of the groups attached to the central atom followed by the name of the central atom, with its oxidation number indicated by capital Roman numerals in parentheses. Thus, $Cr(H_2O)_6^{+3}$ is hexaaquochromium(III)."

It is your responsibility to match up each part of the name according to the rule. In this case, you use the strategy "divide and conquer"; take it step by step.

The rule is given in steps; you are to match

up each part of the name with the proper step in the rule. Here is the example again:

$Cr(H_2O)_6{}^{+3}$

hexaaquochromium(III)

Complex cations are named by giving the number _____

and name of the groups attached to the central atom _____

followed by the name of the central atom _____

with its oxidation number indicated by Roman numerals in parentheses _____.

hexa

aquo [water or (H_2O)]

chromium

(III)

When this compound is written symbolically, the same rule can be followed through:

$Cr(H_2O)_6{}^{+3}$

The central atom is, in symbols, _____.

The name of the group attached to the central atom is, in symbols, _____.

The number of these attached groups is _____.

The oxidation number is indicated by _____.

Cr

(H_2O)

six

+3

Look at this example:

$Cr(H_2O)(NH_3)_5{}^{+3}$

aquopentaamminechromium(III)

Have you noticed that this rule applies to the name rather than to writing the empirical formula?

In the formula the central atom is named _____. In the name the central atom is named _____ except for the oxidation number.

first
last

The name can be untangled by following the rule:

First the number and name of the attached groups are given. In this case there are how many groups? _____

The first attached group is _____.

two
(H_2O) or water

In names the derivative _____ is used for this group.

    aquo

The number of this first group is _____, therefore, no prefix is used.

    one

The name of the (NH_3) group is _____.

    ammine

The number of such groups is _____, so the prefix to use is _____.

    five

    penta

Following the rule that the number and name of the groups attached to the central atom are first named and the central atom is named last, we have now built up the name:

_____.

    aquopentaammine-chromium

The last step in the rule is to indicate the oxidation number, and in this case it will be _____.

    (III)

Given this information:
    Mn = manganese
    (CO) = carbonyl
    (C_6H_6) = benzene
write the name for $Mn(CO)_3(C_6H_6)^+$:

_____.

    tricarbonylbenzene-manganese(I)

Following the rule for naming complex cations is one for naming complex anions.

    "Complex anions, such as $PtCl_6^{--}$, are named by giving the number and name of attached groups followed by the name of the element with an *ate* ending and its oxidation number in parentheses. Thus, $PtCl_6^{--}$ is hexachloroplatinate(IV)."

The strategy to use is that when rules are grouped, always look for similarities and differences. In this case the categories are the same or different? _____

    different

A cation is a positively charged ion; an anion (*an* = not) is a negatively charged ion.

Is the next part of the new rule the same as the first one or different? _____

    same

The number and name of attached groups appear first in the name followed by the name of the _____. That's the same in both rules.

element

The next step marks the difference. In the case of complex anions the name of the element is given an _____ ending.

ate

Last in the name is the oxidation number in parentheses. This last step is the same or different? _____

same

From the example given, $PtCl_6^{--}$, the name can be built up as follows:

The central atom is _____.

platinum

The ending *ate* is to be given to the central atom _____.

platinate

The attached group is _____.

chlorine

The combining form of chlorine is _____.

chloro

There are how many of these groups? _____

six

The Greek designation for this number is _____.

hexa

We build up the name by starting with the number and name of the attached groups: The name is _____, whose oxidation number is four. The complete name is _____.

hexachloroplatinate

hexachloroplatinate(IV)

Reading the names from the formulas is the purpose of this program. If you must also be able to write the formula from the name of still more complex cations and anions, consult a chemistry text for the rules of ordering the groups. Use the same strategy you have used here; namely, match the example to the rule, step by step.

REFERENCE SECTION—PHYSICAL SCIENCES

This reference section covers the prefixes, roots, and numbers especially useful in the technical terminology of physical sciences. Select those terms for which you have immediate use. Add other words you need to the examples. Or you may want to learn these specialized word elements systematically, a few at a time, especially if you plan to take several courses in the same field.

You will also want to practice changing the endings on these terms so that any form will be familiar to you. See Chapter 3 if you need help with suffixes. See pages 169–178 for the suffixes used in chemical nomenclature.

Only the root is listed; the examples show the vowel used in combining the root with other word elements. In a few cases where the combining form (root + vowel) is in common use, that form is given; for example, *aero* as in *aerodynamics*. An asterisk indicates a word element covered in Chapters 1 and 2.

PREFIXES

Word element	Meaning and source	Examples
*a	not, without (G)	aclinic, asymmetric, anhydride
*ab	from (L)	abrasive, ablation, absolute
ab	absolute (abbreviation)	abampere, abhenry, abvolt
*ad	to, toward (L)	attenuate, associative, agglomerate
ambi	both, around (L)	ambient, ambiguous, ambience
amphi	around (G)	amphoteric, amphophilic
an	up, back (G)	anion, anode, analysis
anti	against (L)	anticatalyst, antimatter, antilogarithm
*apo	away (G)	apogee, aphelion, apochromatic
cata	down (G)	catalysis, cation, cathode
circum	around (L)	circumambient, circumscription, circumpolar
cis	on this side (L)	cisatomic, cislunar (*cis* used in contrast with *trans*)
*com	with, together (L)	commutative, covalence, congruent
*contra	against (L)	contraflexure, contraflow, countershaft
*de	down (L)	demagnetize, decant, debug
*dia	through (G)	diamagnetic, adiabatic, dielectric
*dis	apart (L)	dispersion, diffraction, dissociation
*em, endo, ento	in, inside (G)	empirical, endothermic, entropy
*epi	upon (G)	epicycloid, epicenter, epimer
*eu	well, good (G)	eutectic, eutexia
*ex	out (L)	effervesce, evaporator, eccentric

Word element	Meaning and source	Examples
hyper	over (L)	hyperbola, hyperoxide, hyperspace
hypo	under (L)	hypotenuse, hypophosphoric, hypocycloid
*in	in (L)	inductance, irradiation, injector
*in	not (L)	impermeable, inelasticity, irreducible
*inter	between (L)	intersection, interpolate, interferometer
micro	small (G, *mikros*)	microchemical, microhardness, microelectrolysis
*mono	one, single (G, *monos*)	monoxide, monomolecular, monomer
*non	not (L)	nonreactive, nonzero, nonconductor
*ob	against (L)	obverse, oblate, occlude
*para	beside (G)	paradigm, parallax, paramagnetism
*per	through, thoroughly (L)	permutation, permeability, permanganate
*peri	around (G)	peripheral, perigee, perihelion
poly	many (G)	polymerization, polytechnic, polygonal
*pre	before (L)	prestige, precursor, premise
*pro	for, forth (L)	projectile, product, propulsive
proto	first (G)	proton, protein, prototype
pseudo	false (G)	pseudosalt, pseudoscience, pseudoallum
*re	back, again (L)	reagent, reciprocal, refrangible
retro	back, backward (L)	retrograde, retrolental, retro-rocket
*sub	under (L)	subsonic, subtend, suffusion
*super	above, over (L)	superconductivity, superscribe, supersonic
*syn	with, together (G)	asymmetric, synchrotron, syllogism
*trans	across (L)	transporter, transversal, trajectory
ultra	beyond (L)	ultrasonic, ultramundane, ultraviolet

ROOTS

Word element	Meaning and source	Examples
acet	acetic, acid (L, *acetum*)	acetamide, acetous, acetyl
acid	acid, sour, sharp (L, *acere, acidum*)	acidimetry, acidophilic, acidification
acoust	hearing (G, *akoustikos*)	acoustics, acoustician, acoustically
actin	ray of light (G, *aktis, aktinos*)	actinic, actinide, actinoid
aero	air (G, *aer*)	aeronautics, aeronomy, aerothermodynamic
ag, act	to drive or do (L, *agere, actum*)	reagent, radioactive, interaction
ampli	large, ample (L, *amplus*)	amplification, amplidyne, amplitude
amyl	starch (L, *amylum*)	amylopsin, amyloid, amylaceous
angul, angle	sharp (L, *angulus*)	angular, triangle, rectangular
aqu	water (L, *aqua*)	aqueous, aqua, aquifer
astro	star (G, *astron*)	astrophysics, astroballistics, asterism
audi	to hear (L, *audire, auditum*)	audibility, audio, audiometer
aur	gold (L, *aurum*)	auriferous, auric, aurous
bar	weight, heavy (G, *baros; barys*)	barometer, isobar, barite
brom	bad odor (G, *bromos*)	bromine, bromic, brominate
calc	lime, stone (L, *calx, calcis*)	calculus, calcify, calcination
calor	heat (L, *calor, caloris*)	calorimeter, caloric, kilocalorie
*cap, capt, cip, cept	to take or seize (L, *capere, captum*)	reciprocal, capture
carb	coal, carbon (L, *carbo, carbonis*)	carbonize, carbide, carburet
centr	center (G, *kentron*)	centrifugal, heliocentric, eccentric
chem	chemistry (G, *chemeia, alchemy*)	chemic, alchemy, chemotaxis
chlor	greenish yellow (G, *chloros*)	chlorine, bichloride, chlorate

Word element	Meaning and source	Examples
chrom	color (G, *chroma*)	achromatic, chromatography, heliochrome
cycl	circle, cycle (G, *kyklos*)	cyclic, cycloid, cyclotron
dens	to make thick, dense (L, *densare, densatum*)	density, condensation, densimeter
*duc, duct	to lead (L, *ducere, ductum*)	ductility, inductance, deductive
dynam	power (G, *dynamis*)	dyne, thermodynamics, isodynamic
electr, electro	amber (in which electricity first observed) (G, *elektron*)	electrostatic, photoelectric, electron
equ	equal (L, *aequus*)	equilibrium, equidistant, equation
erg	work (G, *ergon*)	erg, energy, synergic
*fac, fic	to make or do (L, *facere, factum*)	saponification, liquefaction, rectification
*fer, lat	to bear or carry (L, *ferre, latum*)	interferometer, circumferential, ablation
ferr	iron (L, *ferrum*)	ferromagnetism, ferric, ferroalloy
flu, flux	to flow (L, *fluere, fluxum*)	reflux, confluent, fluorescence
frang, fract	to break (L, *frangere, fractum*)	refractor, diffraction, frangible
ge	earth (G, *ge*)	geophysics, geodetic, apogee
*gen	birth, race, kind (L, *genus, generis*)	generator, halogen, generation
glyco	sugar (G, *glykys*)	glycogen, glucose, glycoprotein
gon	angle (G, *gonia*)	polygon, isogonic, agonic
grad	to step or walk (L, *gradi, gressum*)	centigrade, gradient, graduate
graph	to write (G, *graphein*)	graphite, barograph, selenographic
grav	heavy (L, *gravis*)	gravity, gravimetric, antigravity
hal	salt (G, *halos*)	halogen, halide, halomorphic
helic	spiral (G, *helix*)	helix, helicopter, helicoid

Word element	Meaning and source	Examples
helio	sun (G, *helios*)	heliograph, heliocentric, perihelion
hetero	different, other (G, *heteros*)	heterodyne, heterosphere, heterocyclic
homo	same (G, *homos*)	homosphere, homolog, homologous
hydr	water (G, *hydor*)	hydroxyl, hydrolysis, anhydride
hygro	wet (G, *hygros*)	hygrometer, hygroscopic, hygrograph
iso	equal (G, *isos*)	isosceles, isomerism, isotope
ject, jact	to throw or hurl (L, *jacere, jactum*)	projectile, ejector, trajectory
kine, cine	to move (G, *kinein*)	kinematics, kinetic, cinematograph
later	side (L, *latus, lateris*)	quadrilateral, equilateral, lateral
lin	line, thread (L, *linea*)	linear, rectilinear, collinear
liqu	to be liquid (L, *liquere*)	liquefy, deliquescence, liquor
*log	word, speech, thought, ratio (G, *logos*)	logarithm, syllogism, homolog
lumin	light, source of light (L, *lumen, luminis*)	luminosity, illuminant, relume
lun	moon (L, *luna*)	cislunar, translunar, luna
lys, lyt	to loosen (G, *lyein*)	catalytic, hydrolysis, electrolyte
magnet	magnetic force (G, *Magnes lithos*, stone of Magnesia where lodestone found)	diamagnetism, electromagnet, magnetic
mer	part (G, *meros*)	dimer, isomeric, polymerization
meter	measure (G, *metron*)	potentiometer, manometer, metric
micro	small (G, *mikros*)	micrometer, microscope, micronucleus
*mit, miss	to send (L, *mittere, missum*)	transmit, emissivity, permittivity

Word element	Meaning and source	Examples
*mo	to move (L, *movere, motum*)	momentum, motion, electromotive
mol, mole	a mass (L, *moles*)	molecular, mole, molar
morph	form or shape (G, *morphe*)	amorphous, enantiomorphs, isomorphic
mut	to change or alter (L, *mutare, mutatum*)	permutation, commutative, mutable
neo	new (G, *neos*)	neon, neoprene, neoarsphenamine
neutr	neither (L, *neuter*)	neutron, neutrosphere, neutralization
nitr	nitrogen (L, *nitrum*)	nitroglycerin, nitrification, nitrogenous
nod	knot, node (L, *nodus*)	antinode, node, nodular
*nomin	name (L, *nomen, nominis*)	denominator, nomenclator, binomial
nucle	kernel of a nut, nucleus (L, *nucleus*)	nucleus, thermonuclear, nucleic
numer	to count (L, *numerare, numeratum*)	enumerate, denumerable, numerator
od	a way, path (G, *hodos*)	cathode, periodic, odometer
oscill	to swing (L, *oscillare, oscillatum*)	oscilloscope, oscillate, oscillogram
pept	to cook, digest (G, *peptein*)	peptone, pepsin, dyspeptic
petr	rock (G, *petra*)	petroleum, petrifaction, petrology
phon	sound (G, *phone*)	phonometer, microphone, phonophorous
phos, photo	light (G, *phos, photos*)	phosphorus, photosphere, photon
*plic	to fold, braid (L, *plicare, plicatum*)	complex, duplicate, replicate
*pon, pos	to put or place (L, *ponere, positum*)	component, transpose, superposition

Word element	Meaning and source	Examples
potent	powerful, capable of (L, *potens, potentis*)	potential, potentiometer, potency
press	to squeeze, press (L, *premere, pressum*)	pressure, compress, pressurize
pyr	fire (G, *pyr*)	pyrometer, pyrite, pyrogenesis
quant	how much, how great (L, *quantus*)	quantum, quantity, quantify
radi	staff, spoke, ray (L, *radius*)	radian, radiosonde, radial
rect	straight, right (L, *rectus*)	rectangle, rectilinear, rectifier
scop	watcher, purpose, aim (G, *skopos*)	oscilloscope, telescopic, radarscope
sec, sect	to cut (L, *secare, sectum*)	trisector, intersection, secant
solv, solut	to loosen (L, *solvere, solutum*)	solute, dissolve, soluble
son	sound (L, *sonus*)	resonance, sonic, ultrasonic
spher	sphere (G, *sphaira*)	spheroidal, chemosphere, spherometer
techn	art or skill (G, *techne*)	polytechnic, technological, technique
tele	distant, far off (G, *tele*)	telescope, telautograph, telemechanic
ten, tens	to stretch (L, *tendere, tensum*)	attenuation, tensile, hypotenuse
therm	hot (G, *thermos*)	thermoelectric, thermosphere, endothermic
*torqu, tors, tort	to twist (L, *torquere, tortum*)	torque, torsion, torsibility
*tract	to draw (L, *trahere, tractum*)	extraction, attract, subtract
trop	turn (G, *tropos*)	allotropy, chemotropic, tropism
vale	to be strong (L, *valere, valitum*)	valence, electrovalence, equivalent
vect, veh	to bear or carry (L, *vehere, vectus*)	vector, convection, vehicular
*vert, vers	to turn (L, *vertere, versum*)	transversal, irreversible, converse

Word element	Meaning and source	Examples
vitr	glass (L, *vitrum*)	vitreous, devitrification, vitriol

NUMBERS

Latin		*Greek*
uni	1	*mono*
uniaxial		monocyclic
unipolar		monobasic
unit		monohydroxy
du	2	*di*
duad		dicarboxylic
duplex		dihedral
duodecimal		dyad
tri	3	Same as Latin
trigonometry		
tricyclic		
trivalence		
quater, quad, quart	4	*tetra*
quaternion		tetramer
quadrilateral		tetraethyl
quartile		tetratomic
quin, quinque, quint	5	*penta*
quincunx		pentavalent
quinquevalent		pentahedron
quintile		pentose
sex	6	*hex*
sexivalent		hexagonal
sextuple		hexane
sextile		hexose
sept	7	*hept*
septivalent		heptane
septillion		heptasulfide
septemfluous		heptode

Latin		Greek
oct	8	Same as Latin
octahedron		
octane		
octillion		
nov	9	*enne*
novemdecillion		enneagon
		ennead
dec	10	Same as Latin
decahedron		
decane		
decibel		

METRIC SYSTEM

Note the differences made between Latin and Greek number prefixes. For example Latin *centum* means "100," as in *centigrade*, but when used in the metric system *centi* means "divided by 100," (0.01), and the Greek prefix *hecto* means "multiplied by 100."

Prefix	Meaning	Example
tera	10^{12} (one trillion)	teraton
giga	10^{9} (one billion)	gigahertz
mega	10^{6} (one million)	megampere
myria	10^{4} (ten thousand)	myriagram
kilo	10^{3} (one thousand)	kiloliter
hecto	10^{2} (one hundred)	hectogram
deca, deka	10^{1} (ten)	decastere
deci	10^{-1} (one-tenth)	decigram
centi	10^{-2} (one-hundredth)	centimeter
milli	10^{-3} (one-thousandth)	milligram
micro	10^{-6} (one-millionth)	micron
millimicro	10^{-9} (one-billionth)	millimicrosecond
nano	10^{-9} (one-billionth)	nanosecond
micromicro	10^{-12} (one-trillionth)	micromicrofarad
pico	10^{-12} (one-trillionth)	picofarad

Chapter 6.
Life Sciences:
Biology, Botany,
Physiology,
Zoology

Like the physical sciences, the life sciences derive technical terminology from Latin and Greek. The difference, of course, is reflected in the application of the classical word elements. In the life sciences, the structure and processes of plants and animals are dealt with. However, as knowledge and technology grow, there is an increasing blending of physical and life sciences. For example, the field of biochemistry relates the study of living processes to chemical substances and processes. Mathematics and physics are both used to further the study of living processes. Therefore, it is not surprising to find some of the word elements in one reference section appearing in another. This makes your task easier, of course. Once the basic meaning is known, you merely have to apply it to the new subject.

This application of word elements to new contexts is the major purpose of this section of this book. The first two sections of this chapter offer you practice in applying these basic elements to the field of life science. A section follows on deriving word meanings from context. This kind of practice should never be slighted. The word elements used frequently in the life sciences are listed in the reference section. Once again, the policy dictating the items selected for this list has been frequency of use. Even though a technical term may be of classical derivation, if its word elements do not appear frequently or have lost all usefulness in helping to remember modern meaning, such a term has been omitted.

The word elements from Chapters 1 and 2 have been combined in alphabetical order. Prefixes begin the practice frames. The reference numbers in parentheses refer to the express or test frames.

PREFIXES
a, an (2-7)
Contrast *aerobic* with *anaerobic*. *Aero* means "air"; *bic* is an adjective form of the root *bio* meaning "life." An aerobic organism lives with _____, whereas an anaerobic

air

organism lives _____ _____.   *without air*

The noun forms are *aerobe* and *anaerobe*.
Note that only the *b* survives from *bio.*

The location of the root *bio* changes. Try
translating *biogenesis.* Literally, "born from
_____." This theory that life is pro-   *life*
duced only by living or once living matter
replaced the theory of spontaneous generation from lifeless matter, or _____.   *abiogenesis*

Other examples of biological terms using
this prefix are *acoelomate, amitosis, aneurism,
anemia, anesthesia, anoxia, asexual, arrhyth-
mia, apodae,* and *aporosa.* All share the prefix
_____ meaning _____. A variant   *a/not or without*
spelling of this prefix is _____.   *an*

ab (2-1)
Abscission literally means "a cutting _____ "   *from*
—a separation. Applied to plants it means
"a natural process where a flower or leaf
is cut _____ the plant."   *from*

Parts of organs or organisms can be located in relation to the axis. A surface turned
from the axis can be described as _____axial.   ab(axial)

If you were required to identify muscles
of the body by function, you could choose
between *abductor* and *adductor* by the prefixes. The muscle which draws a part from
the body is called _____.   abductor

ad (1-5)
A logical word to follow *abductor* is *adductor.*
A muscle whose function is to draw a part
to the body is called _____. The   adductor
prefix means _____.   to or toward
   The nerve impulse which comes to a nerve
center is called _____ferent. The *d* of the   af(ferent)

prefix _____ has been assimilated to _____.

    Some varieties of plants have been accli-
matized to new regions. They have adapted
_____ the new climate.

Since the *d* in *ad* assimilates easily, special
care should be taken to recognize this prefix.
Complete the spellings of these examples:

that which grows to	a_____cretion	c (accretion)
a flowing to	a_____flux	f (afflux)
something glued to	a_____glutinate	g (agglutinate)
something hung to	a_____pendage	p (appendage)
to make similar to	a_____similate	s (assimilate)
tending to draw to	a_____tractive	t (attractive)

Although the above examples display considerable variation in the spelling of the
prefix _____ mean-
ing _____.

apo (2-8)
The combining form *lysis* comes from a
Greek verb meaning "to loosen." The term
apolysis can be translated as "a_____
_____"—a shedding.

    If things are not together, they are sep-
arate, or away from one another. The term
apocarpous indicates that the carpels are
separate, or _____. This information
comes from the prefix _____.

    If apogeny occurs, one can guess that
birth is _____, or to put it in more
usual terms, there has been a loss of repro-
ductive function. Even though literal trans-
lations are often relatively crude, *apogeny*
is an example where literal meanings can
be the clue to a definition stated in more
formal terms.

    Cell division is away from the process of

ad/f

to

ad
to or toward

loosening
from

away
apo

away

meiosis and is called _____ meiosis. That
which is formed without meiosis is called

_____.

apo(meiosis)

apomeiotic

Apo is commonly used in the life sciences,
and its meaning can be the hint you need.
Apospory is without, or away from, spore
formation. *Apogeotropic* translates to "turning _____ from the ground"—in other
words, up.

away

Always try the meaning in the context. Even
a careful examination of the word can save
your making a mistake. If you tried dividing
the word *apodal* into the prefix *apo*, a root,
and then a suffix, you would see immediately that this word *apodal* does not fit such
a pattern. An alternative would be *a + pod
+ al*. Yes, _____ feet (*pod*). In
this instance the prefix is _____ rather than
apo meaning _____.

no or without

a

away

arch (2-9)
Arch used in the prefix position appears
in *archegonium*, the female sex organ which
originates the ova (origin of birth) in mosses
and ferns. Mosses belong to the division
Archegoniatae, a primary division of the
plant kingdom. Mosses may have been
among the first plants to live on land. There
are several ways to associate the meaning
of *arch*: _____, _____, or
_____. Note the variant spelling
arche.

first/original

primary

The roots of *archaecraniate*, *Archaeornithes*,
and *Archaeopithecus* mean respectively
"cranium," "birds," and "mammal," but
all use the word element spelled _____
meaning _____. This spelling is a variation of _____.

archae

first

arch

A term to mean "original life" is _____-*ebiosis.* This term is applied to the first formation of life on earth.

arch(ebiosis)

A designation to show the original cell or group of cells from which microspores develop is _____*espore.* The combining vowel used in this instance is _____.

arch(espore)
e (arche)

Compare *archipallium* with *neopallium*—which evolved first? _____. The spelling *archi* is used as a combining form meaning _____.

archipallium

first

Zo is a combining form usually translated "animal" from *zoion* and is related to a similar Greek word *zoe* meaning "life." The earliest forms of life can be described as _____ic.

archizo (ic)

Two vowels are used in combining *arch*; they are _____ and _____. Did you note these vowels in *zoion* and *zoe*?

i/e

An alternate spelling of the vowel *e* is _____.

ae

com, con (1-6)
One meaning of the form *gen* is "kind." Two plants or animals which belong together in the same genus are _____generous. One such member is a _____gener.

con(generous)
con(gener)

The genus name of the morning-glory family reflects the characteristic of twining or trailing vines—"rolled together," _____-*volvulus.*

Con(volvulus)

Some feature present with birth is termed _____genital.

con(genital)

A contractile cell is one whose drawing _____ causes the rupture of an anther, for example.

together

A contracture means that a muscle or tendon has drawn _____.

together

Conjugation means "a joining _____." In this context, the union, or joining together, of nuclear material as a primitive type of sexual reproduction.

with or together

contra (1-7)
Contralateral is a descriptive term literally meaning "the side _____ or opposite." For example, certain parts of the brain control muscles on the opposite side, that is, _____lateral muscles. The term meaning "same side" is *ipsilateral.*

against

contra(lateral)

The thumb is contraposed to the fingers. Restated: The thumb is placed or set _____ _____ the fingers.

against

A variation of *contra* is *counter.* To counterstain a tissue means to use a contrasting color so that a section may show more clearly. One stain _____ another.
The word *contrasting* is logically assumed to have derived from the Latin verb *stare,* to stand, and the prefix _____ meaning _____.

against

contra
against

de (1-8)
Deciduous trees are those whose leaves literally fall (*cid*) _____ in autumn.

down

An anther dehisces in order to discharge pollen. *De* sometimes serves to emphasize or intensify the meaning of the root to which it is attached. A down action is usually forceful. Such a use is found in *dehisce,* literally meaning "to split _____."
In order to discharge pollen, the anther _____hisces. Ripe fruits and pods also display _____hiscerence. They burst open.

down

de(hisces)
de(hiscerence)

Defoliation, deforest, degrowth, denude, depopulate, depression, detumescence — all use the prefix _____ meaning _____. This meaning may be interpreted as indicating physical direction, as indicating a lessening or reduction (negative), and as an intensive. Apply the meaning according to the context.

de/down

dia (2-10)
Systolic and *diastolic* are terms applied to the contraction and relaxation of muscles, such as the heart or intestines. The diastole of the heart is that phase when the blood can pass _____, as shown by the prefix _____. This is the phase when the cavity fills or empties? _____

through
dia
fills

Also see the prefix *syn* (page 82). Systole is the squeezing together which forces the blood out.

Diaphragm comes from a Greek word meaning "barricade," literally "a fence _____." Applied to mammals it is the partition _____ the body cavities. "A fence through something" also applies to other uses of the term *diaphragm* — insects, a lens aperture, a contraceptive device.

through
through

"Through" is the meaning for the prefix _____.

dia

Compare *diacranterian* with *syncranterian*. The prefixes are the clue. As applied to tooth formation, which term shows that there is a space between the back and front teeth?

_____

diacranterian

"Through" in the sense of "out of," "by way of," or "across" is included in the meaning of the prefix _____.

dia

Caution: Do not confuse *dia* with the prefix *di* meaning "two," as in *diadelphous*. *Di* means "two" and *adelphous* is a form meaning "having stamen fascicles"; hence, *diadelphous* = two fascicles.

Another example is *disporous,* having two spores. Note also that recognizing the prefix provides correct pronunciation: *disporous,* not *disporous.*

dis (1-9)
Disease means literally "_____ from ease."

A discharge is an unloading, a load set _____.

Another way of saying "cut apart" is to use the term _____*sect.*

Disbud, disroot, disforest, disembowel, disinfect, and *dissilient* are other terms using the prefix _____ meaning _____, separate.

em, en, endo, ento (1-19)
An encephalogram is a measure of electric activity where? _____ the head (*ceph*).

The term *embryo* is derived from a Greek verb meaning "to swell" + *em* meaning _____. An embryo is literally a swelling in.

If a foreign particle is suddenly lodged in or literally thrown in a blood vessel, this condition is called an _____bolism.

The prefix *em* has related forms of *endo* and *ento*; these are most often used in technical terminology. *Endocarp, endoderm, endophyte, endoskeleton, endothelium*—look for something _____. *Endo* and *ento* are often interchanged: *endoderm, entoderm.*

The opposing terms are *epi* (2-11) and *ex* (1-10) with its variant *ecto.*

apart

apart

dis(sect)

dis/apart

in

in

em(bolism)

in or inside

epi (2-11)

The epidermis is the covering _____ the true skin, that is, the external covering.

Epiphysis is literally a growing_____, a portion of bone attached to the shaft by cartilage.

This same root (grow) is applied to a plant which grows upon another plant or object. The technical term is _____*phyte*.

An epidemic is a disease _____ the people. A term meaning "a disease upon many birds" is _____*ornithic*.

In learning the terms applied to a plant embryo or seedling, compare *cotyledon* and *epicotyl*. Which one is above the other?

_____

eu (2-12)

If you wanted to form a term meaning "a well-developed head," you could combine *eu* and *ceph* into the adjective _____*alous*. Literally, a _____ head.

The eucalyptus plant was named such because its buds are _____ covered (*kalyptos*).

The Greek word *eugenes* means "_____ born," and from this word has come the term *eugenics*. The eugenicist is especially concerned with the production of_____ offspring.

The prefix *eu* is used in contrast with *dys* meaning "bad." If the light is bad or poor for plants to grow, as in the ocean depths, the term is _____*photic*. However, nearer the surface sufficient light penetrates the water so that growing conditions are good. The appropriate term is _____*photic*.

---

upon

upon

epi(phyte)

upon

epi(ornithic)

epicotyl

euceph(alous)
good

well

well

good or well

dys(photic)

eu(photic)

The prefix *eu* is also contrasted with *pseudo* meaning "false." In English the contrasting term to *false* is _____, which is not too much of a step from *good*. For example, *eucone — pseudocone; eucoelomate — pseudo-coelomate.*

true

The prefix *eu* has two meanings in the life sciences, _____ and _____.

good/true

ex (1-10)
The endocrine glands secrete directly into the blood. Glands which secrete out onto a surface or out to a duct are called _____ocrine glands. The meaning which contrasts to "in" is _____.

ex(ocrine)
out

Cernere and *cretum* are Latin forms meaning "to sift." The process whereby a body sifts out its waste products is called _____.

excretion

To name a nerve fiber which bears or carries impulses from a nerve center out to an organ requires the root *fer* and the prefix *ex* meaning _____. The term is spelled _____ent. The *x* has been assimilated to an _____.

out
effer(ent)
f

Ecchymosis, effector, erectile, exalate, exfoliate, exoskeleton, exostosis, extinction — all illustrate the various spellings of the prefix _____ meaning _____. The *x* may assimilate in order to join smoothly to the root, or the spelling may change to the combining form _____.

ex/out

exo

in (1-11)
If a body appears to have been cut into, it might well be called an _____sect (cut).

in(sect)

Incubate carries the literal meaning "to lie _____," that is, to hatch.

on

Leaves which lie on one another, that is, overlap, are called _____cubous.	in(cubous)
To mix food in the saliva by chewing, or mastication, is to _____salivate.	in(salivate)
A tooth which is adapted to cut into is an _____cisor.	in(cisor)
Another name for the anvil, or middle of the chain of three bones in the ear, means "struck on" or "_____cus."	in(cus)
The prefix *in* carries a second meaning. *Incurable, inedible, indigestible, incaliculate, infertile*—in these words the prefix _____ means _____ .	in not

inter (1-12)

The term *intercellular* refers to the area _____ cells.	between
The portion of a stem between the nodes is referred to as _____node.	inter(node)
The Latin word for rib is *costa*. Name the short muscles which extend between the ribs: _____	intercostal
What is the name of the area between a leaf's ribs? _____	intercostal
Interstices are literally spaces_____ things.	between
The fibrous tissues which bind cells and other tissues are called _____stitial tissues.	inter(stitial)

mal (2-2)

Malformation and *malnutrition* carry the prefix _____ meaning _____ .	mal/bad
If the absorption of nutrients is imperfect or faulty, the term to show this condition is _____*absorption*.	mal(absorption)

Malaria was originally supposed to be caused by noxious substances in the air, in other words, _____ air.

bad

mono (1-36)
Monoploid, monopodium, mononeural, and *monomorphic* are but a few of the many examples using the word form _____ meaning _____.

mono
one

See reference section on numbers, page 189.

non (2-3)
That easy prefix *non* is found in the life sciences.

A plant which is not limited to living in water is called _____ aquatic.

non(aquatic)

Nonmammalian means "_____ mammalian."

not

Nonmuscular, nonmutant, nonporous, and *nonviable* are additional examples of terms using the prefix _____ meaning _____.

non/not

ob (1-13)
A cordate leaf is heart-shaped (*cor, cord*) with the notch as the point of attachment. Where is the leaf attached on the type called *obcordate*? _____

point, tip, or apex

One shape of leaf is ovate or oval with the broader end at the base. An obovate leaf has the rounded end or the point at the base? _____

point

Pyriform means "pear-shaped." If the larger end is up, the term to use is _____ *pyriform.*

ob(pyriform)

per (1-14)
The midrib of a leaf runs through the leaf; it is _____ current.

per(current)

Absorption which is percutaneous takes place _____ the skin.

through

Perdominant, perennate, perennial, per-foliate, perforate, permeate, and *perspire* are called to your attention as examples of terms in this area using the prefix _____ meaning _____.

per

through

peri (2-15)
The prefix *peri* is widely used in the life sciences. This frequent occurrence means built-in practice in use of this prefix.

Tissue which surrounds the heart, is around the heart, is the _____cardium.

peri(cardium)

The sheath or covering around the noto-chord is the _____chord.

peri(chord)

Periglottis is the name of the membrane _____ the tongue (*glottis*).

around

A layer of cells which circles around is called _____cycle, specifically around the stele.

peri(cycle)

The meaning of *peri* helps you to locate a particular area or structure because it means _____. You know where to look.

around

post (2-4)
Post is another prefix showing location.

The body surface which is to the rear, or behind, is _____erior or dorsal surface.

post(erior)

The area behind the abdomen is called _____abdomen.

post(abdomen)

The period following, or after, the ab-sorption of nutrients is the _____absorptive state.

post(absorptive)

A postantennal appendage is located where with respect to the antenna of an insect? _____

behind or after

Postcardinal, postcentrum, postcranial, postembryonic, postfrontal, and *postgang-*

lionic use the prefix _____ meaning _____
in both place and time.

pre (1-15)
Prenatal refers to anything occurring _____
birth.

    Premendelian means "_____ the ac-
ceptance of Mendel's laws."

    The opposite of *posterior* is *anterior* (*ante*
= before). Another way of saying "the an-
terior part of the frontal lobe" is to say "the
_____frontal lobe."

    The part of the insect labium lying in
front of the mentum is logically named
_____mentum.

    Pre means _____ in both place and
time.

pro (1-16)
Prognathism is a state in which the jaws
extend _____; they _____trude.

    The first segment of the thorax—that
which is in front—is the _____thorax.

    That which precedes, is in front of, the
pygidium in beetles you would expect to
be called _____ pygidium. You would look
_____ _____ _____, or
_____.

    "For," "forward," and "in front of" are
meanings to associate with the prefix _____.

    *Proboscis, progeny, reproduction, procrea-
tion, proleucocyte, promorphology,* and *pro-
lagate* are examples of terminology using
this prefix.

re (1-17)
Reproduce means literally "to lead forth

---

post/behind or after

before

before

pre(frontal)

pre(mentum)
before

forth or forward
pro(trude)

pro(thorax)

pro(pygidium)
in front of
forward

pro

_____," that is, another of the same class or kind.   **again**

Some organisms are able to grow a new part again if one is lost, say, a tail. This process of replacement is called _____gen-eration.   **re(generation)**

A cat's claws are retractile; they can be drawn _____.   **back**

A recessive gene is one which can be held _____ by a dominant allele.   **back**

The prefix *re* carries two meanings, _____ and _____.   **again** / **back**

sub (1-18)
Submaxilla is the term for the upper or lower jaw? _____   **lower**

Subpectoral refers to the area _____ the pectoralis muscles.   **under or below**

"Under" refers to place but can also have the sense of "lower" or "less": "less than normal," "less than perfect," or even "a lower division of a larger category."

Complete these terms:
a division of a phyllum _____   **subphyllum**
less than normally
potent _____   **subpotent**
the category above a
family but below an order _____   **suborder**
a leaf which is almost
heart-shaped (*cord*) _____   **subcordate**

Succubous leaves are those arranged so that the upper portion lies (*cub*) _____ those above. This information comes from the prefix _____, in this instance spelled _____.   **under or below** / **sub** / **suc**

super (2-5)
Super is another important prefix in help-

ing to locate organs and structures. Try these:

above a center	_____central	super(central)
above the eye (eyebrow)	_____ciliary	super(ciliary)
above the glottis	_____glottic	super(glottic)

In taxonomic classification a category immediately above a family is _____.

superfamily

Above or *over* also means "excessive."

Excessive infestation by parasites is called _____ism.

superparasit(ism)

An excessive number of eggs produced at one time is called _____ovulation.

super(ovulation)

Related to the prefix *super* is *supra*. Both mean _____. Try these terms:

above or over

above the clavicle	_____clavicular	supra(clavicular)
anything located on the back	_____dorsal	supra(dorsal)
located above the liver	_____hepatic	supra(hepatic)
referring to upper jaw	_____maxilla	supra(maxilla)

syn (2-16)

A synapse is the junction of two neurons. A junction is a coming _____, as shown by the prefix _____.

together
syn

Parasitism is an example of symbiosis— literally, a living _____ of two kinds of organisms.

together

Diastole is that part of the cycle when the blood gets through (*dia,* page 76). That part of the cycle in which the heart contracts, or draws together, is the _____. The prefix is actually _____ but has been assimilated.

systole
syn

Symplasm, symphynote, synapsis, synergid, systolic—all offer the prefix _____ as a clue—referring to a fusion of bone, a muscle contraction, or whatever, always_____.

syn

together

trans (2-6)
When water moves from one location across to another within a plant, the process is called _____location.

trans(location)

Transpiration in plants refers to the loss of water, but in the form of vapor—the water has gone_____ into another form.

across

If you saw the term *transegmental*, you would look for something extending_____ a body segment.

across

Nutrients pass across (hence through) the placenta. This passage is called _____ placental.

trans(placental)

A synonym for *transverse* is _____*wise*.

cross(wise)

ROOTS

All of the prefixes from Chapters 1 and 2 are used in the life sciences, particularly those emphasizing location. Of the roots studied in Chapters 1 and 2 several relate to life processes. These are the ones listed so that you can give them your special attention. Because these roots were practiced indirectly in the prefix section above, only a quick check is needed here. Other roots particularly useful—hence worth learning—are included in the reference section immediately following "Context-clue Practice."

fer (1-23)
A conifer, or coniferous tree, is one which _____ cones.

bears

Spiriferous means "_____ or having a spiral part."

carrying or bearing

Nerve fibers are named afferent and efferent according to the direction in which they_____ impulses. The root is _____ meaning _____.

carry/fer
bear or carry

gen (1-24)
Biogenesis is the theory that all living matter has its _____ from preexisting life.

birth or beginning

Gametogenesis is the process of forming gametes, literally the _____ of gametes.

birth

Congenital, regenerate, eugenic, progeny, generation, metagenesis, parthenogenesis, phylogeny — all share the root _____ meaning _____. The prefixed element tells what is born or begins.

gen
birth, race, kind, or class

spir (1-28)
Breathing in some kind of form is an expected part of the study in this area:

to breathe in	_____
to breathe again	_____
an instrument for measing breathing	_____meter
a breathing hole	_____acle

inspire
respire

spiro(meter)
spir(acle)

Transpiration, respiratory, spirograph — all have some connection with _____, as shown by the root _____.

breathing
spir

Caution: Do not confuse spir meaning "breath" with the form spir meaning "spiral" or "coil." Once again, where there is a choice of meanings, choose the one which fits the context.

CONTEXT — CLUE PRACTICE

Rather than separate practice sentences, excerpts of continuous text are used so that the "flavor" of scientific style can be experienced. This practice may seem overly detailed at times because some of the necessary thought processes are written out in an effort to make clear to you the amount of information provided in any given word — provided you look for it. Especially in scientific writing are words more precise than usual; one word is made to do the work of several. This makes for a formal and tight style which, in turn, makes for difficult reading unless you can appreciate the full meaning of the words used. Only a few of the terms are treated in such detail. You may not be able to supply all of the answers, but by working through these particular frames you will become aware of information you usually overlook and miss out on. Once you are aware of this level of understanding, the whole process goes on quite rapidly;

you will not need to go in a deliberate step-by-step fashion. Here is the first passage.

1   The *compartmentation* of enzymatic activities is readily demon-
2   strated by separating the cell into its various components. If, for
3   instance, one breaks open a batch of liver cells and subjects the
4   broken cell mixture to high-speed *centrifugation*, it is possible to
5   *resolve* the mixture into a *particulate* and a *soluble* fraction. The
6   *particulate fraction* which *is sedimented* to the bottom of the tube
7   during high speed centrifugation is made up of cellular elements,
8   such as nuclei, mitochondria, ribosomes, and the cell membranes.
9   On the other hand, a number of molecules, some large (such as
10   proteins and certain nucleic acids) and others small (glucose,
11   salts, amino acids, and the like) will not be sedimented. This
12   *nonsedimentable* fraction of the cells is called the *soluble fraction.*
13   The soluble fraction contains all of the different enzymes that
14   are not bound in or on one of the particles previously *cited.*

Line 1—Here is a complete translation of the term *compartmentation*: "the making of a state or condition of portions of a whole (taken) together." It is easier and quicker to use the term _____ .

compartmentation

Line 4—*Centrifugation* is a _____ (part of speech) naming an action. What is the more familiar adjective form?_____ . This is a force which literally flees (*fug*) the _____ . It is contrasted with *centripetal*, to seek (*pet*) the _____ .

noun

centrifugal

center
center

Line 5—*Resolve* means "to loosen_____ ." What kind of particle is a *particulate*? _____ . The section of the word providing this information is _____ . (See suffixes, page 129.) The root of *soluble* is *sol,* which means "to loosen." It is a variant form of the root _____ as in _____ .

again

little or minute
ul

solv/resolve

Line 6—What is the noun form of the verb *is sedimented*? _____ . And the result of this process? _____ .

sedimentation
sediment

The name for the part of the cells which
is sedimented is _____ _____ .

particulate fraction

Line 12—Translate *nonsedimentable:* _____
_____ _____ .

cannot
be sedimented

Line 13—Show the connection in meaning
between *soluble* and *not bound:* _____
_____ _____ _____ .

loose
means not bound

Try this passage on photosynthesis:

1   The capacity to conduct photosynthesis is not randomly
2   distributed throughout the body of a plant cell. Like respiration,
3   photosynthesis has its own particular cellular compartment.
4   This compartment contains all of the components required for the
5   capture and utilization of light energy. In photosynthetic bacteria
6   and blue-green algae, photosynthesis takes place in *organelles*
7   called *chromatophores.* In higher plants a more elaborate *organelle,*
8   the *chloroplast,* is the site of photosynthesis. A single cell may
9   contain from one chloroplast (as in the case of some green algae)
10   up to more than a hundred in the cell of a higher green plant.
11   The chloroplast is a highly organized structure. The most prominent
12   aspect of this organization is the network of *lamellae* that traverse
13   the chloroplast. These lamellae, especially the disk-like thickenings
14   called *grana,* contain all of the chlorophyll of the chloroplast.
15   The chlorophyll-free *stroma* contains the enzymes required for
16   CO_2 fixation and other enzymatic processes that the chloroplast
17   is capable of conducting.

Line 5—What is the technical term for "the
capture and utilization of light energy"?
_____

photosynthesis

Line 6—In *organelles,* the suffix *elle* is a clue.
The literal meaning is "_____ organs."

little

An organelle is a specialized part of a cell
functioning as a _____ organ compa-
rable to the organs of many-celled animals.

little

Line 8—The term *chloroplast* is made up
of _____ and _____, literally meaning

chloro/plast,

_____ _____—that is, the site
of photosynthesis.

forming green

Line 12—If you looked at a sketch or electron
micrograph, where would you be expecting
to find something labeled *lamellae* with
respect to the chloroplast—above, below,
across, or scattered through? _____.

across

This information comes from _____ of

tra

the word _____.

traversed

Line 14—If you were asked to identify *grana*
in a diagram, what would you look for?
_____ _____. The

disklike thickenings

word *grana* reminds you of the English word
_____. *Grana* is the plural form

grain, granulate

of the Latin word *granum* meaning "grain."

Line 15—*Stroma* comes from the Greek word
for bedcovering or spread. In a chloroplast
the granules of chlorophyll are dispersed,
or spread through, the stroma. This is a
framework, or matrix. This frame is merely
to complete the terms used in this passage.

REFERENCE SECTION—LIFE SCIENCES

This reference section covers the prefixes, roots, and numbers especially
useful in the technical terminology of life sciences. Select those terms
for which you have immediate use. Add other words you need to the
examples. Or you may want to learn these specialized word elements
systematically, a few at a time, especially if you plan to take several
courses in the same field.

You will also want to practice changing the endings on these terms so
that any form will be familiar to you. See Chapter 3 if you need help
with suffixes.

Only the root is listed; the examples show the vowel used in combining
the root with other word elements. In a few cases where the combining
form (root + vowel) is in common use, that form is given; for example,
aero as in *aerodynamics*. An asterisk indicates a word element covered
in Chapters 1 and 2.

PREFIXES

Word element	Meaning and source	Examples
*a	not (G)	abranchia, anaerobic, apodes
*ab	from (L)	abaxial, abscission, abductor
*ad	to, toward (L)	adductor, accretion, agglutinate
ambi, amphi	both, around (L,G)	amphibian, ambilateral, ambiporous
ante	before (L)	antebrachium, anterior, anteflexion
anti	against (L)	antibody, antigen, antiblastic
*apo	away (G)	apocarpous, apocyte, apogamy
cata	down (G)	catabiosis, catadromic, catagenesis
circum	around (L)	circumcrescence, circumflex, circumnutation
*com	with, together (L)	convolution, compital, contusion
*contra	against (L)	contralateral, contraception, contractile
*de	down (L)	decorticate, decumbent, demyelination
*dia	through (L)	diacoele, diadermal, dialysis
*dis	away (L)	diffusion, dispetal, disjunct
dys	bad (G)	dysgenic, dysgonic, dysostosis
*em, endo, ento	in, inside (G)	embryo, encapsulate, endoskeleton
*epi	upon (G)	epitrichium, epipodium, epithelium
*eu	well, good, true (G)	eugenics, eukinetics, eucoelomate
*ex, ecto	out (L,G)	excrescence, exophytic, ectoplasm
extra	beyond (L)	extracellular, extragenic, extravascular
hyper	over, excessive (L)	hyperchomia, hyperploid, hyperopia
hypo	under, less (L)	hypocellular, hypoblast, hypoglottis
*in	in, into, not (L)	incisura, incretion, impotency
*inter	between (L)	intercellular, interocular, intervertebral

Word element	Meaning and source	Examples
*mal	bad (L)	malnutrition, malformation, malady
meta	between, with, after, (G)	metacarpal, metabolism, metachrosis
*ob	against (L)	obconic, obturator, occipital
pan	all (G)	pancarditis, pangenesis
*para	beside (G)	paramedian, parasympathetic, parathyroid
*per	through (L)	permeate, perennial, perfuse
*peri	around (G)	periblast, periosteum, perimysium
poly	many (G)	polygastric, polycotyledon, polymorphic
post	after, behind (L)	postemergence, postcranial, posttibia
*pre	before (L)	preanal, precordium, precursor
*pro	for, forth, in front of (L)	proboscis, procreate, prothorax
proto	first (G)	protozoa, protoplasm, protogyny
pseudo	false (G)	pseudobranch, pseudopodium, pseudotype
*re	back, again (L)	recapitulation, reflexive, respiratory
retro	backward, back (L)	retrocaval, retrolental, retropubic
*sub	under (L)	subreptary, subphyllum, subesophageal, subcutaneous
*super	over, above (L)	suprarenal, supercrescent, suprascapula
*syn	with, together (G)	photosynthesis, symbiosis, syncraniate
*trans	across (L)	transpiration, transplantation, transection
ultra	beyond (L)	ultrastructure, ultramicroscopic, ultravirus

ROOTS

Word element	Meaning and source	Examples
adeno, aden	gland (G, *aden*)	adenoid, *Adenophora*, adenotrophic

Word element	Meaning and source	Examples
aero	air (G, *aer*)	aerogenic, aerotropism, anaerobic
agri	field (L, *ager, agris*)	agriculture, agricere, agrimotor
agro	of soil, agriculture (G, *agros*)	agrobacterium, agronomy
alb	white (L, *albus*)	albumen, albinism, albino
algia	pain (G, *algos*)	cephalagia, neuralgia, myalgia
all	other, different (G, *allos*)	allele, allosome, allogamy
andr	male (G, *andros*)	androgenesis, androecium, heterandry
angi	vessel, receptacle (G, *angeion*)	angioblast, angiogenesis, sporangium
arbor	tree (L, *arbor*)	arboreal, arboretum, arborize
arthro	joint (G, *arthron*)	arthropoda, arthrostome, arthromere
aur, auric	ear (L, *auris; auricula*)	binaural, auricular, auricle
avi	bird (L, *avis*)	avian, aviary, aviculture
bacter	little staff (G, *bakterion*)	bacteria, bactericide, Aerobacter
bio	life, living (G, *bios*)	anaerobic, biometrics, symbiosis
blast	bud, germ (G, *blastos*)	blastogenesis, blastula, periblast
brady	slow (G, *bradys*)	bradycardia, bradytelic, bradypod
branchi	gill (G, *branchia*)	branchiferous, Branchiata, branchial
card, cardia	heart (G, *kardia*)	cardiac, tachycardia, pericardium
carp	fruit (G, *karpos*)	acrocarp, pericarp, carpogenic
cephal	head (G, *kephale*)	cephalic, cephalothorax, encephalic
cerebr	brain (L, *cerebrum*)	cerebrospinal, cerebroid, cerebriform
chloro	chlorine, greenish yellow (G, *chloros*)	chlorophyll, chloroplasts, chlorosis
chondr	cartilage, grain (G, *chondros*)	mitochondria, chondriosome, chondrogenesis

Word element	Meaning and source	Examples
chord	gut, string (G, *chorde*)	notochord, perichord, chordotonal
chrom	color (G, *chromos*)	chromoblast, chromatin, anisochromia, chromosome
coel	hollow (G, *koilos*)	coelom, hemocoel, coelozoic
cord	heart (L, *cor, cordis*)	cordate, precordium
cost	rib (L, *costa*)	costa, costate, subcostal
crani	skull (L, *cranium*)	craniad, craniometer, pericranial
cresc, cret	to grow (L, *crescere, cretum*)	excretion, crescograph, accrescence
cut	skin (L, *cutis*)	cutin, cutaneal, subcutaneous
cycl	circle, wheel (G, *kyklos*)	*Cyclamen*, cyclic, dicyclic
cyst	bladder, pouch (G, *kystis*)	cystophore, cystic, cystocarp
cyt	hollow vessel, cell (G, *kytos*)	phagocyte, melanocyte, cytoplasm
dactyl	finger (G, *daktylos*)	hexadactylia, dactyloid, dactylus
dendro	tree (G, *dendron*)	dendrophilous, Dendrochirota, *Dendrocopos*
derm	skin (G, *derma*)	epidermis, blastoderm, dermis
entero	intestine (G, *enteron*)	enteron, enteroderm, *Enterobius*
erythro	red (G, *erythros*)	erythrophilous, erythron, erythrocyte
gam, gamet	marriage, united, sexual (G, *gamos*)	gamosephalous, gamete, gametocyte
gastro	belly (G, *gaster*)	gastropod, gastrolith, gastrostege
*gen	birth, race, kind (L, *genus, generis*; G, *genos*)	genoblast, gametogenesis, genesis, antigen
glott, gloss	tongue (G, *glotta, glossa*)	glossa, Glossophora, glottis
gnath	jaw (G, *gnathos*)	prognathism, gnathothorax, gnathocephalon
gon	procreation, seed (G, *gonos*)	gonad, gonocoel, archeogonium

Word element	Meaning and source	Examples
hapl	same, single, simple (G, *haplos*)	haploid, haplocaulescent, haplosis
hem	blood (G, *haima*)	hemal, hematoblast, hematogenous
hepat	liver (G, *hepar*, *hepat-*)	hepatic, hepatogenic, hepatoportal
heter	different, other (G, *heteros*)	heterandrous, heterism, heterozygote
homo	same (G, *homos*)	homozygote, homopetalous, homogametic
ichthyo	fish (G, *ichthys*)	ichthic, ichthyology, ichthyosis
iso	equal (G, *isos*)	isochromatic, isospore, isandrous
kine	motion (G, *kinesis*)	kinesiology, kinetoplast, parakinesia
labi	lip (L, *labium*)	labium, labiate, labial
lact	milk (L, *lac, lactis*)	lactiferous, lacteal, lactation, Lactuca
lepido	scale, flake (G, *lepis*, *lipid-*)	Lepidoptera, Lepidosauria, lepidote
lepto	weak, thin, small (G, *lepein,* to peel)	leptocephaly, leptocercal, leptodactylous
leuko	white (G, *leukos*)	leukocytes, leucoplast, leukon
lys	loosening (G, *lysis*)	lysigenous, lytic, catalysis
micro	small (G, *mikros*)	microfauna, microbe, microscopic
*mito	thread (G, *mitos*)	mitosis, mitosome, mitogenetic
morph	form (G, *morphe*)	morphic, metamorphosis, heteromorphosis
myo	muscle (G, *mys,* mouse)	myophore, myocyte, myosin
nephr	kidney (G, *nephros*)	nephridia, nephric, nephrogenic
neuro	nerve, sinew (G, *neuron*)	neuromotor, neurogenic, neuroblast
ocul	eye (L, *oculus*)	ocular, oculate, oculomotor
odon, odont	tooth (G, *odon*)	mastodon, odontoblast, odontoid
oid	form, resembling, like (G, *eidos*)	hydroid, dysloid, haploid, adinoid
ophthalm	eye (G, *opthalmos*)	ophthalmic, ophthalmencephalon, microphthalmia

Word element	Meaning and source	Examples
ornith	bird (G, *ornis*)	ornithology, ornithofauna, ornithotomy
oste	bone (G, *osteon*)	osteal, osteogenesis, periosteum
oto	ear (G, *ous, ot-*)	otosteal, *Otodectes,* otocyst
ov	egg (L, *ovum*)	ovipositor, ovulation, ovary
ped	foot (L, *pes, pedis*)	quadruped, pedate, pediform
phor	to carry (G, *pherein*)	gametophore, phoresy, Discophora
photo	light (G, *phos, photos*)	photosynthesis, photoperiodism, phototropism
phyll	leaf (G, *phyllon*)	chlorophyll, phylloid, microphyll
phyt	plant (G, *phyton*)	sporophyte, gametophyte, phytomera
plast	form or mold (G, *plastos*)	chloroplast, leucoplast, bioplast
pod	foot (G, *pous, pod-*)	pseudopod, Arthropoda, podilegous
pter	feather (G, *pteron*)	pterodactyl, Pterosauria, pterocarpous
ren	kidney (L, *renus*)	renal, reniform, adrenal
rhin	nose (G, *rhis, rhin-*)	rhinarium, rhinoceros, rhinencephalon
sapr	rotten (G, *sapros*)	saprophyte, saprogen, saprobic
saur	lizard (G, *sauros*)	saurian, saurognathus, Pterosauria
scler	hard (G, *skleros*)	*Scleroderma,* sclera, sclerophylly
som, somat	body (G, *soma, somat-*)	mesosoma, chromosome, somatic
sperm, spermat	seed, sperm (G, *sperma*)	endosperm, spermatogonium, spermatophore
spor	seed, spore (L, *spora*)	sporangium, sporocarp, isospore
stom, stomat	mouth (G, *stoma*)	stoma, stomatous, Cyclostoma
trop	a turning (G, *tropos*)	neurotropic, phototropism, tropism
troph	food (G, *trophe*)	trophoplasm, trophoblast, trophallaxis
zo	life, animal (G, *zoion, zoe*)	protozoa, zoology, zoophyte

Word element	*Meaning and source*	*Examples*
zyg	yoke (G, *zygon*)	zygote, zygodont, zygodactyl

NUMBERS

Latin		*Greek*
uni	1	*mono*
uniparous		monoploid
unipotent		monad
unisexual		monandrous
du, bi	2	*di*
dual		dicyclic
duplicate		didymous
biped		dibranchiate
tri	3	Same as Latin
triceps		
triradiate		
tripetalous		
quat, quart, quad	4	*tetra*
quaternate		tetrapetalous
quarter		tetramerous (4-merous)
quadruped		tetraploid
quin, quinque, quint	5	*penta*
quincuncial		pentamerous (5-merous)
quinquefoliolate		pentadactyl
quintuplet		Pentamera
sex	6	*hex*
Sexostiatae		hexacanth
sextuplet		*Hexanchus*
sexfoil		hexaploid
sept	7	*hept*
septifolious		heptaploid
Septanychus		*Heptranchias*
Caution: Do not confuse		
with *sept* = septum.		heptachlor

Latin		*Greek*
oct	8	Same as Latin
octospore		
Octopoda		
octoploid		
nov	9	*enne*
none		enneapetalous
dec	10	Same as Latin
decacanth		
decimolar		
Decapoda		

NOTE: For large numbers see page 190.

Chapter 7.
Behavioral Sciences: Sociology, Anthropology, Psychology

The behavioral and social sciences do not contain the kinds of technical language which the older sciences present. One reason for this difference is that the behavioral sciences deal in great part with the daily affairs of men, and in the English language words for our daily affairs come from Anglo-Saxon English. However, there remain sufficient terms derived from Latin and Greek to make their study worthwhile. In this chapter notice particularly the words which you may use regularly without appreciating their full meaning. Knowing the derivation heightens the meaning.

This chapter begins with the word elements from Chapter 1 and 2 which are applicable to the behavioral sciences. Next there is a section for context-clue practice, and the chapter ends with a special reference section of the word elements especially used in this subject area. The numbers in parentheses refer to the express frames in Chapters 1 and 2.

PREFIXES
a, an (2-7)
The anonymity of attending a large school can be a serious problem to any student still searching for his own identity. *Anonymity* literally means "_____ name (*onym*)." In this particular context the person is of unknown name; he cannot say who or what he is, so probably no one else can. Note that the vowel *o* was a part of the root.

no

Some student leaders complain that change cannot occur so long as students are generally apathetic. Students who are indifferent literally have _____ feeling (*path*).

no

A person suffering loss of memory is diagnosed as suffering from _____ mnesia.

a(mnesia)

ab (2-1)
Psychology is particularly concerned with behavior which departs from the normal, that is, _____ behavior.

abnormal

In experimental psychology, much knowledge can be gained by selective ablation of various nerve cells, then the consequent behavior of the animal studied. *Ablation* can be translated as "the carrying _____"; in other words, removal.

away or from

Abduction, abstention, abstemious, abscond, abrogate — all share the prefix _____ meaning _____.

ab
from or away

ad (1-5)
Adherence to old customs and beliefs is a mark of the older generation. They literally stick (*her*) _____ the old ways rather than try anything new.

to

The Nazi regime serves as a prime example of forced assimilation to the one ideology permitted by an authoritarian state. Rather than there being diversity among the citizens, all had to become similar _____ the state decree.

to

In the word *assimilation* the prefix is actually _____. The letter *d* has been made similar to the letter _____ of *similation*. This process is called _____.

ad
s
assimilation

Although a primitive culture will probably retain some of its traditions, great changes do occur when primitive peoples are in contact with more advanced peoples. This process of modifying old ways to the new culture is called _____ culturation.

ac(culturation)

The *d* of *ad* assimilates readily. Fill in the correct letters in these terms to replace the *d*:

a_____sociation   a_____commodation

a_____gression   a_____final

a_____trition

s/c

g/f

t

In some cases the *d* is dropped, as in *ascrip-
tion* and *aspirational*. But in all cases the
basic prefix is _____ meaning _____.

ad/to or toward

arch (1-34)
Carl Jung presents the psychological concept of archetypes, that is, universal ideas
that have existed from the _____.

beginning

Nations, like their individual citizens,
usually have an archenemy, even though the
identity changes. Today's enemy may be to-
morrow's ally, but as an enemy he holds
_____ (*arch*) place.

first or chief

Archaeology is the study of ancient or
historical peoples through the remains available such as bones and implements—literally, the study of _____ peoples.

first or beginning

com, con (1-6)
Com is a prefix which carries many spellings, since the *m* must often be assimilated
for ease of pronunciation.

Consanguineal relations are those where
literally the blood (*sanguin*) is _____;
there is a relationship by bloodline from a
common ancestor. Property rights may be
inherited only through consanguineal lines.

together

Concentric zones have been identified as
a pattern of urban development. The zones
are widening circles whose centers are
_____.

together

Either the cohesiveness of the family
unit or the lack of sticking (*hes*) _____
can be a base from which to study a society.

together

Conformity, correlation, competition, collective, consensus —these examples display different spellings of the prefix _____ meaning _____ .

com
with or together

contra (1-7)
Some young people rebel to the extent that they create their own style of life, a contra-culture. This making of a way of life _____ the culture in which they live may provide a temporary way of adjusting to their problems.

against

Although an individual may belong to groups which have overlapping goals, he is not likely to belong to directly *counter-vailing* secondary groups, such as the CIO and the chamber of commerce. He is not likely to belong to secondary groups which are _____ each other in beliefs.
    Counter is a variant of _____ .

against
contra

de (1-8)
The term *decentralization* is used by both political scientists and sociologists. In government, it refers to the power which is moving _____ or _____ _____ (*de*) the central authority. In sociology it refers to the population and industry which are moving _____ or _____ _____ (*de*) the central city.

down/down from

down/down from

In the behavior of human beings, both as individuals and as groups, certain actions veer from the normal course, or path (*via*). The technical term is _____*viant behavior.*

de(viant)

Some critics of present American society use the term *decadent,* meaning that there has been a falling (*cad*) _____ from established norms.

down

One reply to this view is that such criticism merely serves as a demarcation of the old from the new; that is, the criticism clearly marks _____ the division separating the old and new generations — popularly called "generation gap."

down

Many *de* words are found in the social area: *depopulate, deterrent, delinquency, descent, debility, degeneracy.* All share the prefix _____ meaning _____ in the sense of "lessening and lowering." Quite a negative prefix!

de/down

dis (1-9)
What changes would result if voters cast ballots on a dispassionate basis, that is, _____ from passion or strong emotion?

apart

The disprivileged position of minority groups must be considered as one of the causes of social unrest and revolt. What position? _____ from the privileges enjoyed by the majority group.

apart

The fact that minority groups cannot enjoy certain of the privileges of the majority group must be considered as one cause of social unrest. The minority group is set apart from privileges; it is in a _____priv- ileged position.

dis(privileged)

Like *de, dis* also carries a negative sense and appears frequently in terms describing human behavior: *discrimination, disputant, disorganization, cognitive dissonance, disunite.*

In the words *differentiation* and *diffusion* the prefix is _____, but the *s* has been as- similated to _____.

dis
f

em, en (1-19)
The enslavement of a nation means that the citizens are _____ slavery.

in

Endemic literally means "_____ the people (*dem*)," in other words, native or indigenous.

in

Related to *em, en* is the prefix *endo* meaning "within."

A society may require marriage only within certain specified groups. This custom is called _____gamy (*gam* = marriage).

endo(gamy)

Psychology has a long history of attempts to classify human personality by body build. Sheldon used the term *endomorph* for the soft, round build, with highly developed digestive viscera. This "within" visceral development can be associated with the prefix *endo* meaning _____, as a way of remembering. Technically *endomorph* is the chosen term because the functional elements of this internal structure are developed primarily from the endodermal embryonic layer. But "within" helps make an association here, also.

within

See *mesomorph*, page X.

epi (2-11)

In 1840 the Whigs nominated a folk hero for President, Gen. William Henry Harrison, and they called him by the affectionate epithet of "Tippecanoe." The meaning of *epithet* can be figured out from knowing that *epi* means _____, hence something extra or added to characterize or describe. In this case, an affectionate nickname, but "you lowdown cur" is also an _____thet.

upon

epi(thet)

"Stewart Alsop characterized the White House as the epicenter of world power." Although *epicenter* is a technical term for that part of the earth's surface directly _____ the center of an earthquake, Alsop's use was a legitimate metaphor. The White House

upon or over

figuratively sits _____ the center of
world power.

ex (1-10)
The founding fathers relied upon their back-
ground and broad education to solve the
exigent problems then existing, that is, the
problems which stood _____ as most
needing attention.

   In minority groups men tend to practice
exogamy more often than women. Another
term for *exogamy* is _____marriage.

   The ability to educe relationships is an
important factor in estimating intelligence;
in fact, such ability defines intelligence,
according to some psychologists. *Educe*
means "to lead _____ or draw _____."
The prefix of *educe* is _____, but the letter
_____ has been dropped.

   *Extortioner, exorcism, egregious, evert, ex-
patriation, expedience,* and *emasculate* all
share the prefix _____ meaning _____.
The prefix is spelled two ways, _____
and _____.

in (1-11)
"The steady influx of immigrants helped
to maintain the new communities as an
intact minority group." Translate these
terms from the sentence:
   influx = a flowing _____
   immigrants = those who are coming

_____

   intact = _____ touched

   The imbalance in sex ratio in the Western
states possibly explains the fact that the first
woman legislator was elected from Montana
in 1916. The sex ratio was _____
_____.

Answers (right column):

upon or over

out

out(marriage)

out/out
ex
x

ex
out
ex/e

in

in
not

not
balanced

The prefix *in* carries the meanings _____ and _____.

in
not

inter (1-12)
Interaction of one group with another produces a flow of behavior which can then be analyzed by the sociologist. What kind of action produces behavior? Action _____ groups, as shown by the prefix _____.

between
inter

Interpersonal relations are sufficiently active that even the psychologist conducting an experiment with his students must be considered as a variable. Relations _____ the experimenter and his subjects must be accounted for.

between

The entire field of social study seems concerned with "between":
The area between two ecological zones is called the _____stitial area.

inter(stitial)

Killing between group members, or mutual slaughter, is called _____necine.

inter(necine)

To "speak between" the doer and his action is to _____dict, whether by formal administrative order or by taboo.

inter(dict)

The word *interdict* has been heard frequently in the Vietnam war, a special kind of "speaking _____"—firepower to stop enemy movement.

between

mal (2-2)
One cause of severe social problems is the malassignment of highly competent people —for example, a black physicist working as a technician. Such an assignment is _____.

bad or evil

Even more of a social problem is the malevolence of bigots—their wishes for certain other persons are _____ to the extent of visciousness.

bad or evil

"If hope for a change exists, then there will be a limit to the evil treatment people will endure." One word to substitute for "evil treatment" is _____ .

maltreatment

mono (1-36)
In contrast to their Mediterranean neighbors, the Jews were monotheists from a very early date. They believed in _____ God, as shown by the prefix _____ .

one
mono

The practice of allowing only one mate at a time is called _____gamy.

mono(gamy)

A person who is otherwise normal can become deranged concerning a single idea. Such a person is called a _____maniac.
Monopolistic, monasticism, and *monarchical* are other behavioral science terms indicating _____ of something.

mono(maniac)

one

non (2-3)
In order to control for previous knowledge, meaningless combinations of letters are used to study verbal learning. These syllables make no sense; they are_____ syllables.

nonsense

In contrast to the previous generation's attitude of conformity, present young people make an effort at not conforming. They are _____conformists to socially prescribed behavior.
The prefix *non* means _____ .

non(conformists)

not

per (1-14)
Social interaction pervades even the animal laboratory.
Social interaction extends_____ to even the animal laboratory, and must be considered in interpreting experimental data.

through

A percept is the result of perception—a recognized object. The *per* indicates that the stimulus object goes beyond visual response and _____ to brain centers for recognition.

through

Person, personality, persona—all derive from *per* + *sonare*, meaning literally "to sound _____." This literal meaning comes from the masks (*personae*) used in ancient times by an actor, through which he spoke. *Persona* is now a technical term denoting the "mask" all of us assume at times in order to present a desirable image.

through

Perversion literally means "a turning _____" in the sense of "thoroughly." For example, a sexual pervert has turned thoroughly from normal sexual activities and seeks abnormal kinds of sexual gratification.

through

pre (1-15)
The theory of instincts in human beings no longer holds popularity, but has, in part, been replaced by the notion of a predisposition to react in a certain way. Predisposition means that a person is inclined or disposed to respond to a particular stimulus situation _____ he encounters the situation.

before

Another word for foresight, or knowing beforehand, is _____*science* (*scire* = to know).

pre(science)

A term meaning "knowing events before they happen" is _____*cognition*—a part of ESP.

pre(cognition)

Precocity means "development (literally, ripening) _____ the normal time."

before

In addition to "before" in time, the meaning "before" also refers to place. The United States government official who "sits before" all others is the _____sident. In other countries this official may be called the _____mier.

Pre(sident)

Pre(mier)

A preliterate society is so termed because a written language has not yet developed; the society is literally a society _____ letters.

before

Prejudice, prestige, preschool, and *pre-active (inhibition)* are other current terms sharing the prefix_____ meaning_____.

pre/before

pro (1-16)
Projective tests are a widely used technique to gain insight into personality. Ambiguous stimuli, such as inkblots, are used so that the person throws (*ject*) _____ his own interpretations of the pattern, thus revealing his inner perceptions and strivings.

forth or forward

A procurer promotes business for a prostitute. Translate the prefix *pro* in the sentence:
   procurer = one who cares _____
(takes care of)
   promotes = moves _____
(advances)
   prostitute = one who is stationed_____
(is available)

for

forward

before

Pro also means "for" or "in favor of."
During the Civil War one who was in favor of slavery was called a_____slaver.
Proponents of black power by force are called militants. They support, or place themselves_____ _____ _____, the idea of gaining power for blacks by forceful means.

pro(slaver)

in favor of

Pro is contrasted with *anti,* as in *anti-American* and _____*-American.*

pro(-American)

re (1-17)

Repression is a part of Freudian theory. Any of our behaviors which cannot be tolerated consciously are pressed _____ into the subconscious as a defense mechanism.

back

A theory which "leads" complex data "back" to an overly simple form is called _____ductionism, criticized as a dangerous procedure.

re(ductionism)

Relearning is the name of a technique used in studying the phenomenon of forgetting. The number of trials originally required to learn a task is compared with the number of trials needed at a later time to learn the task _____. The difference in number of trials is called savings; not everything must be _____learned.

again

re(learned)

Reaction, regression, reflex, renomination, repeople, rejuvenation, retaliatory—all share the prefix _____ meaning _____ or _____.

re/back

again

sub (1-18)

The subjugation of minority groups is a continuing social problem. Minority groups are literally _____ the yoke (*jugum*), enslaved.

under

The study of our complex American society can better be managed by studying the smaller groups categorized under the term *American society*. These smaller groups are technically called _____societies.

sub(societies)

Social positions can be ranked from higher to lower according to several factors, such as influence or money. The higher positions are superordinate, while the lower ranks are _____ordinate.

sub(ordinate)

Persons who occupy subordinate positions are called _____lings.

under(lings)

Subcommittee, sublimation, subculture, subversion, surrogate, suspicion, and subliminal are additional social terms using the prefix _____ meaning _____. Notice that the b of sub assimilates.

sub/under

syn, sym (2-16)
The study of a single aspect of behavior may be necessary for research, but eventually the data from such studies must be synthesized with the entire field of interacting factors. The single factors must be put _____ to understand the entire field of behavior.

together

The several signs, or symptoms, occurring together in a particular kind of abnormal behavior are called a _____drome.

syn(drome)

Hearing a sound may also arouse a sensation of color. For such a sensation, or feeling, to occur along with another is called _____esthesis.

syn(esthesis)

If the Latin for "with" is used instead of the Greek syn, the above sensation would be called a _____comitant sensation.

com(comitant)

Synchronous, sympathy, systemize, syndicalism, and syllable are other social behavior terms using the prefix _____ meaning _____. Notice the assimilation of the letter _____.

syn
together or with
n

trans (2-6)
When the feelings about a father are carried across to the psychoanalyst, the process is called _____ference.

trans(ference)

A transitional area in a city is one which is in the process of going _____ from residential to business use.

across

Some cultures believe that at death the soul passes across to another person or animal. This is called _____*migration*. This term also applies to any going across, say, moving from a plains area to a mountain region.

trans(migration)

The term *tradition* is derived from *trans* + *dare* meaning "to give _____," hence to hand over from one generation to another.

across

ROOTS
cept, cap, cip (1-20)
Perception is a major topic of study in psychology. Our responses to physical stimuli are _____ through to brain centers for identification. The fact that we can be wrong (misperceive) for a variety of reasons is what makes this a major topic for study.

taken

Intellectual capacity is another major area in the study of behavior. *Capacity* means "the ability to _____ in information."

take

The meaning "seize" (take by force) comes into use in such words as *capture, captivity,* and *captivate.*

dict (2-17), *duct* (1-21), and *fact* (1-22)
The roots *dict, duct,* and *fact* are in such common use that the terms lose a technical sense, but for review purposes:
  A dictator is one who _____ with absolute authority.

speaks

  Reductionism is the error of _____ back complex data to a too simple explanation.

leading

  Artifact is the term reserved for objects such as tools which are man-_____.

made (man-made)

fer, lat (1-23)
In order to understand a person's behavior, one should know his reference group, that

is, the group he _____ back to   carries
for identification and guidance.

   In a complex society individual members
show various characteristics. Instead of all
individuals developing in identical ways,
their various social experiences carry them
apart or separate. This process is called
dif_____erentiation.   fer (differentiation)

   Fertility rites are an important aspect of
cultural studies. These are the rites signify-
ing the age of _____ offspring.   bearing

The term *ablation* uses the fourth principle
part of the Latin verb *ferre, latum.*
   For research purposes a part of the brain
is destroyed, literally _____   carried
away, and the consequent behavior is observed.

gen (1-24)
It is hardly surprising that birth and race
are major areas of interest in social behavior.
   Laws of inheritance can be established
by the order of birth: *Primogeniture* means
the estate goes to the first _____;   born
ultimogeniture means the last _____.   born

   Miscegenation is the term used for a marriage between mixed (*miscere*) _____.   races
The advertising for the movie *Guess Who's
Coming to Dinner* merely showed the picture
of the racially mixed couple instead of using
the technical term *misce_____ation.*   gen (miscegenation)

   Generation is the term applied to individuals who are _____ at about the same   born
time, arbitrarily set within a thirty-year
period.
   The descendant generation consists of
those _____ later, e.g., a son.   born

Gene flow theory and gentic drift are terms related to the _____ or begetting of _____ .	birth races
mo (2-19) What prompts us to behave or move in certain ways is called a _____tive, an as yet little understood area of behavior.	mo(tive)
People move around. This ability to change social rank or physical location is termed _____bility. The direction of change in social rank may be horizontal or vertical.	mo(bility)
A society which permits easy change in kinds of work displays occupational_____ .	mobility
The root *mo* means_____ or_____ _____ _____ .	move/set in motion
nasc, nat (2-20) In a historical view certain ideas are seen to revive or be born again. This phenomenon is called re_____ence.	nasc (renascence)
The Renaissance is the name of the period in Europe marked by a _____ of classical influence.	rebirth
The fact of birth is an important factor in human development. Try these: Neonatal studies are those concerned with the new_____ .	born (newborn)
The land of your birth is your _____ land.	native
Although a nation is technically a political division, it is based on the fact that most of its citizens have been _____ there.	born
patr, matr (2-22) The human concern with birth implies concern with parentage and the family group. The state of being a father is _____nity; that of being a mother is _____nity.	pater(nity) mater(nity)
Lines of descent may be patrilineal or	

matrilineal—respectively, through the _____ or the _____.

father
mother

A society in which the father dominates (inheritance, residence, and control) is termed a _____iarchate.

patr(iarchate)

Although less common, a society in which the female or mother dominates is called a _____iarchate.

matr(iarchate)

The place of residence of married couples may be determined by the male, in which case the practice is called _____local.

patri(local)

sent, sens (2-25)
Extrasensory perception (ESP) is gradually gaining status as a legitimate area of investigation. *Extrasensory* means "perception beyond the usual five senses or_____."

feelings

When a group "feels together" and agrees upon a common pattern of action, the term to use is *con_____us.*

sens (consensus)

Bodily activity which combines both feeling and movement is called _____-orimotor.

sens(orimotor)

tend, ten (1-30)
The root of *attenuation* literally means _____, hence thin or weak. Experimental data may be corrected for attenuation by statistical means; the data have been contaminated or weakened by other measures.

stretched

Tension is a commonplace psychological ailment of our present society. Nerves or emotions are _____ to the breaking point.

stretched

One cannot learn what one has not

stretched his mind to. Restated: One cannot
learn what one has not at_____ to.   tended (attended)

The state of applying or stretching one's
mind to an object is called at_____.   tention (attention)

tain, ten, tin (1-29)
To keep, or hold back, in memory is a capacity desired by all students. The proper
term for this holding back is *re_____tion.*   ten (retention)
To hold back is to re_____.   tain (retain)

The 1968 federal housing law was designed to stop the containment of minority
groups in ghettos. The minority groups
have been _____ together in a limited   held
area.

Supreme Court justices need not worry
about tenure in office. They _____ the   hold
office, or position, for life.

theo (1-37)
In the history of religious beliefs polytheism
preceded monotheism. The belief in many
(*poly*) _____ preceded a belief in one   gods
_____.   God

Priests control the government in a theocracy. Such a form of government indicates
that the sovereign, or ruler, is _____,   God
as shown by the root _____.   theo

Washington and Lincoln have at times
been lifted from human to almost divine
status. Such apo_____sis was also accorded   theo (apotheosis)
Martin Luther King at the time of his as-
sassination.

tract (2-28)
One theory of society is called the contract
theory, which states that individuals_____   draw

together for mutual protection and in return give up their right to force.

Cultures vary in procedures used by females to attract mates — to _____ mates to them.

draw

The goal of social scientists is to be able to draw from their raw data certain theories or principles which can be generalized. The social scientists try to abs_____ principles to explain social behavior.

(abs)tract

ven, vent (1-31)
Social conventions mean that there are certain behaviors on which there has been a _____ together, an agreement, as to acceptability. Disregarding the conventions can be shocking to the older generation.

coming

The advent of atomic warfare has had profound psychological and sociological effects. Another word for *advent* is *arrival*, literally the _____ to.

coming

The "coming upon," or finding, a new way of doing something is called an in_____.

(in)vention

Standards of living have been raised to extremely high levels by inventors, men who _____ upon new solutions.

come

vert (1-32)
In times of stress a person may revert to former, more immature behaviors — may _____ back to.

turn

Aversive stimuli are those to which our reaction is to _____ away.

turn

Pervert, conversion, versatility, and *vertigo* are other social behavior terms containing the root _____ meaning _____. This root is also spelled _____.

vert/turn
vers

CONTEXT — CLUE PRACTICE

You may want to refer to Chapter 4 for a review of the six kinds of context clues if you find you are missing some of the information to help you decide on the meaning of a word in the following practice. The examples given permit you to apply your context skill in the area of behavioral science.

Social and economic democracy in America was expected to mitigate competition for social status, but rather it was observed to intensify it.

Mitigate means _____.

alleviate, make less severe

Not everyone deplores the changes in our racial relations; many think we have not gone far enough.

A substitute word for *deplore* is _____.

regret, lament

Many congressmen spend most of their energies working for parochial rather than national interests.

The term *parochial* is used in the sense of _____.

local, provincial

In behavioral decision theory a difference is made between the microeconomics of information (individual criteria) and macro-economics of information (group criteria).

Micro means _____, and *macro* means _____.

individual, small group, large

Until recently American blacks have been almost completely apolitical.

Apolitical translates to _____ _____.

not political, without politics

Close physical proximity is a characteristic of modern urban society.

This _____ makes conflict very likely.

closeness, nearness

Not everyone agrees that television is a bad thing for children; some psychologists feel that a certain amount may even have a salutary effect.

Salutary means _____.

healthful, beneficial

It was of great practical value that early man had hands with which to carry things —bipedal walking was thus encouraged.

What kind of walking? _____.

on two feet, upright

The church prohibited usury (the lending of money at interest), but the canon law did permit Jews to lend to non-Jews.

Canon law is law of_____ _____.

the church

We have been discussing various factors involved in human interaction. These are not dormant factors, but rather very active.

A substitute word for *dormant* is_____.

inactive, sleeping

If we cannot accept the true explanation of our behavior, we tend to accept pseudo-explanation.

Pseudo means _____.

false, untrue

Merely providing jobs for the unemployed will not satisfy the need; the jobs must be challenging, not stultifying.

A stultifying job is _____.

dull, stupid, debasing

We identify with a glamorous movie star or outstanding athlete in our search for prestige, since a vicarious experience can serve just as well as real achievement.

Prestige means "to stand _____."
Vicarious means _____.

before, first
substituted, imagined

Male hormones are paradoxically responsible for the growth of hair as well as for the loss of scalp hair.

A paradox is a _____.	contradiction
Prejudices contain an affective, or emotional, quality. An affect is an _____.	emotion
"My country, right or wrong" is considered chauvinistic in some current views, ordinary patriotism in others. *Chauvinistic* indicates _____ _____.	excessive pride or loyalty
The best example of a true social isolate is the feral child, or would be, if a child actually could be found who had been totally reared by animals. *Feral* means _____.	wild, savage
John Foster Dulles coined the term *brinkmanship* to mean the ability to come to the verge of war without getting into a war. Another word for *verge* is _____.	brink
The early effect of the Fourteenth Amendment was largely vitiated by the Court decision to permit separate but equal treatment of racial groups. *Vitiated* means _____.	weakened, debased

REFERENCE SECTION — BEHAVIORAL SCIENCES

This reference section covers the prefixes, roots, and numbers especially useful in the technical terminology of behavioral sciences. Select those terms for which you have immediate use. Add other words you need to the examples. Or you may want to learn these specialized word elements systematically, a few at a time, especially if you plan to take several courses in the same field.

You will also want to practice changing the endings on these terms so that any form will be familiar to you. See Chapter 3 if you need help with suffixes.

Only the root is listed; the examples show the vowel used in combining the root with other word elements. In a few cases where the combining form (root + vowel) is in common use, that form is given; for example, *aero* as in *aerodynamics.* An asterisk indicates a word element covered in Chapters 1 and 2.

PREFIXES

Word element	Meaning and source	Examples
*a	not (G)	anonymity, anarchical, anomie
*ab	from (L)	aborigine, abduction, abstention
*ad	to, toward (L)	addiction, ascribe, appointee
*ambi	both, around (L)	ambivalence, ambidextrous, ambiversion
ante	before (L)	antenatal, antecessor, anticipate
anti	against (L.	antisocial, antislavery, antipathy
cata	down (G)	cataleptic, cataplexy, cathexis
circum	around (L)	circumcision, circumnavigation, circumscribe
*com	with, together (L)	comity, consanguineal, cohesiveness
*contra	against (L)	contravene, contraposition, countermovement
*de	down (L)	deviance, demobilization, debility
*dia	through (G)	diagnostic, diachronic, diametric
*dis	apart (L)	disqualification, disputant, diffusion
*em, endo, ento	in, into (G)	embedment, engram, endogamy
*epi	upon (G)	epidemical, epilepsy, epicritic
*ex	out (L)	expurgate, exogamy, emasculate
extra	beyond (L)	extrasensory, extradite, extracurricular
hyper	over, excessive (G)	hypergamy, hypermnesia, hypertension
hypo	under (G)	hypogamy, hypothesis, hypochondriac
*in	in (L)	inflationist, indoctrinate, immigrate
*in	not (L)	incompatibility, insatiate, illegitimacy

Word element	Meaning and source	Examples
*inter	between (L)	internecine, interstitial, interpersonal
*mal	bad (L)	maltreatment, malevolence. maladministration
*mono	one (G)	monotheism, monogamist, monopolistic
multi	many (L)	multilateral, multimillionnaire, multipartite
*non	not (L)	nonconformity, nonsense, nonaggression
*ob	against (L)	obsolescent, obstruction, occupancy
pan	all (G)	pantheistic, pandemonium, Pan-American
*para	beside, resembling (G)	paranoia, parasympathetic, paranormal
*per	through (L)	percept, perversion, permissive
poly	many (G)	polygyny, polyandry, polycentrism
post	behind, after (L)	postmortem, post hoc, posthypnotic
*pre	before (L)	preactive, preliterate, predisposition
*pro	for, forth (L)	proponent, projection, promiscuity
proto	first (G)	prototype, protolithic, protohistory
*re	back, again (L)	regression, recidivism, relearning
retro	backward (L)	retroactive, retrograde, retrospective
se	apart (L)	segregation, secretive, secessionist
*sub	under (L)	subculture, subliminal, surrogate
*super	above, over (L)	superpower, superego, superordination
*syn	with, together (G)	synesthesis, sympathetic, systemize
*trans	across (L)	transitional, traditionalist, transmigration

Word element	Meaning and source	Examples
ultra	beyond (L)	ultraism, ultraconservative, ultramontane
vice	in place of (L)	vice-regent, vicarious, vice versa

ROOTS

Word element	Meaning and source	Examples
ag, act	do or act (L, *agere*, *actum*)	agency, preactive, interaction
alter, altr	the other (L, *alter*)	alter ego, altruism, alternative
andr, andro	male (G, *andros*)	androphobia, polyandry, androgen
anthropo	human being (G, *anthropos*)	anthropology, anthropocentric, Pithecanthropus
*arch	first, chief, beginning (G, *archein*, to rule)	patriarchate, archetype, oligarchy
auto	self (G, *autos*)	autointoxication, autocracy, automation
*cap, cept, cip	to take or seize (L, *capere, ceptum*)	capacity, percept, reciprocity
cast, cest	pure, chaste (L, *castus*)	caste, incest, castigate (*agere*)
ced, cess	to go (L, *cedere, cessum*)	succession, ancestry, progressive
centr	center (L, *centrum*)	concentric, polycentrism, decentralization
cephal	head (G, *kephale*)	cephalocaudal, brachycephalic, electroencephalograph
civ, civit	citizen (L, *civis*)	civics, uncivilized, incivility
col, cult	to till, inhabit (L, *colere, cultum*)	colonize, culture, acculturation
cracy, crat	strength (G, *kratos*)	democracy, theocrat, bureaucratic
dem	people (G, *demos*)	endemic, democratize, demography
*duc, duct	to lead (L, *ducere, ductum*)	reductionism, educe, ducal
dyn, dynam	power (G, *dunamis*)	dynamic, dynast, dynasty
ego	I (L, *ego*)	egocentric, superego, egoistic
equ	equal (L, *aequus*)	equipotentiality, equilibrium, equation

Word element	Meaning and source	Examples
ethn	race, people (G, *ethnos*)	ethnic, ethnocentrism, ethnography
*fac, fact, fic	to make or do (L, *facere, factum*)	artifact, factor, somnifacient
*fer, lat	to bear or carry (L, *ferre, latum*)	transference, fertility, oblation
fin	end, border (L, *finis*)	affinal, finalization, finance
flex, flect	to bend (L, *flectere, flexum*)	reflex, inflexible, reflective
frater, fratr	brother (L, *frater, fratris*)	fratricide, confraternity, confrere
fus	to pour (L, *fundere, fusum*)	diffuseness, confusion, profusion
gam	to marry (G, *gamein*)	endogamy, heterogamous, monogamist
*gen	birth, race, kind (L, *genus, generis*)	miscegenation, genital, ultimogeniture
gnos, gni	to come to know (L, *gnoscere, gnotum*)	diagnostic, cognitive, cognize
grad, gress	to go or step (L, *gradi, gressus*)	aggression, degradation, regress
graph	to write (G, *graphein*)	electroencephalograph, demography, graph
greg	herd, flock (L, *grex, gregis*)	segregation, egregious, aggregate
gyn	woman (G, *gyne*)	gynocracy, polygyny, gynecoid
habit, hib	to have or hold (L, *habere, habitum*)	habitudinal, habitus
her, hes	to stick to (L, *haerere, haesum*)	inherent, hesitancy, cohesiveness
hetero	different (G, *heteros*)	heterogamy, heterosexual, heterogeneity
hom, homin	man (L, *homo, hominis*)	homicidal, hominoid, Homo sapiens
homo, homeo	same (G, *homos*)	homogeneity, homeostasis, homogamy
ideo	idea (G, *idea; idein,* to see)	ideology, ideomotor, ideograph
it	to go (L, *ire, itum*)	transition, initiative, initiation

Word element	Meaning and source	Examples
ject, jact	to throw or hurl (L, *jacere, jactum*)	jactation, projective, ejaculation
kine	to move (G, *kinein*)	autokinetic, kinesthetic, kinematics
leg	law (L, *lex, legis*)	illegitimacy, legality, legislative
lin	line, thread (L, *linea*)	lineage, lineal, patrilineal
loc	a place (L, *locus*)	patrilocal, localism, allocation
*log	word, thought, reason (G, *logos*)	ideology, criminology, dialogue
mani	madness (G, *mania*)	monomania, maniacal, manic
*matr	mother (L, *mater, matris*)	matriarchate, matrix, matricide
mega, megal	great, large (G, *megas*)	megascopic, megalopolis, megalomania
meso	middle (G, *mesos*)	mesomorphy, mesocephalic, mesic
mo	to move, set in motion (L, *movere, motum*)	mobility, motivational, sensorimotor
morph	form or shape (G, *morphe*)	ectomorphy, endomorph, isomorphic
mut	to change (L, *mutare, mutatum*)	mutation, immutable, mutafacient
neo	new (G, *neos*)	neolocal, neoteric, neonatal
neur	nerve (G, *neuron*)	neurasthenia, neuromotor, psychoneurosis
nom	law (G, *nomos*)	anomie, autonomy, nomological
*nomen, nomin	name (L, *nomen, nominis*)	denomination, nominal, nominative
norm	rule, standard (L, *norma*, carpenter's square)	norm, normative, abnormality
nov	new (L, *novus*)	innovation, renovate, novation
oid	appearance or form (G, *eidos*)	Caucasoid, humanoid, eidetic
onym	name (G, *onymos*)	teknonymy, anonymity, homonym
ord, ordin	order, row, series (L, *ordo, ordinis*)	subordination, superordinate, ordinal

Word element	Meaning and source	Examples
paleo	long ago (G, *palai*)	paleontology, paleolithic, paleoethnic
*pater, patr	father (L, *pater, patris*)	paternity, patristic, patrilocal
path	feeling or suffering (G, *pathos*)	apathetic, empathy
polis	city (G, *polis*)	megalopolis, necropolis, Indianapolis
potent	powerful, capable of (L, *potens, potentis*)	equipotentiality, potential, impotent
prim	first (L, *primus*)	primitive, primogeniture, primary
psych	breath, life, soul, mind (G, *psyche*)	psychodrama, psychophysics, psychedelic
pub	signs of puberty, youth (L, *pubes, pubis*)	pubescent, puberty, pubic
sanc, sanct	to make holy (L, *sancire, sanctum*)	sanction, sanctuary, sanctify
sangu, sanguin	blood (L, *sanguis, sanguinis*)	consanguinity, sanguine, nonsanguineal
*scrib, script	to write (L, *scribere, scriptum*)	ascribed, conscription, scrip
sec, sect	to cut (L, *secare, sectum*)	sect, sector, dissection
*sent, sens	to feel, perceive, sense (L, *sentire, sensum*)	extrasensory, consensual, sensorimotor
soc	companion, ally (L, *socius*)	socialize, antisocial, association
somat	body (G, *soma*)	somatotype, psychosomatic, somatology
soror	sister (L, *soror*)	sororate, sorority, sororal
sta, stat	to stand (L, *stare, statum*)	status, stateless, static
*ten, tend, tens	to stretch; weaken (L, *tendere, tensum*)	neoteny, tenuous, attenuation
*theo	God or gods (G, *theos*)	polytheism, theocratic
val	to be strong (L, *valere, valitum*)	ambivalence, value, validity

Word element	Meaning and source	Examples
vert, vers	to turn (L, *vertere, versum*)	ambivert, conversion, aversion
volv, volut	to roll, revolve (L, *volvere, volutum*)	involution, revolutionary, evolvement

NUMBERS

Latin		*Greek*
uni	1	*mono*
unilinear		monandry
union		monogamic
unicameral		monotheism
du	2	*di*
duopoly		digamy
duad		digraph
duplicate		dyad
tri	3	Same as Latin
triad		
triarchy		
trichotomous		
quater, quadr	4	*tetr*
quaternary		tetrarch
quadroon		tetragram
quadrigamist		tetrapartite
quin, quint	5	*penta*
quintuplet		pentagonoid
quincentennial		pentapolis
quintile		pentarchy
sex	6	*hex*
sexennial		None
sextipara		
sexcentenary		
sept	7	*hept*
septemvirate		heptarchy

Latin		*Greek*
septennate		
septennial		
oct	8	Same as Latin
octarchy		
octennial		
octad		
nov	9	*enne*
None		None
dec	10	Same as Latin
decile		
decathlon		
decade		

NOTE: For large numbers see page 190.

Chapter 8.
Humanities:
Literature,
Fine Arts,
and Music

One can enjoy literature and the arts without having a highly developed vocabulary—although that enjoyment is limited to the extent that vocabulary is limited. But for the *student* of literature and the arts, technical vocabulary is as necessary as in any other discipline. Added to the technical aspects, the student of literature is also reading content which ranges from simple talk to highly elaborate and difficult word level.

Although originality in the use of language may be desirable in an artist and even be the mark of an artist, there still remains a fairly stable pattern for coining new terms. There also remains the body of terms used in literary criticism. Each of these sources uses words of classical derivation.

Art and music display their heritage by continuing to use terms formed from Latin and Greek. In the case of music, the terms may be directly from Italian, but the original Latin derivation shows through. As in literature, the newly coined words in art and music frequently use old word forms in new ways.

This chapter offers practice in application of the word elements presented in Chapters 1 and 2, then practice in context clues applied to text material in this area. A reference list including additional useful prefixes, roots, and numbers for this subject area ends the chapter. The numbers in parentheses refer to the express frames in Chapters 1 and 2.

PREFIXES

a, an (2-7)

A novel is frequently developed with strict adherence to the time sequence; however, an author may choose to follow a pattern where events are not in order of time, _____chronological treatment.

a(chronological)

A composer may deliberately avoid the use of traditional tonality in creating his music. If he does, his composition is called

atonal, _____ tone in the traditional sense.	no or without
Substitute one word for "not harmonic": _____.	anharmonic
Perfect symmetry may be the ideal in some cases, but a design that is asymmetric can be more interesting—a design which is _____ symmetric.	not

ab (2-1)

To some viewers abstract art is merely an aberration, a wandering _____ the natural state. But to the abstractionist, he is	from
drawing _____ the natural state the very essence of his subject, whether it be a tree, a building, or his own personality.	from
Ablative is the name of a grammatical case showing separation. In Latin the preposition *ab* denotes motion from a fixed point. The phrase *fuga ab urbe* would be translated "flight _____ the city." The case used	from
with the preposition *from* is appropriately called _____lative.	ab(lative)

ad (1-5)

On my bookshelf is a book entitled *Lewis Carroll, The Annotated Alice*. The annotator, Martin Gardner, added explanatory notes _____ Carroll's text.	to
The prefix in the word *annotate* is really _____, but assimilation has changed the	ad
_____ to _____.	d/n
In the phrase "a study of the poet Milton," *Milton* and *poet* have been placed next to each other so that *Milton* can explain or limit the term *poet*. *Milton* is in _____position to *poet*.	ap(position)

The modifier of a verb is placed next to

or near to the verb. The name of this modifier is _____ *verb.*

                                       ad(verb)

Accidental, accentuation, afflatus, alliteration, allusion — all share the prefix _____ meaning _____.

                                       ad
                             to or toward

apo (2-8)

The literal meaning of *apostrophe* is "a turning _____." This meaning applies both to letters omitted in words and to the device of addressing a person not present. In either case there is a turning _____ from the ordinary procedure, as shown by the prefix _____.

                                      away

                                      away

                                      apo

    Even though in type the mark indicating an apostrophe is often a straight line ('), I was first taught to make a curved line, one which "turned away." Were you?

    An apology is literally "a speaking _____," perhaps of some criticism? Possibly, since a synonym for *apology* is *excuse* or *justification.* When the justification takes on literary quality, the speaking away becomes an _____ logia.

                                      away

                                 apo(logia)

    The cutting away of final sounds or letters in a word is properly termed _____ cope.

                                 apo(cope)

arch (2-9)

Universal themes in literature dating from the beginning of man or perhaps even of creation are called _____ etypes. They are the original models (*typos*).

                               arch(etypes)

    An architect is literally the _____ builder (*tekton*). This literal meaning is literally true, since the architect's ideas are responsible for the finished building.

                               first or chief

    The first, or lowest, part of an entablature

is the _____itrave. An entablature? The section between the column and the roof in classical-style buildings. The architrave is _____, next the frieze, then the cornice.

arch(itrave)

first

As explained in Chapter 2, *arch* is used both as a prefix and a root. To remind you of its use as a root, try this frame:
Archaic art, archaic speech, archaic writing —all are old-fashioned, antiquated. This information comes from _____ meaning _____.

arch
first or beginning

com (1-6)
The term *complex sentence* means that a minor thought has been folded (*plic*) _____ a major thought. However, if one major idea has been placed with another major idea, the sentence is called _____pound.

with

com(pound)

A *composition*, a *compilation*, a *compendium* —all show by the prefix that several things have been treated _____.

together

Consonance is a term which is widely applied. Its literal meaning, "sounding (*son*)_____," applies directly to music, indicating sounds that produce a satisfying, harmonious effect. This literal meaning of "pleasing sound" also applies to words, which are, of course, nothing but sound patterns.

together or with

A broader use applies to anything which is harmonious, or in agreement. For example, if a theory agrees with the evidence, it is said to be _____sonant.

con(sonant)

Since an artistic product is made up of several things treated together in a special way, the prefix *com* appears frequently in this area. Consider *concerto, connotation, collaborator, concordance, concatenation,* and *coordination.*

contra (1-7)
Characters, singers, designs—whatever—are of more interest if there is opposition: one thing placed *contra,* _____, another. In fact, the storyteller has no tale if there is no problem: one factor against another.

against

In depicting the human figure, the vertical axis may be twisted so that hips, shoulders, etc., go in different directions, one direction against another. The term for this treatment is _____*pposto.* The spelling of the term may be Italian, but the prefix is pure Latin!

contra(pposto)

Contrapuntal, contraoctave, contrabass, and *contralto* are examples of musical terms using this prefix. In literature there are *contrast* and *contradiction.* But add the variant spelling *counter.* A counterplot is one plot placed _____ another.

against

de (1-8)
In Latin *crescere* means "to grow up, to increase." If you need a word to indicate a reversal of this process, use *de* meaning _____. The musical direction meaning "to play with a decreasing volume" is _____*crescendo.*

down

de(crescendo)

The depiction of the human body may be done in any fashion according to the artist's idea. But regardless of style or medium, if the likeness has been depicted, it has been put _____ (*de*) in some kind of concrete form.

down

The final task of a novelist is to "untie

the knot" of the skein of events he has developed. This outcome of "bringing the knot down," or unraveling, is called the _____ nouement. The term is French but derived from Latin *nodare,* to tie or knot, with the prefix *de* showing reversal.

de(nouement)

The general meaning for *de* is _____, and it is used in both a literal and a figurative sense.

down

Demonstrative, delineate, dependent, and *declamatory* are other words in which the prefix meaning helps to clarify the term.

dia (2-10)

An octave in music literally means eight notes. If you play or sing these eight notes straight through without deviation to other notes, you are using the _____tonic scale.

dia(tonic)

Diapason is the name of an organ stop, taken from the Greek phrase *dia pason cordon symphonia,* meaning "concord_____ all the notes." An obsolete meaning of *diapason* is "the interval _____ an octave," hence harmony or concord— perhaps a useful piece of information if you are reading music history.

through

through

Dialectics as used in literature applies to any systematic exposition or reasoning which seeks to resolve conflicting ideas. The purpose of this dialectical form is to argue _____ to a solution of the conflict.

through

Dialogue is another term for *discourse* or *conversation.* Literally, _____ words or speech people exchange ideas.

through

dis (1-9)

Music deviating from, or apart from, harmony is called _____harmony.

dis(harmony)

The opposite of consonance is _____ so-nance. Please note the help it is in spelling to distinguish prefix from root: in *dissonance* there must be two *s*'s. To distinguish? To tell them _____.

dis(sonance)

apart

Sounds or ideas that are together are consonant, but dissonance prevails when they are _____ from each other. Discord is the result.

apart

If resemblance to the truth is lacking, if something is apart from truth, the word to use is _____*emblance.*

dis(emblance)

Simulare is a Latin verb associated with the Latin adjective *similis*, to be like, to re-semble. In English, to dissimilate means to become unlike, _____ from being similar, while to dissimulate means to be _____ from truth, to give a false appear-ance. Watch the spellings to distinguish the two English verbs: *ilate* and *ulate.*

apart

apart

em, en (1-19)
"Figures from Greek mythology were en-chased on the stone." They were carved as an ornament or decoration. The literal meaning of *enchased* is "_____ a case," which is exactly what we do with things of value—put them in a case or proper setting for ornamental display.
"The ruby was enchased in platinum." In this English sentence the preposition *in* appears how many times? _____

in

two (en and in)

Enharmonic keys are those which are the identical notes on a piano but can be writ-ten two different ways, e.g., F sharp major and G flat major. This is one sense of the literal meaning "_____ harmony."

in

A design applied to a surface so as to put protruberances, or bosses, into the surface is called an _____bossed design.

em(bossed)

epi (2-11)
Epigram means literally "something written _____." In literary usage *epigram* refers to a saying or short poem written _____ a single thought or point, and it is often satirical.

upon
upon

A final word to conclude or round out a literary work is an epilogue. The literal meaning of *epilogue* fits ordinary usage: "a word _____ the rest of the writing" — an additional word.

upon

A literary term meaning "a coming upon" is _____*sode.* This term refers to a brief action which is a part of a larger action but remains distinct and separate. In your travel (sod, *hodos,* way), you come upon a distinctive but related event. Episodes add variety.

epi(sode)

eu (2-12)
A writer pays special attention to the sound effects of his words. If he is striving to convey harshness, even his words may be harsh, out of harmony. The term for this device is *cacophony.* But ordinarily the writer wants his words to produce a pleasant, harmonious sound — an artistic use called *euphony,* literally _____ sound.

good

Euphemism and *euphuism* are two words often confused. Both use the prefix _____, which means _____. Both use the suffix _____. Only the roots are different.
   Pheme is a Greek word meaning "speech." *Euphemism* then carries a literal meaning

eu
good or well
ism

_____ _____, the good words we
use in place of unpleasant or harsh ones.
For example, we no longer have poor folks
—only underprivileged or disadvantaged
ones. Also, we don't die—we pass away.

Euphuism comes from a character named
by John Lyly in his *Euphues, the Anatomy
of Wit,* 1579. The term applies to an affected
style of speaking and writing, one that has
grown beyond accepted usage. But where
did Lyly derive the name for his character?
From a Greek word meaning "_____
grown."

By the way, the first erroneous case of
substituting *euphuism* for *euphemism* is
dated 1865 by the Oxford dictionary. Things
haven't improved much!

ex (1-10)
Expletive carries two meanings in literary
usage. One is "to fill (*plet*) _____ a
line or phrase without adding to meaning"
—only a filler.

The second meaning of *expletive* is "a
word or phrase exclaimed or shouted _____
as an oath." This meaning especially refers
to obscene or profane words. Our good old
Anglo-Saxon four-letter words, for example.

Exegesis, exposition, explicit, exeunt—all
share the prefix _____ meaning _____.

in (1-11)
Many literary and other artistic words are
of an inspirational nature. Their purpose
is to help us breathe (*spir*) _____ a new
hope, a new spirit.

An intaglio carving is one which has been
cut _____ the stone. The figures and
designs are hollowed out, so that if an impression into another surface were made,

good speech	
well	
out	
out	
·	
ex/out	
in	
in or into	

the result would be a relief, raised figures.

The prefix of *intaglio* can help you to remember this technical term. "If an impression into another surface were made"? The intaglio is pressed _____ the other surface. The prefix of *impression* is actually _____, but the _____ has been assimilated to _____.

> in or into
>
> in/n
> m

An innovator is one who brings _____ new (*nov*) ideas.

> in

Incisive language is the kind which cuts _____ the matter. It is pointed and sharp.

> in or into

The second meaning of *in* is used in the following words: *insensitive, indefinable, illegible, inartistic, inharmonious.* The second meaning of *in* is _____.

> not

inter (1-12)
Intermissions are the breaks _____ the acts of a play.

> between

In melodrama, at the point in the action when the villain is about to overcome the heroine, the hero intervenes and saves the day. The hero comes _____ the villain and his victim.

> between

The Latin word *intervallum* referred to the spaces between the ramparts. The derived word *interval* and its meaning have broadened from reference to fortifications to include the space _____ any series, whether physical or space of time.

> between

Musically, an interval is the difference in pitch _____ any two tones.

> between

Intermezzo is an Italian term which retains the Latin prefix. A serious drama may have some light work presented between the acts. A symphony or larger work may have a movement presented between major sections. The term for this part which comes between is _____*mezzo*.

inter(mezzo)

mono (1-36)
Speaking in monosyllables is characteristic of the stereotyped strong, silent hero. He speaks in words of only _____ syllable.

one

The metrical aspects of poetry receive much attention. If you heard the term *monometer* you would know that the line of verse contained _____ foot, or measure.

one

Mono is a word element widely used throughout the arts. Consider *monochrome, monophonic, monotone,* and *monody.* In whatever specific field the term applies, you at least know that they all share the idea of _____.

one

non (2-3)
Non is such an easy prefix that only a reminder is needed. Translate:

nonharmonic	_____ harmonic	not
nonbook	_____ a book	not
nonpareil	_____ equal (*par*)	not

ob (1-13)
Although the derivations of *obscene* and *obscure* are not certain, the meaning of the prefix *ob* helps in understanding these words. Take *obscene* at the simplest level of meaning: *ob* + *scene* means "_____ the scene or view." An obscenity is _____ the values or view generally held, and so *obscenity* becomes a term meaning "filth" or "foulness."

against
against

So with a passage whose meaning is obscure to you. You know something is _____ your understanding. It may be your own

against

ignorance, or it may be that the author did not understand clearly what he was trying to write.

Opprobrium means "disgrace," "infamy," or "shame." The prefix is actually *ob* meaning _____. The idea of "against" can supply the clue you need to comprehend this sentence: "Opprobrium is always attached to ignorance." Yes, indeed, we hate to show our ignorance even if justified and pardonable.

against

per (1-14)
One style of drawing is to use perspective, literally the look (*spect*) _____ from a particular point of view. This may be an objective view of reality or the subjective view of the artist.

through

The characters of a novel or play are called *personae*, the plural form of *persona*. *Persona* is the Latin term for the mask worn by an actor, and literally means "sound _____." The voice of the actor came through the mask of the character being played. The term has broadened to include the mask or social front we all assume upon occasion. Our ordinary word *person* also comes from this same source—as does *personate*, meaning "to act the part of another."

through

Perfunctory means "in a routine manner, lacking interest." *Per* still carries the basic meaning _____ but in the sense of completion, getting _____ with the action or situation.

through
through

peri (2-15)
Rather than answer a simple "Yes," some speakers prefer, "My answer to your question is stated in the affirmative." *Periphrasis*

is the name for this style of language and simply means "the long way _____," as shown by the prefix _____.

around
peri

Peripeteia and *peripety* are synonyms referring to the sudden reversal of circumstances in a literary work or in actual affairs. A sudden reversal toward good or bad can create high dramatic interest. The literal meaning of *peripety* is "a falling _____." Can that meaning help you to remember? One set of circumstances surrounds the hero; suddenly it all falls _____ his feet, so to speak, and everything is changed.

around

around

A peristyle may be a part of the new design for a government building, a modern adaptation of a Roman peristyle. A peristyle is an open space with roof-supporting columns or pillars (*stylos*) _____ it.

around

As with all prefixes, the meaning of *peri* can be a clue to your working out the meaning of words whose roots you may not know. In some kind of connection, a *peri* word has something _____.

around

pre (1-15)
In either a dramatic or musical work, the main action is seldom the starting point. An introduction comes before the main section, a _____lude to the main action.

pre(lude)

Unfortunately, students seldom read the prefatory matter in books. Such information comes _____ the main text and contains valuable guides as to purpose and organization of the text.

before

Precentor is the name for the person who leads the singing _____ the congregation. He may lead the choir or the congrega-

before

tion, but he performs (*pre*) _____ the congregation in either case.

before

The meaning "before" applies to either time or place. Consider *presentiment, prestige, pre-Raphaelite, prescient, presage,* and *prerogative.*

pro (1-16)
Is *forestage* a synonym for the *proscenium* of a modern stage? You can answer by looking at the prefix of *proscenium,* which is _____. The proscenium is that part of the stage in front of or behind the curtain?

pro
in front of

The literal translation of *prolix* is "a flowing _____." *Prolix* applies to lengthy and drawn-out speech or writing. The words literally flow _____. "Prolixity was his weakness at a time when economy of words was in vogue."

forth or forward

forth

Pronounce, proclaim—both mean "to speak _____."
Occasionally an adverb may become a pronominal. That is, it may be used as a pronoun, literally, a word which stands _____ a noun.

forth

for

A prolated style of speaking is appropriate for especially solemn occasions. Each sound is carried (*lat*) _____, that is, extended or drawn out.

forward

re (1-17)
In the late 1960s, styles from the 1920s and 1930s underwent a renascence—literally, were born _____.

again

A repertory theater is made up of a company of players brought together for one special occasion. True? _____ because

no

the prefix in *repertory* means _____;
therefore, such a group of players is prepared
to play many times. *Repertory* and *repertoire*
both mean "a storehouse or stock ready to
be used."

*Rebuttal, recantation, redolent, reflexive,
reflective* — all share the prefix _____ meaning _____ or _____.

sub (1-18)
The subdominant tone is the one next
_____ the dominant.

Books often carry subtitles which may
help to explain the main title. The subtitle
appears _____ the main title.

Subtle, suffix, subtext, and *supplicate* are
terms using the prefix _____ meaning
_____. Notice that the *b* assimilates.

syn, sym (2-16)
Although a symphony may be a complex
and difficult kind of music to write and ar-
range, the literal meaning of *symphony*
remains its goal: the many instruments must
"sound _____" to produce a
harmony of sounds.

To communicate in English, one must not
only know the correct words but also know
the syntax of the language, that is, how
words are put _____ to convey
the intended meaning. Dog bites man. Man
bites dog. It does make a difference syn-
tactically.
A synopsis is the whole work taken_____
for a brief general view (*ops*).

The field of English has developed highly
technical terms for some of our common

Right column answers:
again or back

re
back/again

below or under

under or below

sub
below or under

together

together

together

speech habits: *s'prise* for *surprise* is an example of a *syncope*; saying *seest* as one
syllable is a *syneresis*; *th' elephant* for *the
elephant* is called *synaloepha*. The *syn* can
help you to remember these terms as re-
lating to sounds put _____ with   together
the result that the total number of sounds
is reduced.

trans (2-6)
Examples of *trans* are easy to find:
   A transitive verb shows action going
_____ to an object.   across
   Transitional sentences carry the thought
_____ from one paragraph to the next.   across
   Trans words show up in music and art
also: *transposition, transcription, transept,
transcent, transfigure.*

ROOTS

Relatively few roots have wide technical application in this area, but
they will serve as review and, perhaps, to intensify meanings of words
you use so often that you have forgotten their full meanings.

dic, dict (2-17)
Dic is a commonly used root in the field of
English. So common, in fact, that you need
only be reminded:
   A place for words is a _____ionary.   dict(ionary)
   Words spoken (a statement) are a
_____um.   dict(um)
   Choice of words or verbal expression is
_____ion.   dict(ion)

fac, fic (1-22)
The suffixes *ify* and *ification*, meaning literally "to _____," are commonly used   make
to show what the author or artist was at-
tempting: to personify, clarify, typify.

   Something lacking in naturalness, ob-
viously made, is arti_____ial.   fic (artificial)

An author who failed to represent a naturalness of dialogue and made up his own version would be accused of arti_____iality.

fic (artificiality)

Facile, facsimile, and *factitious* are examples of words using the root *fac* or *fic* meaning _____.

make or do

pon, pos (1-26)
Pon is an example of meanings we forget in words in common use. Putting or placing can actually represent great effort and struggle.
Composition—verbal, musical, or pictorial —can be translated literally as "something _____together." Planning, even dreaming may be the start of the process, but the work gets done by the actual putting together of the ideas into concrete form.

put or placed

Exposition, transposition, apposition, and *compound* are reminders of terms using some form of *pon* meaning _____.

put or place

scrib, script (2-24)
How many ancient scribes deserve our appreciation for their painstaking care! Scribes are _____.

writers.

A tool used to write on metal is called a _____.

scriber

In a medieval monastery a room was especially set aside for the scribes. It was a writing room, a _____orium.

script(orium)

sent, sens (2-25)
An insensate audience is to be avoided by the performer if at all possible. He cannot perform well if his audience has no_____, is indifferent.

feeling

The great artist has great sensitivity to the human scene. By interpreting his own _____, he is able to express the universal.

feeling

Sentience is only the beginning; perception and ideation must follow. The root of *sentience* is _____ meaning _____.
In the context of the above sentence, literally, pure _____, nothing more.

sent/feeling

feeling

CONTEXT—CLUE PRACTICE

In order to make this context practice as realistic as possible, the following material has been taken from various texts in the field. Be alert for the clues. They are not always easy, but they are there.

Style is one aspect of literary study which deserves our attention. By style we mean the way in which an author uses language.
 An author's use of language defines _____.

style

The artist stands as a bulwark against the dehumanization of man in a scientific age.
 A bulwark is a _____.

protection, defense

Formerly the writer interspersed the scenes and action with his own comment, but the modern writer is more self-effacing.
 The modern writer tends to _____ himself.

remove, eliminate

Much of the lexicon of music has been borrowed from Italian.
 A lexicon is a _____.

dictionary, vocabulary

The bold distortions of the human form in modern art do not find favor with the ordinary man. The artist _____ and elongates the body in his attempt to communicate.

twists

Future artistic forms by unknown methods now lie dormant in the minds of the very young.

A synonym for *dormant* is _____.

sleeping, inactive

Blues, in its most refined form, permits the performer to express his innermost feelings more than any other idiom.

In this context *idiom* means _____ _____.

musical style

It is customary to use six lines to represent the six strings in guitar tablature.

Tablature is the name for _____ _____.

musical notation

A writer may choose names for his characters that are in some way descriptive; on the other hand, the names may be mere appellations so as to distinguish one from another.

Appellation is another word for _____.

name or designation

In order to avoid long explanations, an author can locate his story in time by supplying details of the social customs of the given period. A close scrutiny will reveal these details to the reader.

A substitute for *scrutiny* is _____.

examination, inspection

In the arena theater the audience is seated around the stage on raked platforms. This arrangement gives each spectator a full view.

Raked means _____.

sloped, slanted

On the surface the action in a story may seem straightforward and realistic, but interfused with this seemingly simple treatment may be a deeper meaning which changes the story.

Interfused means _____ _____.

blended in, literally poured between

Enjoyment in reading is a primary goal,

but it is only worthwhile when one can recognize the difference between the genuine and the spurious.

Spurious is another word for _____.

false, counterfeit

Plot is the organization of drama, not merely an arrangement of incidents. It is the architectonic element.

Architectonic indicates that plot is the _____ part of the drama.

chief or first

A novel thus organized in terms of a theme may become primarily didactic. Its teaching may be moral or social.

Didactic is explained by the word _____.

teaching

The generation of World War I artists did not view Western culture as sacrosanct. They felt free to attack the civilization of which that horrible butchery was a part.

These artists did not feel that Western culture was _____, therefore immune to attack.

sacred

If a character develops within the story, is the change plausible? Can you believe it?

Another word for *plausible* is _____.

believable

The author's style is at odds with his story; it is distracting rather than subserving his characters.

Reworded: "distracting rather than _____ _____ his characters."

useful for, helping promote

The solo material herein presented is playable by all who know drum rudiments. A review of the proper sticking of each rudiment is carefully explained in Section One.

Rudiments means _____ _____.

Sticking in this context means _____ _____ _____.

basic skills
handling
of drumsticks

A sense of pitch is indispensable to the musician.

Reword the sentence to translate *indispensable* to plain English: A musician _____ _____ _____ a sense of pitch.

cannot do without

REFERENCE SECTION—HUMANITIES

This reference section covers the prefixes, roots, and numbers especially useful in the technical terminology of literature, fine arts, and music. Select those terms for which you have immediate use. Add other words you need to the examples. Or, you may want to learn these specialized word elements systematically, a few at a time, especially if you plan to take several courses in the same field.

You will also want to practice changing the endings on these terms so that any form will be familiar to you. See Chapter 3 if you need help with suffixes.

Only the root is listed; the examples show the vowel used in combining the root with other word elements. In a few cases where the combining form (root + vowel) is in common use, that form is given; for example, *aero* as in *aerodynamics*. An asterisk indicates a word element covered in Chapters 1 and 2.

PREFIXES

Word element	Meaning and source	Examples
*a	not (G)	achronological, anhemitonic, asymmetric
*ab	from (L)	ablative, abstract, absonant
*ad	to, toward (L)	alliteration, annotation, ad nauseum
ambi	both, around (L)	ambidexterity, ambiguity, ambisyllabic
ante	before (L)	antecedents, anteclassical, antepenult
anti	against (L)	antiphonal, antistrophe, antagonist
*apo	away (G)	apostrophize, apocryphal, apotropaic
auto	self (G, *autos*)	autobiographical, autotelic, autocriticism

Word element	Meaning and source	Examples
cata	down (G)	catachresis, catacomb, catalectic
circum	around (L)	circumlocution, circumflex, circumvolution
*com	with, together (L)	compendium, conjunction, concrete
*contra	against (L)	contrapuntal, counterplot, contrapposto
*de	down (L)	decrescendo, denotation, delineate
*dia	through (G)	diabolic, pandiatonic, diagonal
*dis	apart (L)	dissonant, dissimulation, display
*em, en	in, inside (G)	emblazonry, enharmonic, encomium
*epi	upon (G)	epitomize, epigram, epistrophe
*eu	well, good (G)	eulogium, euphony, euphemism
*ex	out (L)	expletive, exegesis, exotic
extra	outside, beyond (L)	extravaganza, extrados, extrascientific
hyper	over, excessive (G)	hyperbole, hypercritic, hypermetry
hypo	under (G)	hypostyle, hypodiapason, hypotaxis
*in	in (L)	inspirational, impressionable, intaglio
*in	not (L)	improvisation, illiberal, incognito
*inter	between (L)	intermezzo, interval, interrogatory
*mal	bad (L)	malapropism, malediction, malposition
meta	change, beyond (G)	metaphysical, metaphor, metalanguage
*non	not (L)	nonharmonic, nonverbal, nonextant
*ob	against (L)	obscenity, opprobrium, occult
pan	all (G)	panegyrist, pandiatonic, panoramic

Word element	Meaning and source	Examples
*para	beside, resembling (G)	paradox, parable, paraphrase
*per	through (L)	perpendicular, perspective, perlative
*peri	around (G)	periphrastic, peripety, peripatetic
poly	many (G)	polymeter, polyglot, polyrhythm
post	behind, after (L)	postconsonantal, postclassical, postlude
*pre	before (L)	precursor, preconsonantal, prelude
*pro	for, forth, in front of (L)	prologue, proscenium, protasis
*re	back, again (L)	refrain, resonance, recantation
retro	backward (L)	retrograde, retrospective, retrochoir
*sub	under (L)	suffix, subtlety, subtext
*super	above, over (L)	supercolumnar, supercommentary, supertemporal
*syn	with, together (G)	symphonist, syncopation, syndetic
*trans	across (L)	transcription, transdialect, translucent
ultra	beyond (L)	ultramodern, ultramarine, ultracritical

ROOTS

Word element	Meaning and source	Examples
ag, act	to do or drive (L, *agere, actum*)	agent, act, inaction
agon	contest, struggle (G, *agonia*)	protagonist, antagonist, agony
aqu	water (L, *aqua*)	aquatint, aqueduct, aquafortis (strong)
*arch	first, chief, ruler (G, *archein*, to rule)	archetype, architrave, archaism
art	art or skill (L, *ars, artis*)	artistry, artisan, artifice
aster, astr	star (G, *astron*)	asterisk, disaster, astral
aud, audit	to hear (L, *audire, auditum*)	audition, auditorium, auditory

Word element	Meaning and source	Examples
biblio	book (G, *biblion*)	bibliophile, bibliographical, bibliopegy
cad, cas	to fall (L, *cadere, casum*)	cadence, cadenza, cascade
calli, kali	beautiful (G, *kalos*)	calligraphy, kaleidoscope, kalon
cant, cantat	to sing or play (L, *cantare, contatum*)	cantata, cantor, recantation
ced, cess	to go (L, *cedere, cessum*)	antecedents, procession, precede
chrom	color, modified tone (G, *chroma*)	monochrome, chromo, chromatic
chrono	time (G, *chronos*)	achronological, anachronism, chronogram
climax, climact	high point, critical point (G, *klimax,* ladder)	anticlimax, climax, climactic
cresc	to grow, increase (L, *crescere, cretum*)	crescendo, descrescendo, concretion
cycl	circle, wheel (G, *kyklos*)	cyclic, cyclorama, Cyclopic
dox	opinion, belief, glory (G, *doxa*)	paradox, orthodoxy, doxologize
*fac, fact, fic	to make or do (L, *facere, factum*)	facile, artificiality, personification
fig	to invent, shape, feign (L, *figurare, figuratus; fingere, fictum*)	figurine, figurative, fictional
flex, flect	to bend, modulate (voice) (L, *flectere, flexum*)	reflexive, inflection, reflection
*gen	birth, race, kind (L, *genus, generis*)	gender, genre, ingenious
ger, gest	to bear, act (L, *gerere, gestum*)	gesture, gesticulation, gerund
glot, gloss	language, tongue (G, *glotta, glossa*)	polyglot, glossary, glottal
grad, gress	to step, walk (L, *gradi, gressus sum*)	retrograde, transgression, egress
graph	to write (G, *graphein*)	calligraphic, serigraphy, lithography

Word element	Meaning and source	Examples
harmon	harmony (G, *harmonia*)	enharmonic, nonharmonic, harmonious
hier	powerful, holy (G, *hieros*)	hierography, hieratic, hieroglyph
homo	same (G, *homos*)	homophonic, homonym, homophone
iso	same (G, *isos*)	isorhythm, isocephalic
ject, jact	to throw, hurl (L, *jacere, jactum*)	adjective, projection, conjecture
junct	to join (L, *jungere, junctum*)	conjunction, juncture, disjunct
libr	book (L, *liber, libri*)	libretto, library, librettist
lig	to tie, bind (L, *ligare, ligatum*)	ligature, ligative, ligation
lingu	tongue (L, *lingua*)	lingual, linguist, linguodental
liqu, locu	to speak (L, *loqui, locutus sum*)	soliloquy, obloquy, circumlocution
liter	a letter (L, *litera*)	literati, alliterative, literacy
lith	stone (G, *lithos*)	lithographer, monolithic, cyclolith
luc, lumin	light; source of light (L, *lux, lucis; lumen, luminis*)	luminism, lucidity, translucency
lud, lus	to play (L, *ludere, lusum*)	prelude, allusion, postlude
mega	large, great (G, *megas*)	megaron, megalith, megaphonic
melo	song (G, *melos*)	melodic, melisma, melodramatic
meter, metr	measure (G, *metron*)	hexameter, polymeter, trimetric
mim	imitate (G, *mimeisthai*)	pantomimic, mimic, mimesis
*mo	to move, set in motion (L, *movere, motum*)	mobile, motive, movement
neo	new (G, *neos*)	neoclassic, Neo-Gothic, neo-impressionism
not	to mark, note (L, *notare, notatum*)	denotation, connotation, note

Word element	Meaning and source	Examples
onym	name (G, *onyma*)	antonym, pseudonym, metonymy
op, opt	eye; opening, hole (G, *ops; ope*)	metope, optical, Cyclops
oper	work (L, *opus, opera*)	opera, operetta, opus
ortho	straight (G, *orthos*)	orthography, unorthodox, orthostyle
os, or	mouth, (L, *os, oris*)	orate, peroration, osculation
*pend, pens	to hang, to weigh (L, *pendere, pensum*)	dependent, perpendicular, pendentives
phon	sound (G, *phone*)	homophony, antiphonal, phonetic
phras	to speak (G, *phrazein*)	paraphrase, periphrasis, phrase
pict	to paint (L, *pingere, pictum*)	picture, depict, pigment
*plic, plex	to fold, plait (L, *plicare, plicatum*)	complicate, explicit, complex
poet	composer, poet (G, *poete*)	poetic, poesy, poetaster
*pon, pos	to put or place (L, *ponere, positum*)	appositive, exposition, composer
rhythm	rhythm, measure (G, *rhythmos*)	isorhythm, polyrhythm, rhythmicity
scen	stage (L, *scena*)	proscenium, scene, scenographic
sens, sent	to feel, sense (L, *sentire, sensum*)	sensual, sentimentality, sensationalism
simil	like (L, *similis*)	simile, assimilate, similitude
sol	alone (L, *solus*)	soliloquy, solo, solitude
son	sound, noise (L, *sonus*)	consonance, sonnet, assonance
styl	pillar (G, *stylos*)	hypostyle, peristyle, amphistylar
terr	earth (L, *terra*)	terra cotta, terrazzo, terre verte
text	to weave (L, *texere, tectum*)	textile, texture, subtext
ton	tension, tone (G, *tonos*)	atonal, pentatonic, pandiatonic

Word element	Meaning and source	Examples
tract	to draw (L, *trahere, tractum*)	abstract, retraction, tract
verb	word, verb (L, *verbum*)	verbosity, verbatim, adverbial
ver, verit	true; truth (L, *verus; veritas*)	verism, verisimilitude, verity

NUMBERS

Latin		*Greek*
uni	1	*mono*
unison		monophonic
unity		monotype
unicorn		monochromatic
du	2	*di*
duologue		disyllabic
duple		diaeresis
duet		dichromatic
tri	3	Same as Latin
trichromatic		
tricornered		
trilogy		
quater, quadr	4	*tetra*
quaternion		tetrachord
quatrefoil		tetralogy
quadrilingual		tetrapla
quin, quint	5	*penta*
quinte		pentacle
quincunx		pentalogy
quinible		pentameter
sex	6	*hex*
sexisyllable		hexastyle
sexfoil		hexasyllable
sextuplets		hexastich
sept	7	*hept*
septet		heptachord

Latin		*Greek*
septfoil		heptameter
septicolored		heptatonic
oct	8	Same as Latin
octave		
octavo		
octapodic		
nov	9	*enne*
None		enneastylos
		enneasyllabic
dec	10	Same as Latin
decameter		
decastich		
decasyllabic		

NOTE: For large numbers see page 190.

Chapter 9.
Occupational Fields:
Agriculture, Business,
Auto Mechanics,
and Nursing

Unless you are studying or working in a basic field, such as physics, biology, or language, then you are working in areas where the basic field has been put to use, that is, applied. For example, agriculture draws its knowledge, hence terminology, from botany, zoology, physics, mathematics, etc. It represents a cross section of such subject areas and takes what is useful for agriculture from these areas.

This chapter presents material like the kind you find in your textbooks and covers many of the word elements from Chapters 1 and 2. The coverage is not exhaustive but is intended to serve as specific practice in popular areas not already covered.

Because applied fields draw from several subject areas, no reference section is given. Rather, use the general and specialized reference sections already presented according to what you need.

AGRICULTURE

The breeding quality of an animal is learned by the kind of progeny it produces. For example, although hogs may be similar in appearance, they may differ in their ability to transmit these qualities to their offspring.

A synonym for *progeny* used in this excerpt is _____ .

offspring

Notice also *produces*, *differ*, and *transmit*, all covered in earlier chapters.

A large, symmetrical udder is desirable in a diary cow.

Symmetrical means "measure _____ ," in other words, the same rather than lopsided.

together

Perennials are plants living more than 2 years. Some of the most troublesome weeds are perennials.

The prefix of *perennial* is _____, and the word translates to _____ the years (*enn*, *ann*).

per
through

Farmers use picker-shellers or "corn combines"—a machine so named because it picks and shells the ears _____, as shown by the prefix _____.

together
com

To achieve good quality hay, crops must be handled so that the leaves are retained.

Translate *retained*: _____ _____

held back

Preemergent sprays are applied to the surface of the ground after the seeds of the crop have been planted but _____ (pre) the plants of these crops "have come _____" of the ground.

before

out

Land-tenure reform played an important role in agricultural development after World War II.

Land tenure translates to "land _____ ing."

hold(ing)

The County *Extension* Agent is so called ·because his work _____ _____ to all residents of the county.

stretches out

Many farmers have achieved a worthwhile supplemental income through improved forest management.

The farmers have switched to forest management as their livelihood? _____ (yes/no) This is shown by the prefix _____ meaning _____.

sup(sub)
under

Hog breeders were motivated to produce an animal with more meat and less fat because of consumer demands.

In other words, the consumers _____ | moved
the breeders to new action.

Additional Words for Study

You already know and use some of these words, but perhaps not in connection with agriculture. For example, *capacity* literally means "the power or ability to take." On a farm perhaps you think of silos. How much grain can they take?

Or you may find words new to you. Do you know *lactiferous*? *Fer* means "bear or carry," *lact* means "milk,"—so, milk bearing? What bears milk on a farm? Cows and goats, of course, but so do *milk*weeds.

Study the remaining words in the same way. Decide what they mean, then think about what connection they have with agriculture.

lactiferous	eccentric	cooperative
parasite	respiratory	impermeable
malformation	photosynthesis	liquefaction
postermergence	transplant	capacity
perimeter	defoliate	paternity

BUSINESS

An unprecedented expansion in the size of business occurred in the post-Civil War years.

In the word *unprecedented* can you recognize two prefixes and one root? _____ meaning _____, _____ meaning _____, and _____ meaning _____.

      Un/
no/pre/before
ced/go

You know that expansion means an increase because *ex* means _____.

      out

After or before the Civil War? _____
The word providing this information is

_____.

      after

      post

The United States is considered an affluent society, although the consequences are controversial.

An affluent society has goods and benefits flowing (*flu*) _____ it, as shown by the prefix _____, which is actually the prefix _____.

      to
af
ad

The consequences may be good or bad?

_____ , as shown by the prefix _____ meaning _____ . In other words, more than one viewpoint.

Both/contro
against

Consider the italicized words in this paragraph:

Consumer information can *promote* a better understanding of business. For example, research shows that in a *supermarket* there are two best *positions* on which to *display* high-*profit* items for *attracting* the consumer's eye: shelves at eye level or near the checkout counter.

Consumer means the one who takes _____ , in the sense of completely, uses up.

with or together

Promote means to _____ _____ .

move forward

Supermarket means a store _____ the size of a mom and pop store.

above or over

Positions contains the root _____ meaning _____ .

pos
place

Attracting contains the prefix_____ meaning _____ and the root _____ meaning _____ .

at
to/tract
draw

Display uses the prefix _____ meaning _____ . The *play* part is derived from *plic* meaning _____ , thus a display is goods set out so as to catch your eye rather than to be lost within a group of many items.

dis
apart
fold

When you read *profit*, did you wonder about the *pro*? If so, then you are becoming aware of word elements. *Profit* comes from a Latin verb meaning "to go _____ ," which is certainly the direction for profits to go.

forth or forward

In the century from Marshall Field and R. H. Macy to Ralph Nader, the American consumer seems to have moved from *nominal* king to king in *fact*. At least the knowledgeable consumer can be in command of his buying habits.

Nominal means in _____ only, not in practice.

Fact means _____, hence actual, real.

name

done

The expansion of world trade has created *unparalleled export* opportunities for both large and small businesses. For many firms export sales can mean the difference between an *adequate* and an *unacceptable* sales year.

Unparalleled literally means _____ _____ one another, hence, nothing to equal.

not

beside

Export literally means _____ _____, hence goods sold to other countries.

Adequate translates equal _____.

Unacceptable translates to *un* meaning _____, *ac* meaning _____, *cept* meaning _____, hence rejected.

carry out

to

not/to

take

Management by objectives is a method of *translating* organizational goals into terms that will *motivate* and *elicit* teamwork from all members of the organization.

Translating means _____ _____ goals from one kind of language to terms that _____ (motivate) and draw _____ (elicit) teamwork from everyone.

carrying

across

move

out

A salesman who desires *repeat* business will certainly not misrepresent his product. He may even do *post*sale follow-up to be sure of customer *satisfaction*.

The prefix of *repeat* is _____ meaning _____ or _____.

The first prefix of *misrepresent* is _____ meaning _____.

*Post*sale follow-up means a follow-up _____ the actual sale.

re

back/again

mis

bad or wrong

after

Satisfaction means "enough (satis) has been _____," the meaning of the root _____.

done
fact

Additional Words for Study

Figure out the literal meaning of the word, then think about how that meaning applies to business. For example, *supercargo*. "Over the cargo?" Yes, the officer on a merchant ship in charge of (over) the cargo.

countersign	import	repossess
deferred charges	malpractice	subdivision
dictating machine	monopoly	supercargo
disbursements	portage	syndicate
ejectment	preferred stock	transcript

AUTO MECHANICS

Compression is one method used to raise a fuel's temperature. *Compression* is the *reduction* of space in which the fuel is *confined*.

Compression literally means "pressed ____ _____."

together

Reduction carries the prefix _____ meaning _____ and the root _____ meaning _____. In other words the area is lessened.

re
back/duct
led

Confined carries the prefix _____ meaning _____ and the root _____ meaning _____. The fuel is in a space_____ _____s.

con
with/fin
end or limit/with
limit(s)

A too advanced spark will rob the engine of an *excessive* amount of its *momentum* and can even kill the engine.

Excessive carries the prefix_____ meaning _____ and the root *ces* meaning _____, a variant form of the root_____. An amount "gone out of" indicates beyond the correct amount, out of the limit.

ex
out/go
ced

The root of *momentum* is _____ meaning _____ and serves as your clue to the more precise definition of "force of motion."

mo
move

Under power, a piston sets up a one-sided

strain in the crankshaft. To counteract this strain, counterbalances are built into the crankshaft opposite each throw. The shaft runs smoothly because a counterbalance develops an inertia at the opposite shaft side, thus relieving the strain.

There are five words in the above passage containing a prefix meaning "against." What are they?_____ _____

_____ _____

_____

counteract/ counter-balance
opposite/counter-balance/opposite
in/not

Also from the above passage, the prefix of the word *inertia* is _____ meaning _____ and can be a clue to the technical definition. *Inertia* comes from a Latin word meaning unskilled, idle, or motionless.

The force of a shaft's rotation is called *torque*, a _____ing force.

twist(ing)

If two liquids having different boiling points are mixed, they can also be separated by boiling, that is, by distilling.

Two of the above words carry a prefix meaning "apart." They are _____ and _____. For your information, the *se* of *separated* is also a prefix meaning "apart."

different
distilling

During combustion, if there are too many carbon atoms for the amount of available oxygen atoms, only one carbon atom combines with each oxygen atom.

This gas with one carbon atom is called carbon _____xide.

mono(xide)

Hard carbon deposits are a part of the residue resulting from poor combustion.

Deposits contains the prefix _____ meaning _____ and the root _____ meaning _____.

de
down/pos
put or placed

Residue contains the prefix _____ meaning

re

_____ and the root _____ meaning _____. Besides hard carbon, black smoke and soot also result from poor combustion.

back/sid
sit

Heavy-duty oils contain large amounts of protective additives to make them highly detergent.

   Contain translates to _____ _____ _____ .

hold together

   Pro in *protective* means _____ , in the sense that a problem is avoided _____ it can happen.

before
before

   You already know that a detergent is a cleanser, but why that particular word? The root *terg* means "wipe," so *de* plus *terg* literally means "wipe _____ or away," hence cleanse.

down

The engine block is usually provided with two or more expansion plugs. If the coolant in the block should freeze, these plugs can "spread (pans) _____ ," thus relieving the ice pressure.

out

   Did you notice *provided*? *Pro* plus *vid* means _____ _____ . In time or place? _____

see before
time

The blocker ring was an improvement for manual transmissions. It prevented the possibility of the two members of the clutch contacting each other before their speeds were synchronized.

   The transmission is the mechanism by which engine power is literally " _____ _____ " to the live axle.

sent
across

   Synchronized means that the gears are "timed (chron) _____ " so that they mesh smoothly.

together

   Did you also notice *prevented* and *contacting*?

   Just a question of interest: Can you simultaneously operate the accelerator pedal, the clutch pedal, and the gearshift lever? In other words, can you operate a manual, or standard, transmission?

Additional Words for Study

Have you ever wondered why some things are called what they are? Consider these automotive terms using word elements you have learned. For instance, consider the word *automobile*: *Auto* means "self," and *mo* means "move." "Self-moving?" Yes. Remember that the automobile was named in the days when vehicles needed horses to pull them.

Now go through the list, figuring out why these terms are used instead of some other word.

independent suspension	generator
reverse gear	inhibitor
fluid reservoir	distributor
torsion bar	compact car
tension and compression	monocoque

NURSING

Nursing and the other health professions use a highly technical vocabulary, thus requiring special attention to the reference section for Life Sciences, p. 191. But to give a sample of the application of word elements you have learned thus far, the following excerpts are offered.

Emetics are given to make a patient vomit.

Emetics literally "get" the contents of the stomach "_____."

The prefix is actually _____, but in this word the letter _____ has been _____.

out
ex
x/omitted

Sympathetic and parasympathetic are the two divisions of the autonomic nervous system. Not one system but a second one _____ (para) the other.

beside

They work in opposition to each other. For example, the sympathetic nerves speed up the heart. In contrast, the parasympathetic nerves slow the heart rate.

What are the three words in the above

paragraph which use the prefix meaning "with" or "together."

_____ _____

_____

sympathetic/
parasympathetic
system

Two of the words carry a prefix meaning "against." They are _____ and
_____ .

opposition
contrast

The nurse can predict that if a stroke patient is kept in good alignment, he is more likely to develop contractures than one who is not.

How does the word *contractures* come to be defined as a shortening of muscle or tendon? The prefix is _____ meaning _____
_____ and the root is _____ meaning
_____ , hence shorten.

con
together/tract
draw

Probably the oldest theory of the causation of *disease* is that it is caused by the *malign* influence of *supernatural* power.

Analyze the italicized words:

Disease means "_____ from ease."

Malign means "_____ ."

Supernatural means "_____ the natural power."

apart
bad or evil
over or beyond

But then what is natural power? The root *nat* means _____ , thus natural can mean inborn or innate, the normal power of the physical world.

birth

If *sublethal injuries* are *prolonged*, cells are able to adapt to the *presence* of *abnormal* stimuli by new or altered steady states.

Sublethal: death or less than death?
_____ because _____ means _____ .

Injuries literally means "_____ right (jur)," hence damages or hurts.

In *prolonged*, the prefix _____ shows that time has been drawn _____ , or lengthened.

Less/sub/under
not

pro
forward

In Latin the verb included the preposition needed to express the meaning, but in English the preposition follows the verb as a separate word. For example, the phrase "adapt to." The English word "to" is used because of the Latin prefix _____.

ad

Contrast *presence* with *absence*. To be _____ (before) as contrasted to be _____, not present. Here *before* means place or time?

pre

from

_____

place

Abnormal also used the prefix _____ and translates to _____ normal.

ab

from

Additional Words for Study

Think about the words in the list below. Is it the prefix, the root, or both which help you to understand the meaning of the word and to remember it? For example, consider *hepatogenic*, a cancer which originates, is born (*gen*), in the liver (*hepat*).

epidemic	respiratory	pre-Nightingale
infusion	parathyroid	rehabilitation
malignant	eugenics	transfuse
epithelium	permeability	subcutaneous
endothelium	pathogenic	contralateral

WORD LIST

All the words used for study in this chapter are listed here. Select the section or sections you studied and use the words for review. You should be able to recognize the word elements you have learned and be able to supply their meaning. The next step in your mastery is to be able to use each word in a sentence or phrase.

AGRICULTURE

capacity	impermeable	perennials
combines	lactiferous	perimeter
cooperative	land tenure	photosynthesis
defoliate	liquefaction	postemergence
differ	malformation	preemergent
eccentric	motivated	produces
extension	parasite	progeny
genetics	paternity	respiratory

AGRICULTURE (cont'd.)
retained
supplemental
symmetrical
transmit
transplant

AUTO MECHANICS
automobile
carbon monoxide
compact
compression
confined
contain
counteract
counterbalance
deposits
detergent
different
distilling
distributor
excessive
expansion
generator
inertia
independent suspension
inhibitor
momentum
monocoque
opposite
protective
reduction
reservoir
residue
reverse
synchronized
tension
torque
torsion

transmissions
system

BUSINESS
adequate
affluent
attracting
consumer
controversial
countersign
deferred
dictating
disbursements
display
ejectment
elicit
expansion
export
import
malpractice
misrepresent
monopoly
nominal
portage
positions
post-Civil War
postsale
preferred stock
profit
promote
repeat
repossess
satisfaction
subdivision
supercargo
supermarket
syndicate
transcript
translating

unacceptable
unparalleled
unprecedented

NURSING
abnormal
absence
adapt
contractures
contralateral
contrast
disease
emetics
endothelium
epidemic
epithelium
eugenics
infusion
injuries
malign
malignant
natural
opposition
parasympathetic
parathyroid
pathogenic
permeability
pre-Nightingale
presence
prolonged
rehabilitation
respiratory
subcutaneous
sublethal
supernatural
sympathetic
synchronized
system
transfuse

Part 3.
A Final Word

Chapter 10.
A Final Word

Contrary to the commonly understood definition that reading is deriving meaning *from* the printed word, this book has tried to offer the skills necessary to accomplish what reading actually is: the bringing of meaning *to* the printed word. This definition applies equally to listening, the aural equivalent of reading.

If you already have an appropriate meaning to associate, then there is no problem. If not, then you must be able to use all of the clues available to join with what you already know to make some kind of meaningful association. This book has covered the meanings of word elements which are repeatedly used in various combinations and has also covered the use of context clues so that you can make a choice of meaning appropriate to the passage. The techniques have been explained and practiced. Additional reference material has been supplied for you to expand your vocabulary skills.

One remaining aspect of vocabulary mastery should be acknowledged. Some words do go in and out of fashion. Some words even undergo an abrupt change in meaning. The skillful user of words not only knows meanings but is aware of when and how to use words. The following excerpt was chosen to illustrate this aspect of words. It is hoped you will also find it amusing as a reward for your hard work in mastering vocabulary skills.

These are not the only ways of a man with a word. Recently I was traveling in rugged country with friends of mine from abroad. We had car trouble and camped near an isolated ranch, although the rancher was a bit surly, probably fearing we might be careless with fire. The next day we drove to the neighboring town, without seeing much of our host, who had left early, but later in the day I noticed two women of our party talking to him. They were eminently respectable women, happily married, and consequently I was not unamused when one of them reported their conversation, beginning, "We were talking to the man we slept with last night. I was glad to find out he's a nice man."

The good lady had forgotten for the moment that *sleep* often does not mean "to sleep," if followed by *with*. This sort of colored use of an innocuous word arises frequently. We need delicate ways of referring to matters which local customs have branded indelicate, and accordingly we find innocent, general, vague words, preferably from a foreign language. Words associated with bodily functions, for instance, are likely to go through rapid changes in respectability. What was once delicately called *toilette* — after all, a lady had to make her toilette — and is now with a new delicacy sometimes called a *powder room*, has run through hundreds of words. The Anglo-Saxons called it respectably a *gong*, that is, a place you go to; currently children say that they *have to go*. But the word *gong* became crude, and was replaced with the Latin *necessarium*. If Shakespeare wanted to be a bit vulgar, he called the place a *jakes*, that is, a *Jacks*, the literal equivalent of the modern *John* or *Johnny*. Later the establishment became a *water closet*, as it is now a *bathroom*—what could be more innocent than pure water? But not for long. Soon one had to use the letters, *W.C.* Meanwhile, French slang developed the phrase *lieu de l'anglaise*, that is, *place of the English woman*.

Thus words run afoul of our taboos and when they do, several changes are likely to occur. Words shift in respectability and even lose old meanings or acquire new ones under pressure of the taboo. When there is a taboo against speaking a word, we find another way of saying what we mean. We find a noa-word, *noa* meaning "profane" in Polynesian as *taboo* means "sacred." Thus *gosh, darn,* and *Codfish Mighty* appear so that we shall not take the name of the Lord or mention His words in vain, and in order that the devil may not appear when he is named we refer to *the Dickens* and *Old Nick*.

Conversely, words with a bad odor sometimes become deodorized. *Jazz,* for instance, was formerly a crude term for indulging in an action which in polite society is referred to, if at all, only with such vague Latin terms as *intercourse* and *cohabitation*. There was nothing vague about *jazz* in those days. Most good girls never heard the word and if they did, they never used it. Meanwhile the word had enjoyed a respectable if limited use, mostly among Negroes and Creoles apparently, in connection with music. When Negro music became popular, the respectable use of the word crowded out the vulgar use, though for a time bad boys about the age of puberty could be heard to snicker when a nice girl spoke of *jazzing* something.

Index